CHILDREN OF PRIVILEGE:
STUDENT REVOLT IN THE SIXTIES

Why did a student movement arise in the early sixties? Why did it take the course it did? And why did it begin to decline in the late sixties? Cyril Levitt provides answers to these questions by examining the changing conditions of life facing middle class youth in the fifties and sixties and the changing role of the universities. His book is based in part on extensive interviews with former student leaders in the United States, Canada, and West Germany.

In all three countries students in general, and student activists in particular, were from middle and upper income and status families. They had been promised that university studies would provide an entrance into a small, influential, and powerful élite. But the massification of higher education led to the devaluation of the university degree and to the massification of the intellectual élite itself. These 'children of privilege' interpreted this process as a breaking of the promise that society had made to them.

After taking up the causes of others – among them civil rights and peace – in the middle of the decade the student radicals gradually became concerned with student syndicalism, student power, university reform, the war in Vietnam, and anti-draft activism. But their isolation in society and the rejection they had experienced in their attempts to move beyond the campus led them to develop a politics based upon a fantasy. This was accompanied by a growing concern with ideology and especially with a variety of forms of Marxism. By means of Marxist ideology the student radicals sought to establish the élitist claims that had been denied them by the process of élite massification. The student movement began to decline as a result of the slowing of the boom in higher education, the increase in graduate underemployment and unemployment, and the widening gap between the activist leadership and the mass of students.

Levitt demonstrates that the student movements in all three countries were remarkably similar in their trajectories despite national differences, and that they were 'revolts of privilege against privilege, for privilege in a society in which the character of privilege had been changing.'

CYRIL LEVITT is an associate professor in the Department of Sociology at McMaster University.

Children of

CYRIL LEVITT

Privilege

STUDENT REVOLT IN THE SIXTIES

A Study of Student Movements in
Canada, the United States, and
West Germany

UNIVERSITY OF TORONTO PRESS
Toronto Buffalo London

378,198
L 666

© University of Toronto Press 1984
Toronto Buffalo London
Printed in Canada

ISBN 0-8020-5636-9 (cloth)
ISBN 0-8020-6537-6 (paper)

Canadian Cataloguing in Publication Data

Levitt, Cyril, 1946–
    Children of privilege : student revolt in the sixties

    Bibliography: p.
    Includes index.
    ISBN 0-8020-5636-9 (bound). ISBN 0-8020-6537-6 (pbk.)

    1. College students–Canada–Political activity.
    2. College students–United States–Political
    activity. 3. College students–Germany (West)–
    Political activity. 4. Student movements–Canada.
    5. Student movements–United States. 6. Student
    movements–Germany (West). I. Title.

LB3610.L48 1984   378'.1981   C83-099135-2

Quotations from 'Of Vietnam and Gold and the Cauldron of '68' by John M. Lee © 1978
by the New York Times Company. Reprinted by permission.

Und tatsächlich, was bringen doch Bildung und Intelligenz für grosse Dinge hervor? Wie will einer ohne sie zu den besseren Leuten gehören?

Brecht, *Der gute Mensch von Sezuan*

Zwei Seelen wohnen, ach! in meiner Brust,
Die eine will sich von der andern trennen.   Goethe, *Faust*

Here we may reign secure, and in my choice.
To reign is worth ambition, though in Hell:
Better to reign in Hell, than serve in Heav'n.   Milton, *Paradise Lost*

O, what a world of profit and delight,
Of power, of honour, of omnipotence,
Is promised to the studious artizan!   Marlowe, *Dr Faustus*

Contents

Part 4 Ideology

Preface

The idea for this book first arose in a series of conversations with Lawrence Krader at the Freie Universität Berlin (FU) in the spring of 1976. After the collapse of the student movement in 1970, I had turned my back on activist politics and thrown myself into my studies. Like many of my erstwhile comrades, as I later discovered, I had slammed the door on a turbulent period of my life without having come to terms with it.

Having completed a master's degree in sociology, I left Canada for Germany in the fall of 1972. Unlike the situation at universities in North America at that time, where the left political sects were insignificant dots on the campuses, sectarian strife at the FU and other major centres of higher learning in Germany was highly visible. I was often provoked to reflect upon the struggles which raged among the German students and between the students and the authorities, but I did so from afar, for my resolve to pursue my studies without distraction was firm.

I completed my doctoral dissertation in 1975, and for the first time in five years I temporarily disengaged from my academic pursuits. It was at that point that I began to feel a certain uneasiness about the New Left years. To use a psychoanalytic metaphor, the student movement was a 'point of fixation' in my life, and I was determined to go back and work it through.

While still in Berlin, I began to sift through the enormous literature on the New Left and to discuss the idea of a book on the topic with my friend and teacher Lawrence Krader. The theoretical underpinning of this work is based upon a careful study of his writings and upon numerous discussions and years of correspondence with him. In a world full of academic hustlers and professorial charlatans, it was my extremely good fortune to have found a scholar's scholar for a teacher and collaborator.

Having decided to pursue this project, I questioned my friends in Berlin about the student movement in Germany. To Andreas Baudis, Jürgen Ebeling, Lutz Flöth, Klaus Hesse, Heinz and Hildegaard Immendorf, Fritz and Barbara Paalzow, José Ripalda, Heinz-Peter Seidel, Ingrid Sommerkorn, Klaus Tetzlaff, Wolfgang Winkler, Ray Wolf, and Sylvia Zacharias I owe my first impressions of the character of the German New Left. At the same time, correspondence with my good friend Tony Hyde in Ottawa was helpful in determining the scope of the undertaking and the general thrust of the research. Indeed, without Tony's help at every step, this book would have been much poorer in form and content. To Tony and to Cathy Moses go my heartfelt thanks for their generosity and friendship through it all.

In the summer of 1976 I returned to Canada to assume a position at McMaster University. At McMaster I found colleagues and friends who not only were immensely supportive generally but provided information, insight, and constructive criticism throughout the endeavour. I would like to thank Howard Brotz, Richard Brymer, Ellen Derrow, Berkeley Fleming, Jack Haas, Roy Hornosty, Frank Jones, Graham Knight, Victor Marshall, Ralph Matthews, Peter Pineo, Gerry Rosenblum, Bill Shaffir, and Jane Synge for their input and encouragement. I would also like to thank Dean Greg McIvor and Dean Peter George of the Faculty of Social Science at McMaster for their constant material support and expressions of confidence in me and my work.

The Arts Research Board at McMaster provided the funds which enabled me to spend several weeks conducting further research on the German New Left. It was during this trip in December 1976 that I met Ulf Kadritzke and Bernd Rabehl, two former student leaders in Berlin, and conducted a series of interviews with them concerning the history and dynamics of the German movement. In addition, Kadritzke and Rabehl provided me with the names and addresses of former movement members whom I eventually interviewed in Germany the following year. During that first trip I spent a great deal of time working up bibliographies in the Universitätsbibliothek and the Staatsbibliothek. I also rummaged through the alternative bookstores of Berlin's student bohemia looking for relevant sources.

By this time I had decided to conduct a series of interviews with former New Leftists. I was convinced of the necessity of this by the appearance of a spate of one-sided and superficial articles in the popular media about the movement. In addition, I had learned that many former activists had also shut the door abruptly on their past. And so, I began to conceive the book, in part, as a forum for these people to re-examine that period of their lives.

Bob Ross, whom I met at the 1977 American Sociological Association meetings in Chicago, provided me with the addresses and phone numbers of most of the Students for a Democratic Society (SDS) people I interviewed in the United States. Peter Stein was helpful in locating former activists in the New York City area, and Douglas Kellner and Jim Miller put me in touch with former SDS members in Austin. In Canada Peter Warrian supplied the missing addresses of several former leadership people in the Combined Universities Campaign for Nuclear Disarmament (CUCND) and the Student Union for Peace Action (SUPA), and Stewart Saxe gave me the addresses of several former key Canadian University Press (CUP) leaders.

Helen Garvey kindly made available to me copies of the papers delivered at the American SDS reunion in 1977. Although I had originally planned to incorporate analysis of this material in the book, I felt that it should not be made the object of public scrutiny, at least not at the hands of an outsider.

Several archival and personal collections having to do with the student movement proved to be of invaluable assistance in writing this book. The CUCND-SUPA and Canadian Union of Students (CUS) archives at the Mills Library at McMaster University were easily accessible. Tilman Fichter and Siegward Lönnendoncker at the Zentralinstitut für sozialwissenschaftliche Forschung at the FU provided me with important material from the German Sozialisticher Deutscher Studentbund (SDS) archives on microfilm. Tony Hyde, Niels and Ulf Kadritzke, Don McKelvey, Tom Patterson, Michael Rowan, Ingrid Sommerkorn, and Peter Warrian gave me material from their private collections. Hildegaard and Heinz Immendorf and Barbara Krader sent items related to the study of the German New Left.

It was my good fortune indeed to have found so many people to read the manuscript in whole or in part whose suggestions have made for a better book. My thanks in this regard go to Richard Allen, Philip Altbach, Richard Brymer, Berkeley Fleming, Louis Greenspan, Rod Hay, Roy Hornosty, Tony Hyde, Greg Kealey, Lawrence Krader, Victor Marshall, Ivar Oxaal, Robert Pike, Bob Ross, and Peter Warrian. A conversation with Malcolm Spector gave me new insight into a number of issues. Discussions with Peter Dreitzel and Wolf Lepenies clarified a number of matters concerning the German New Left. Of course, any errors of omission or comission are solely my responsibility.

This work could not have been completed without the secretarial assistance of Marg Belleck, Helen Bennie, Isabelle Brymer, Chris Downey, Cornelia Hornosty, Shirley McGill, Ilene Millington, Brenda Nussey, Brigitte Pantis, Karen Poxon, Marcella Rollman, and Jackie Tucker. Members of the staff of the McMaster University Library were also most helpful. Special thanks go to Joanne Marshall and Charlotte Stewart for their concern and assistance. I would also like to thank Peter Coleman and Rick Hazell at the McMaster Information Processing and Academic Computing Services for their technical assistance on matters concerning word processing software.

There were so many others who supported my work in so many different ways: my old teachers and friends Ted Abel, Gerard DeGré, and David Kirk always had words of advice and encouragement; colleagues at Rutgers and the City University of New York were very helpful during the early stages of the research; Andrew and Myra Fell opened their home in London to me on my way to and from Germany; Morris and Susan Zoladek allowed me to make their Toronto home my headquarters in that city; Andreas Baudis and Sylvia Zacharias provided lodging for me in Berlin; my students and friends critically evaluated my ideas and participated in the production process by proofreading and checking references. Limited space precludes me from naming them all. I would, however, like to express my gratitude to Rod Hay and Donna Samoyloff, who proofread the typeset copy with great care.

I wish to thank the Canada Council and the Social Sciences and Humanities Research Council for bearing the costs of the interviews and their transcription. This book has been published with the help of a grant from the Social Science Federation of Canada, using funds provided by the Social Sciences and Humanities Research Council of Canada, and a grant from the Publications Fund of the University of Toronto Press.

My deepest gratitude is extended to all those who shared their experiences, afterthoughts, analyses, and judgments with me. Thanks are due as well to Philip Altbach for permission to reprint material from my article 'The New Left, the New Class and Socialism' which appeared in *Higher Education* 8, 1979.

I wish to express my deep gratitude to Mr Virgil Duff, editor at the

University of Toronto Press, who supported this work from the beginning and made the difficult process of evaluation and preparation as painless as possible. I would also like to thank Margaret Parker for her expert editing of the copy and for her patience and understanding.

My late parents prepared the foundation for my intellectual and social development, which took an unexpected turn after their untimely deaths.

To my wife, Angelika, go my apologies for the material and spiritual costs which the writing of this book exacted, as well as my deepest gratitude for her support through it all.

Finally, this book is dedicated to Shoshale, whose recent appearance filled an empty part of my heart with much joy.

CHILDREN OF PRIVILEGE

Introduction

An old Yiddish tale describes the predicament of the elders of a small *stettl* who were required by tradition to ensure that all members of the community upon their passing were buried honourably in accordance with religious law. It came about that one of their number, a soul bereft of kin, a man who was famous for his general misanthropy, passed away. The elders went to consult their learned rabbi about the burial, for none of them could find anything positive to say about the departed as custom required. After hearing their problem, the wise teacher agreed to deliver the eulogy himself: 'Let us remember the positive contributions made by the deceased,' he implored. 'It is true that he was a liar and a cheat, a thief above all else. Nevertheless, his father was an even greater thief and rogue, and this fact alone does honour to the departed!'

The sins of the father put the lesser faults of the sons in a better light. In the eulogies composed by the mass media in recent years, the New Left of the sixties has been portrayed much more favourably than the Old Communist Left of the thirties and forties had been – at any time (Gordon 1976:11–66; Kristol 1977:42–57; Langguth 1976:74–7; Mauss 1971:1–20; Newfield 1967:109–30; Young 1977:298–323; *Monthly Review* 1969:3–11; Weinstein 1972:3–60). Ex-Stalinists were moved to denounce the 'God that failed,' Trotskyist intellectuals abandoned socialism for sociology, and radical social democrats sought accommodation within the political consensus. The most gifted of the former radicals and revolutionaries of the thirties and forties admitted to themselves and to the world that they had been wrong and misguided, in varying degrees. The economic success of capitalism, the passivity of the working class, Stalinist butchery, and the organized repression of McCarthyism (and its counterparts outside the United States) decimated the ranks of the Old Left and removed the question of socialism from the agenda in the West for more than a decade. The New Left, however, in spite of the obvious excesses of the radical fringe, appeared to have been right about the war in Vietnam, East-West accommodation, the threat to the environment, the oppression of women and minority groups, illegal police practices, and the smugness and corruption of the political process.

By and large the radical students of the sixties did not break with their political past. Research has shown (Fendrich and Tarleau 1973; Fendrich 1974, 1976, 1977; Krauss 1974; Levitt 1979, 1981) that the majority of former activists have maintained a basic social and political commitment which is continuous with their previous New Leftism. In opposition to this, the media have generally emphasized the discontinuity of past and present[1] by uncritically portraying the invariably 'middle class' career and living conditions of former prominent members of the student movement.[2]

The New Left student movement is the concern of this book.[3] Baldly stated the thesis maintains that the student movement was a revolt of privilege against privilege, for privilege in a society in which the character of privilege had been changing. Empirical sociology has presented overwhelming evidence of the material privilege enjoyed by the student activists.[4] Many of the former activists interviewed during the course of this study testified that, in retrospect, they were acutely aware of their relatively privileged positions. As one former American student radical observed:

That whole 'baby-boom,' post-World War II generation was in fact people growing up in a world in which in a limited sense there was a material base for being concerned about democracy. I had time to think of the quality of life in politics, whereas my father, who worked six days a week, twelve hours a day, didn't. On some levels it was as simple as that. I actually was in college and could think about the options I had and with the generation of people. I mean, we used to be attacked all the time ... 'These kids are spoiled.' It looks like this is what happens when you're given too much freedom, and have too many options, and so on, and I think they were right. In fact, we were kids who'd grown up with a sense of options that nobody else in the world had ever had before [so] that we could actually think about defining our lives; and so that when we began to come of age we began to do that.

The oppositional character of the relatively privileged has been a topic of interest for many neo-conservatives (Bruce-Briggs 1979:ix–x;

Kirkpatrick 1979:45). That the relatively privileged students of the sixties should have turned against the social and political order which was the source of that privilege is a puzzle to Norman Podhoretz:

> Among the many puzzles thrown up by the disruptions of the 1960's in the United States, none seemed more perplexing than the virulent hostility toward their own country which was evidently felt by some of the most privileged elements of American society ... Why should young people from prosperous families who had been given – as the saying used to go – 'every advantage,' who were enjoying what to all outward appearances was a life of luxury, indulgence, and ease, and who could look forward with relative assurance to positions of comparable status and reward in the years ahead, characterize themselves as 'niggers'? (1979:19)

During the early years of the movement, the activists responded truthfully that theirs was a revolt of the spirit, of conscience and will. On moral grounds they condemned striving after material privilege as an obstacle in the search for spiritual authenticity. But if the student movement did not stem from conditions of material want, it was nonetheless a product and expression of specific material conditions.[5] The precise way in which the movement developed out of these specific conditions is the central concern of this work.

The New Left considered the problem of the material conditions of its existence only during the period of its disintegration. One position adopted at that time represented a variety of the 'new working-class' thesis which had been imported from France. Translated into the student idiom it was mixed with elements of student syndicalist ideology to produce the 'youth-as-class' position. Accordingly, students were seen to be part of a new youth proletariat exploited by capital and manipulated by the state. Thus, the student movement was held to be a response to the exploitation of youth in general, students in particular. Privilege thus gives way to 'proletarianization.'

By means of such theoretical constructions, the New Left posed anew the question of the transition to socialism in the advanced, industrial, capitalist societies. Yet the question was raised in a context of weakness and inner-movement strife; the important role accorded to students in the great historical transformation represented a fantastic inversion of their actual impotence. At the same time, the 'Marxism' which emerged out of the New Left found a home in academic life and has become an influential intellectual paradigm in the seventies and eighties.[6] The growth of Marxism in the New Left of the sixties and in the academies of the seventies is based not upon the developing class consciousness of social labour but upon its weakness and lack of solidarity. The radicalization of the students and intellectuals was a response to the changing character of privilege in the sixties. In this case, it is as Laufer and Bengston suggest, that 'generationally based movements for social change arise when the criteria for social and economic positions of leadership change' (1974:187; cf Scott and Lyman 1970:24).

To consider the student movement as an undifferentiated whole is to consider it speculatively and falsely. The early period of the New Left, the 'period of glory,' differed from the periods of transition and disintegration which followed it. The movement was born of a concern with pressing moral issues: nuclear testing and disarmament, militarism, civil rights. The early New Leftists fervently believed that these problems could not be solved on the basis of political ideology, that political ideology itself was an obstacle to achieving an effective solution.[7] Moral considerations were to replace political and ideological ones as a guide to action. Right and truth were on one side, wrong and calumny on the other. Little theoretical knowledge was required to understand the issues. Slogans such as 'Black and white together,' 'Peace in the world or the world in pieces,' and 'Help the poor to help themselves' were to offer at one and the same time an analysis and a program for action. Each individual was deemed to be morally responsible for the existence of immoral conditions, for it was in the power of each person armed with the 'Truth' to combat iniquitous social and political practices. The great emphasis was thus placed upon personal commitment in moral protest (Altbach 1967:22; Ericson 1975:10; Haber 1967:40; Hyde and Rowan 1967:3; Young 1977:18). 'Speak truth to power and the truth shall set you free' expresses the sentiment which inspired the early New Left activists. They did not challenge society's cherished values; in fact, they were the most ardent champions of these values. They were not sinners and outcasts, but saints and martyrs, the keepers of the social conscience.

Like Robin Hood of old, they were prepared to steal from the rich to give to the poor. And, like Robin, they were more honest, more devout, and more socially conscious than hypocritical clerics and officials:

Robin is at once an embodiment of honour and an agent of retribution. He corrects the evil which flows from the greed of the rich clerics and the corruption of royal officials. But he does not seek to overturn social conventions. On the contrary, he sustains those conventions against the machinations of the wicked and the powerful who exploit, flout and undermine them. He keeps his word, unlike the treacherous sheriff. He is devout, unlike the avaricious abbot. He is courteous, unlike the churlish monks whom he entertains to dinner. *He makes his world conform to the principles which are supposed to underlie it.* (Emphasis added; Holt 1982:10; on students see: Flacks 1967, 1970, 1971; Keniston 1968, 1971; Mehnert 1977:viii; Parkin 1967; Soloman and Fishman 1963, 1964a, 1964b)

The movement first arose as a moral criticism of specific social and political practices and policies which were taken to be violating traditionally held and publicly professed ideals. Somewhat later, the New Left began to develop a global or 'holistic' critique of modern society (which it variously referred to as 'corporate-liberal,' 'bureaucratic,' 'capitalist,' 'imperialist,' 'de-humanizing,' and 'materialistic'). At the same time, there was a shift in the movement away from issue-oriented protest to radical politics. This represented the transitional middle period of the New Left and it marked a significant turning-point in its history. Moral criticism and political analysis entered into an erratic alliance which was given expression by the conflicts which developed between the 'personalists' and the 'politicos,' the 'wheelies' and the 'feelies,' the 'libertarians' and the 'authoritarians.' Finally, during the last two years of the decade, the moral attitude was consciously suppressed by some in favour of varying forms of immanentist historical analysis and critique. If non-violence and participatory democracy were central facets of the early movement, vanguardism and terrorism were the 'new' elements in the process of its disintegration. It appeared as if whole sections of the late New Left had moved into direct opposition to everything which the early movement cherished (see Young 1977:336–41). 'Humanism,' 'personalism,' 'moralism,' 'pacifism' gave way to 'scientific socialism,' 'Marxism-Leninism,' 'Maoism,' 'Stalinism,' and terrorism.[8] These major changes in the late movement were not purely fortuitous; they were an expression of the antagonistic cross-pressures bearing upon the student generation of that time and of the ambivalent reality of the youth of the broad middle strata.

The movement was a phenomenon which belonged to the decade of the sixties; it was born with it, just as it died with it. It was a movement of youth led by students from the universities and colleges. It was a global phenomenon, even though international attention was drawn to the movements in the powerful industrial countries of the West and Far

East. Yet, in spite of its international ambience, the New Left was a polycentric social movement, the various national leaderships having had only sporadic and furtive contact with one another (Pinner 1969:61; Shils 1969:31). The impact of this new activism on the national political scenes varied greatly from case to case, just as the responses of the various governments to the revolt of their youth varied. Where the New Left gathered strength, it challenged the three major politically organized forces on the left: liberalism, social democracy, and Moscow-oriented communism. Paradoxically, the New Left grew and prospered only when it espoused and acted on the vision and values of liberalism, social democracy, and, abstractly, of communism.

There always had been a small number of communists – Stalinists and Trotskyists for the most part – in and around the New Left. They had little impact as communists upon the early movement and were tolerated as long as they abided by group norms, which they generally did. Most of them had been 'red- or pink-diaper babies,' that is, children of communist or socialist parents respectively. Since the thrust of the early New Left critique was moralistic, the ideological adherence of individual members was considered to be irrelevant. A communist and a Christian would both be welcomed if each were willing to engage in moral action for peace and civil rights wherever and whenever they were threatened. It was this seeming acceptance of communists in the ranks which deeply disturbed the adult liberal and socialist groups with which New Left organizations were affiliated. As a former member of the American SDS from New York who was active in the mid-West during the early sixties put it:

Moreover, the fact that we said openly that we weren't communists – disarmed liberals to a certain extent, or even Marxists, forget about communists – they had so attuned themselves to the debate of the fifties and the McCarthyist environment, even the more liberal ... and the liberals had so ingrained their conceptions and categories within that vein that intellectually, I think, they were somewhat disarmed by the fact that we openly proclaimed ourselves not to be Marxist and had no interest in that. Basically we had an interest in some plain issues, clear-cut issues, and we were not going to get into a historical debate about the Soviet Union, which is constantly what they pushed.

In a strange way, the New Left was a response in part to the cold war propaganda of the late forties and early fifties. In the West, unrealistic expectations were created among school-aged youth concerning the promise of 'democracy.' As a former student leader in Southern Ontario explains: 'The lack of democracy in liberal democracy was important in the "radicalization" of a lot of people. And I wondered too then, whether the intense anti-Soviet, pro-democratic propaganda of our youth, you know, may have made an impression on a lot of us about how the world is supposed to work.'

The movement died organizationally at the end of the sixties, yet the general political and social commitment of the New Left survived in different forms. The feminism, environmentalism, committed journalism, and academic radicalism of the seventies and early eighties owe their existence in no small measure to the generation of the New Left, for they are highly dependent upon the leadership and support of former New Leftists and of those who were influenced by the student movement. Recent studies of these former New Left activists (Fendrich 1974, 1976, 1977; Fendrich and Tarleau 1973; Levitt 1979, 1981) have shown that they have moved into very specific employment areas – teaching, social work, the media, government and state bureaucracies, trade union work – while remaining faithful to their past political and social values.

The contents of this book have been greatly influenced by a series of interviews I conducted with former activists who were centrally involved with the most prominent New Left groups in Canada, the Federal Republic of Germany (FRG), and the United States.[9] (The similarities among the three national groups were as striking in the late seventies as they had been throughout the sixties.) Much of the analytic material which follows was developed as a result of the scores of interviews conducted with former activists in these countries. Those who were interviewed were not treated as mere sources of data but were partners in the analysis; they were agents as well as patients. In this way, what follows can be understood as a self-analysis of the student movement.

Some may take exception to the choices of these three national movements; surely those in France and Japan were more powerful and influential than the one in Canada. This is not to be denied. Yet I knew the Canadian movement from the inside,[10] and it was selected for this reason. The German students in the SDS and SHB were the most theoretically 'advanced'; if one can conceive of an international division of labour in the student movement, then the German students were the theoreticians and strategists and the American activists were the tacticians (although the contributions of the Dutch, French, and Japanese students in this regard were recognized and widely acclaimed).

In addition, the trajectory of the New Left in the three selected countries was remarkably similar. The American and German organizations were originally student groups affiliated with parent social democratic bodies. The same kinds of issues in both countries led to similar kinds of strains and hostilities between the 'adult' and student groups. The pacifist ideological influence was considerable in all three cases during the formative period. Furthermore, the Moscow-oriented communist parties in Canada, the FRG, and the United States were extremely weak, whereas their counterparts in France and Italy were politically very powerful. The student activists in these latter countries were forced to confront influential 'proletarian' parties which had been the keepers of 'revolutionary' orthodoxy.

There is no magic in the number three. More cases could have been examined. Yet the massive literature on the student movement in dozens of countries and in many languages cannot be thoroughly absorbed by any single study.

If the student movement has been the object of such detailed analysis, why have I found it necessary to place yet another book on the topic before the reading public? Could a new work offer the reader fresh empirical information or a new approach to the material? In fact this book attempts to do both. Material taken from the interviews with former New Left activists will provide the reader with new information and, I hope, new insight. In addition, the book lays claim to originality on the basis of its particular grasp of the historical character and meaning of the student movement.

There have been hundreds of insightful studies of the student activism of the sixties. Indeed, many of their findings have been extremely useful in developing the analysis which follows. However, to the best of my knowledge, none of the previously published works has pursued the trajectory of the student movement as an intrinsic expression of the material social and economic conditions and relations of that student generation. Many have made reference to the privileged class background of the students; many have called attention to the moral character of the early movement and the ambivalent factions of its decline. Some perspicacious few have even discovered a material interest given expression in the New Left. Yet no one has attempted to follow the inner connection linking the changing material conditions of the sixties' student generation, the form and content of protest and revolt, and their ideological expressions.[11] Without this kind of analysis, every history of the movement must necessarily be uncritical and every attempt to grasp the real historical significance of the student revolt must remain superficial.

PART ONE: SOURCES

1

The cradle of the New Left

Introduction

> ... all science would be superfluous, if the form of appearance and the essence of things immediately fell together.   Karl Marx

It seems as if each decade interprets the past and pictures the future differently. The composition of *Zukunftsmusik* (music of the future) is just as much an activity of the present as is the reconstruction of past history. The difference between critical and uncritical writing has less to do with a formal commitment to objectivity than it does with an actual striving towards self-critical honesty. No one is capable of leaping over his own time; yet not everyone apprehends his own time in thoughts (Hegel 1967:11, 295).

The New Left of the sixties was both an expression of and a protest against the times of which it was a part. It was a living movement, a genuine manifestation of the life experiences and conditions of an entire student generation. Times have changed, however, and the conditions of the sixties no longer exist. The New Left cult of the late seventies is both a testimony to the rootedness of the movement in the generation of the sixties and an affirmation of the movement's historical obsolescence. 'A man cannot become a child again, or he becomes childish.' It is time to relinquish the ghosts of the past, to let the dead bury their dead. It is time for a generation to begin the process of self-clarification in earnest.

A tale of two generations

The New Left student generation of the sixties emerged out of the cauldron of the fifties. In many ways the relationship between the post-war generation and that of its parents was one of beauty and the beast. Adults raising children after 1945 themselves matured in times of depression and war; the prosperity of the fifties was seen by them as a welcome change from the want and deprivation of the thirties and forties. Their children, however, accepted the relative material abundance in their lives as the normal state of affairs, in spite of the moral lectures which they received from their parents concerning the hard times of depression and war and the starving children in India.[1] Who could blame the children for not taking the sermons of their elders seriously? How could the reality of hunger in the bellies of millions of children in poorer regions be transmitted to the scions of the well-fed, especially when these moral messages were only designed to trick the finicky eaters into finishing their spinach?

The young generation in the fifties was given a series of double messages. On the one hand, children were to be pampered and coddled, kept from the evils which plagued earlier generations of youth. It would not be out of place to suggest that the children of the fifties were being used by their parents, who vicariously sought to experience a happy (or what they thought of as a happy) childhood. There are few persons alive today born between 1945 and 1950 into the middle class in North America who did not hear from his or her parents the expression 'I want you to have everything that was denied to me as a child.' On the other hand, children were fed a pablum of apparently outmoded 'words of wisdom' concerning 'survival in the cold, grey world,' a world which was never experienced by the children themselves but was for ever (embarrassingly) present as a conjuration of the parents, especially of the fathers. It was that very abstract world and its rules of conduct which was to become a target of New Left rage.

The child-bearing and child-rearing generation of the fifties was cautious and conformist.[2] It was not as interested in independence as it was in status and security. The corporatization and bureaucratization of economic life imposed its own regimen upon the 'organization man' at every rung of the corporate career ladder. Non-conformity was generally considered to be both unpatriotic and neurotic. The conservatism of the middle class, however, was not of the know-nothing, populist variety. It was a sophisticated doctrine of *amor fati*:

Once people hated to concede that their behavior was determined by anything except their free will. Not so with the new suburbanites; they are fully aware of the all-pervading power of the environment over them. As a matter of fact, there are few subjects they like so much to talk about; and with the increasing lay curiosity about psychology, psychiatry, and sociology, they discuss their social life in surprisingly clinical terms. But they have no sense of plight; this, they seem to say, is the way things are, and the trick is not to fight it but to understand it. (Fromm 1955:160–1)

If the price to pay for material success, status, and security was the acceptance of the 'anonymous authority' which went along with the grey-flannel suit, the young adults of the depression and war generation were prepared to pay it without protest.

Thus, the middle class was fruitful and multiplied in the new suburbia. Suburban life gave expression to the economic boom which occurred from 1947 to 1957:

Families in great numbers moved to the suburbs. New developments sprouted up around the outskirts of all the big us cities. Supermarkets and shopping centers were built to serve these new developments, on a multi-billion dollar scale. Drive-in restaurants, banks and movies became commonplace. Family shopping often shifted to the new centers where parking space was available. Serve-yourself techniques changed the appearance of retail stores. Discount houses appeared, took a sizeable share of the retail business.

Most of the 11 million new homes built during the decade were of the new rambler or split-level designs. More and more had two-car garages. Nearly all had picture windows of some kind. For the first time, the majority were heated by gas or oil rather than coal, had 'revolutionized' kitchens. Many had new wall refrigerators, built-in vacuum-cleaning systems, even built-in intercom arrangements.[3]

It was in this suburban paradise that the New Left generation was nurtured. Its members didn't feel that they were particularly privileged or fortunate to live in such a comfortable environment, although they were continually reminded of their good fortune by their parents. For them, middle class suburbia was the state of nature, the home of 'normal man.'

Although the children were suburbanites, their position within that world differed radically from that of the older generation. They were prized by their parents. They were to be that which their parents were not. The revolution in child psychology of the post-war era, the new permissiveness in child-rearing wisdom gave vent to this deeply rooted desire of middle class parents to give their children everything. The young were the centre of attention in the family, a reflection of the growing affluence. These relationships were dramatically different from those of preceding decades: 'It is the children who set the basic design; their friendships are translated into the mother's friendships, and these, in turn, to the family's. Fathers just tag along.'[4]

The children of the 'organization men' were encouraged to be creative, to be expressive, to be themselves. Treatment of and expectations for the young were no longer sexually specific. Girls were looked upon as boys who were not expected to go quite as far. Yet the encouragement of independence on the part of the young by their parents was explicitly circumscribed by the existing relations of middle class life. In theory, self-expression was to allow well-adjusted young adults to make their way in the given society. For the older generation the creativity and independence accorded the young were functional prerequisites in a society with an increasingly complex division of labour. And along with the encouragement of these traits in their children, the parents of the fifties made a promise to them, a promise which remained unfulfilled in the eyes of their progeny. The latter were assured that they would become successful in life if only they followed the course prescribed for them. If they completed their university education, the centres of social and economic power would readily open to them. They would literally inherit the earth.

The children came to believe the official and unofficial claim in the fifties that the university was the royal road to success.[5] It was the tacit breaking of this promise in the process of élite massification which fuelled the student revolt of the sixties.

It is important to note that success was not primarily defined in strictly monetary terms by the children or by their parents (although it was clearly more important for the latter than the former). It was more often a question of achieving an élite position to do good: to create jobs for others, to make humane policy decisions, to discover a cure for cancer (Jonas Salk was the role model for this). When mothers boasted about 'my son the doctor' they expressed the sentiment of this élitist altruism which was shared between the generations.

Politics

Historically, political idealism has been the prerogative of the affluent and the destitute. It has also been the privilege of the young, who have not yet become part of the process of social production. The children of the fifties accepted and affirmed the political values and ideals of their respective countries as easily and as naturally as they accepted and affirmed the relative material abundance around them.[6]

The depression and war generation was able to take the civil and political ideals of the country with a grain of salt; it was able to maintain the distinction between reality and those shiny ideals which were not realized in practice without becoming 'neurotic' about it. Moreover, it was satisfied that the gap between the ideals and the social actuality was slowly being closed. But this very ability to live with a separation of the real and ideal was itself a product of the experiences of the older generation in the 'cold, grey world' under depression and wartime conditions. The vaguely comprehended fact that negroes would not be served in restricted cafeterias in North Carolina was at best mildly disconcerting to liberals in comparison to the evils of the depression and Hitler. Under conditions of rising affluence, permissive child rearing, and filicentral if not filiarchal family life, the children of the fifties never had to develop the capacity to tolerate public hypocrisy.

The great international political reality in the fifties was that of the cold war. There were two components to this in the popular mind: the fear of communism, journalistically portrayed as the 'Red Menace' or the 'Yellow Peril,' and the fear of nuclear annihilation. Internally, socialism had become downright subversive. As the working class continued faithfully to pledge allegiance to the flag, the trade unions were purged of leftists: socialists, liberals, and ex-Marxists competed with each other in a race to retreat from any and every radical critique of society. Intellectuals proclaimed the end of ideology; history had at last come to an end, and we were left with only technical problems to solve. The western part of Germany had its economic miracle and became politically and militarily part of the NATO bloc. The Sozialdemokratische Partei Deutschlands (SPD) completed its move from *Klassenpartei* (a party of the working class) to *Volkspartei* (a popular party), and the ghost of Marx was exorcized by the party hierarchy. Anticapitalism became synonymous with Moscow communism.

Political leadership in these countries was in the hands of the 'old guard': Eisenhower in the United States, Adenauer in Germany, Louis St Laurent in Canada. The tone of these administrations was cautious, conservative, and conformist:

Politically, North America was locked in the legacy of the Second World War. In the US, Eisenhower, Dulles and happy Republicanism held the country; in

Canada, C.D. Howe's benevolent civil service managers continued administering Mackenzie King's solution to our political problems. Geo-political strains within the nation were hidden by the *modus vivendi* worked out between Maurice Duplessis, Leslie Frost and the federal Liberal Party. Walter Harris handed down successive 'balanced budgets' – he was much too complacent to bring in Keynes – and Canada remained a sound investment. Internationally we thought ourselves to be moderates, 'trusted by everyone,' and the nation glowed through the Suez Crisis. (Hyde and Rowan 1967:1)

But the first cracks began to appear in the monotonal landscape of the fifties: the Hungarian revolt in 1956 and the sputnik shock of 1957 linked scientific development and cold war politics in a way which contributed to the rapid expansion of university education in the sixties; the US Supreme Court decision against segregated schooling in 1954 and the bus boycott in Montgomery, Alabama, in 1955 were forerunners of the civil rights movement of the next decade. The growing popularity of the drop-out culture of the beats, the attraction of the 'deviant' music form of jazz, the literature of vagabonds and non-conformists, such as Jack Kerouac's *On the Road*, the poetry of Allen Ginsberg and Lawrence Ferlinghetti, and the rise in the popularity of rock'n'roll among the youth of the white middle class all represented the first stirrings of a counter-culture in the United States which would eventually spread around the world and become the environment in which the student movement would thrive. Finally the recessions of 1954 and 1958 sent a shiver of fear through the depression generation and put temporary crimps in the unbroken chain of progress in the economy.

This, then, was the world which the children and adolescents of the fifties never made. It was a world of television, of long-playing records, of Dr Spock, of General Motors and Krupp. It was a world of conformity, mediocrity, hypocrisy, and the Bomb. It was a world of black and white, of red and true blue, a world full of promise for the young, but at the same time it was incapable of making good on that promise. It was a world in which the largest generation in North American history was coming of age. And in unheard of numbers the 'privileged' of that generation were moving inexorably towards the doors of the universities.

2

The crucible of the student revolt

The world which the radical students sought to revolutionize was divided into hostile camps. The political, legal, administrative, philosophical, and ideological differences between the Soviet system and the bourgeois societies of the West and Far East were the focus of international attention during the cold war years. Yet both the Soviet system and capitalist society are founded upon an economic formation based upon the production of capital (Krader 1979).

Over the course of the last two decades the interpenetration of the two forms of capital production has proceeded apace through barter practices, the selling of licences, joint ventures, and bi-lateral co-production.[1] Although both sides have 'benefited' from the growing economic symbiosis – capitalists in the West have been able to export capital to areas containing pools of cheap labour, state managers in the East have benefited from the acquisition of Western technology and the import of 'scientific' management from the West – it has been estimated that in 1980 the COMECON countries (together with Yugoslavia) owed the OECD countries approximately $100 billion US (Levinson n d).

From the centres of capital to the universities is a long step, yet changes in the system of capital production had a major impact upon higher education. In fact experts in the sociology of education have described a post-war global explosion in education at all levels. It has been demonstrated that 'between 1950 and 1970, education ... has everywhere expanded independent of the constraints and stimuli that economic, political, and social structures provided in previous times' (Meyer et al 1977:225). The authors of this study were led to conclude 'that the causes of this expansion lie in the characteristics of the contemporary world system, since such characteristics would affect all nations simultaneously' (225). Economists had informed policy makers that a strong correlation existed between the wealth of a nation and the level of education acquired by its population. Advanced technology would be next to useless without the skilled operatives to organize, run, maintain, and supervise the processes of production. The great explosion in education went hand in hand with the general expansion of the capital-producing economy.

The changes which occurred side by side with the expansion of the economy in the post-war period were both technical and organizational in character. There was an unprecedented growth of the class of mediate producers,[2] of those who largely organize, plan, supervise, and manage the production process, who 'labour with their heads.' This necessitated the creation of a more highly qualified class of social labour. It is not surprising, therefore, that education, and especially higher education, became of interest to business, industry, commerce, the military, and the government. For different reasons, which are explored in the following section, it became of interest to the broad middle class as well.

'Human capital' was the economic theory which expressed the confluence of interests of business, government, and the middle class in the sixties. According to this theory, capital was not only money, machines, raw material, and finished commodities; capital could also be something non-material – knowledge and skill. And because knowledge and skill were attributes of human beings, this form of 'capital' was christened 'human.' Since economists making international comparisons noticed a correlation between economic productivity and the level of national educational attainment, they concluded that the increase in the educational attainment was responsible for the increase in productivity. Of course they were not slow in bringing this to the attention of their respective governments. Thus the expansion in the educational sector which occurred in the sixties came to be justified and rationalized on the basis of the 'discoveries' of the 'human capital' school of economics.[3]

The theory itself was a most apt expression of the alliance of interests outlined above. It considered the wants of capital for highly qualified labour and for 'scientific' management, maintenance, and support of the system of production. The middle class rejoiced in the coincidence of the 'national' interest with the career wants of its children. The human capital theory was welcomed by the agencies of the state as a justification for the augmentation of state control over a growing system of education, and by a military-industrial complex seeking hardware during the cold war. 'Human capital' was a magical phrase which meant different things to different people.[4]

Human capital theory was a theory not of capital, but for capital. Fundamentally it was a theory concerning the qualification of human labour, of increasing skill and technical ability, of the scientific and rational understanding of social labour. The expression of a theory of labour in the form of a theory of capital is at once a reification of the former, the fetishization and hypostatization of the latter.[5] Yet it is not a mere trick of the conjurer, but a reproduction in theory of a distorted reality,[6] for the active power in society appears to be the power of capital (the alienated power of social labour past and present). The attribution to the mediate producers in modern society of the power of capital is an attempt to flatter a part of social labour at the expense of the other part, and the acceptance of the mantle of capital is at once a self-aggrandizement and a false consciousness on the part of the actual or potential mediate producers. Human capital theory supposedly allowed these 'intellectuals' or 'head' labourers to develop within themselves the social power of capital, from which they were excluded outside themselves. With the corporatization of economic life, the growing dependency of the middle class was ameliorated by this apparent 'democratization' of capital. The differences between the personification of 'material' capital and the 'human' capital of the mediate producers were understood as ones of degree, but not of kind. Subjectively, the man of 'material' capital might secretly, or even openly, covet the knowledge or 'human' capital of the learned, and the latter might look down upon the owner of 'material' capital as a philistine. Throughout the history of civil society the relationship between the dominating classes and the class of mediate producers has been an ambivalent one (Goldhammer 1978; Sohn-Rethel 1978).

The general tendency for all countries to expand their systems of education represented an attempt to develop the skills and capacities of the class of social labour, a precondition for the rapid expansion of production in the postwar period. Therefore it was directly related to the training and qualification of skilled labour, of the immediate and especially of the mediate producers. But those who have alluded to the necessary connection between education and the wants of capital have only seen the coercive side of the relation (Bowles and Gintis 1976; Farber 1970; Leibfried 1968; Lockhart 1971; Rowntree and Rowntree 1968a, b, c). They have brought out the image of the school as prison, the student as 'nigger,' education as a means of class control and socialization, as a means of providing educated labour-power for the capitalist class at public expense. But education has traditionally been employed by the middle class as an instrument for achieving what sociologists call social mobility. Higher education has always been, and still remains, the preserve of the middle and upper classes.[7] Education is not capital, but historically the two have grown together.[8] The wealthier classes in the underdeveloped areas have aped the middle classes in the countries of capital who have made the attainment of formal education into a cardinal virtue. But our concern here is not with the question of education and class in the capital-poor areas of the world. We want to explore the social context of the changing nature of education in general, higher education in particular, in those 'advanced' countries where the student revolt occurred in the sixties.

For most industrial countries the period 1950–8 was one of incredible economic growth. The Americans emerged from the war unscathed as the most powerful economic and military power in the world. The Canadians were content to reap the benefits of an economy dependent to a large extent on the 'productivity' of us capital. The West Germans entered the period of the so-called economic miracle (*Wirtschaftswunder*), even though there was nothing 'miraculous' whatsoever in their success.[9] It was a period of change and of consolidation. Real wages were rising, the absolute living standard of most classes was also rising, even though the relative distribution of wealth remained generally stable. Industrial strife was not unknown, and at times it was bitter, but for the most part the fifties can be characterized by the co-operation of 'big business,' 'big labour,' and 'big government.'

The vicissitudes of the middle class

Although a social and economic history of this period is beyond the scope of the present study, it is important to note a significant trend that gained strength during that post-war period – the bureaucratization of economic life and the concomitant squeezing of the middle class so that its possibilities for manoeuvring were more limited. In the FRG, for example, the percentage of 'independent' producers in the economy fell from 31.6 in 1950 to 16.6 in 1970, while the number of Germans working for some employer rose correspondingly (Kommission für wirtschaftlichen und sozialen Wandel 1977:50). During this same period the contribution to the GNP from construction, service industries, and the state sector rose most rapidly, whereas that of mining, forestry, and farming decreased most rapidly (62). Expenditures in the state sector rose from 28,141 million marks in 1950 to 196,330 million marks in 1970 (74). Between 1962 and 1977 the percentage of those employed in farming and forestry, energy and mining, manufacturing, and construction declined, that in trade and commerce remained steady, and that in communications, service occupations, and the state sector in general increased (319).

In Canada a similar tendency is seen in the changing character of the occupational structure. Since 1945 the share of employment falling to the primary industries has declined from 28 per cent to 9 per cent, their share of total production declining from 15 per cent to around 5 per cent (Economic Council of Canada 1970:14). At the same time, a counter-tendency is apparent in the rapid growth of service industries:

In contrast to the relatively slow rates of growth or declines in most of the goods industries, employment has increased more rapidly than average in all of the service industries except transportation, storage and communication, which are not only linked to many activities in the goods-producing industries but also share some of their characteristics ... The largest part of the increase was in community services, including education and health services, which now employ about four times the number employed in these activities in 1946 ... The Canadian service industries now account for close to 60 per cent of total employment ... Total employment in Canada increased from 4.8 million in 1946 to nearly 7.3 million in 1966. Of the increase, 2.1 million were in the service industries and only 400,000 in the goods industries. (Economic Council of Canada 1968:67–9)

This tendency is not as strong in the United States. Between 1950 and 1968, however, the percentage of the labour force employed in white collar occupations increased from 36.6 to 46.7; the percentage for blue collar occupations decreased from 41.9 to 36.3; and the percentage for agriculture decreased from 11.8 to 4.6[10] But for our purposes the most important trend is the decline in the number of self-employed persons as a percentage of the US labour force from 21.6 in 1940 to 17.3 in 1950 to 13.7 in 1960 to 9.1 in 1969.[11]

In all three countries we find a rapid and pronounced growth in professional, technical, service, community, and state employment, a drop in the percentage of employees in the primary sector (especially agriculture), a marked decline in the percentage of the labour force which is self-employed, and a corresponding increase in salaried or wage labour. In other words, the number of those who were 'independent' and worked outside bureaucratic and corporate structures as a percentage of the total labour force fell noticeably over the course of the period, whereas the number of those working within these structures increased dramatically (Knight 1982:1–17).

For the youth of the middle class in the 1950s and early 1960s current trends heralded a future course which led it to the great public and private bureaucracies. And sociological research has shown that the educational qualifications for positions within the latter were beginning to rise just as the massive baby boom generation was preparing itself to enter the labour market.[12] In previous decades university attendance was a nicety of life available for sections of middle class youth, one way among many to achieve 'upward social mobility.' By the beginning of the sixties the attainment of a university degree had become a matter of life and death for a broad cross-section of middle class high school students.[13]

Observing higher education in 1958, Wilson Woodside described the rapid growth in demand for trained engineers by industry as the 'fever of 1956.' At the same time he identified the so-called brain-drain of Canadian graduates to the United States (partly because of the lack of graduate facilities at Canadian universities) and the Soviet challenge as spurs to the further development of tertiary education in Canada during that decade. On Soviet competition Woodside writes: 'Should we require our high school students to take science and mathematics? Yes, if the Soviets do. Should we offer higher pay for teachers, to secure enough first-class ones for our schools? We must, or the Soviets will catch us. Already the competition has a title: The Cold War of the Classroom' (1958:32).

The West Germans were, of course, affected by the 'Soviet challenge' much more directly than the Canadians. The FU in West Berlin was founded in 1948 as a direct response to the changing character of the old Humboldt University in the city's eastern sector. In the mid- and late fifties the Federal German authorities began to encourage scientific and technical training at all levels of the educational system and the Wissenschaftsrat investigated ways of rationalizing and modernizing the university (Schumm 1969).

The student revolutionaries of the sixties were 'silently' moving through the primary and secondary schools during the fifties. Home and school, state and media collaborated in singing the praises of the university and extolling its grand promise to the younger generation. For most middle class primary and secondary school youth, future university attendance was an accepted fact, part of the nature of things. The growth of enrollments and the movement toward universal higher education had made enrollment in college increasingly obligatory for many students, and their presence there increasingly "involuntary"' (Trow 1970:25). The flow of students into the universities became a flood as the great wave of middle class 'baby boomers' moved, quietly at first, but inexorably and irreversibly, towards the doors of the academy, not knowing just what was awaiting them inside but thoroughly conscious of the fact that, whatever it was, it was to be one of the most important things in their lives.

The description of the relations of education and the economy to this point may have given rise to the notion that the middle class was a victim or at best a pawn in a game orchestrated by the agencies of capital and the state. Granted that it was the state which was responsible for changing policy and funding for education, and granted that an expanded tertiary sector was supported and encouraged by industry and the military. Yet the government was extremely sensitive to the educational wants and aspirations of the middle class; and make no mistake about this fact: the middle class wanted higher education for its children. The following excerpt from an editorial in a popular liberal Canadian magazine shows how the pressure to expand higher education was manifested at the time:

In 1961 the presidents of Ontario's universities were called to a meeting with the premier and various other officials of the provincial government. The presidents were asked what total enrolment they expected in ten years. They said they expected 58,000. *Wrong*, they were told. Very wrong. Robert Jackson, the government's advisor on such matters, said they could expect between 90,000 and 110,000 students. 'You can't build fast enough,' said one of the government people. As it turned out, in 1971 there were 134,119 students in Ontario's universities. (*Saturday Night* 1978)

The middle class recognized that the post-war conditions of its existence demanded university training or credentials for its children.[14] Governments did not respond slowly to the demand for an expansion of the university system, especially since such a course was in full harmony with business and military interests.

The university as an instrument of mobility and security

During the post-war years, the children of the baby boom generation in Canada and the United States were moving up and through the school system. (For a variety of reasons there was no corresponding baby boom in Germany, although a mini-boom did occur there somewhat later, between 1957 and 1967.) In Canada the number of births increased steadily from 228,730 in 1945 to 405,527 in 1952. The average birth rate per thousand of population increased from 23.4 during the period 1941–5 to 28.0 during the period 1951–5. In the United States 2,735,456 babies were born in 1945 (an average birth rate of 19.5 per thousand of population), whereas in 1952 3,846,986 babies were born (an average birth rate of 24.7 per thousand of population).

Universal primary school attendance was achieved in all three countries, and in the United States (and to a lesser degree in Canada) universal secondary attendance was in the process of being realized.[15] Education had always served at least a part of the middle class in North America as a means for securing its position or for achieving upward social mobility. For the working class in general, education historically meant primarily technical training and apprenticeship. Before World War II it was a smaller part of the middle class which coveted the high school diploma as an entrance (one of several) into a middle class occupation. Historically, the university served a rather narrow section of middle and upper class youth, in part as a 'finishing school' for the social élite, in part as a means for maintaining an élite position through occupational accreditation.

Of course there were national differences among the systems of education. The German system was more élitist than the Canadian, the Canadian more élitist than the American. The *Gymnasium* was the preserve of the middle class (it was attractive to the lower middle class in particular), the university, the centre of the intellectual élite.[16] The Canadian universities had been for the most part church-affiliated institutions with a strong classical orientation. After 1906, however, they began to pay attention to the wants of industry and society by developing science faculties and by supporting professional training. Eventually the universities became public institutions, relinquishing church control for increased state financial assistance. The university in Canada was traditionally a finishing school for the élite, a training ground for the clergy, the legal, the medical, and other classical professions,[17] and one means of maintaining class position or of achieving a higher one.

The modern university in the United States has its roots in the transformation of higher education which took place during the last quarter of the nineteenth century. Men such as Eliot, Gilman, and

White were instrumental in fashioning the distinctive character of the American academy. To the plan of the German university constructed by Humboldt which combined research and teaching in an atmosphere of *Lehr- und Lernfreiheit*, they added the professional schools and the practical spirit of intellectual training typical of Yankeedom. Unlike those of Canada and Germany, American universities, in theory, were not designed to serve a small, aristocratic élite. In the words of Gilman: 'It is neither for the genius nor for the dunce ... but for the great middle class possessing ordinary talents that we build colleges' (Bledstein 1976:293). But it was not the youth of the 'great middle class' which entered the universities before World War ii, but rather only a portion of that cohort. (It was, of course, true that the middle class was overrepresented as a proportion of the student body.)

The distinguishing feature of the university in all three countries prior to the war was not the ivory-tower character of the institution, its detachment from the surrounding society, but rather its training and certifying function for a relatively small, educated social élite. In other words, the air of detachment surrounding the hallowed halls of ivy was precisely representative and expressive of its social role. The university did serve as a means of class maintenance or advancement for the middle class, but it was not the only, and certainly not the primary, means to this end. There were several roads to middle class security and mobility, only one of which was the university. A secondary school diploma, a high school degree, or the *Gymnasiumabschluss* were sound credentials which provided access to positions in both the public and private spheres. They often allowed direct passage into many professional programs which were available entirely or in part outside the aegis of the university. But even the secondary school diploma was not a matter of life and death for the scions of the middle class. Small shopkeepers, craftsmen of all kinds, lesser professionals could take their children into the family business and train them on the job. Alternatively, the young person could start an enterprise of his own in a market which was more enticing to the small, independent craftsman or businessman than it was after the war.[18]

The object of the foregoing was not to provide a detailed picture of the changes in higher education which occurred in the three countries. However, it should be made clear that massive expansion in enrolments, funding, faculty, and physical plant took place in Canada during the sixties, and to a significant but somewhat less dramatic extent in the FRG and in the United States as well. Above all the concern here is with the social significance of this expansion, the agencies which were involved in setting the changes in motion and which were most directly affected by them, the economic context of these changes, and the relation of the students of the sixties to these new conditions.

There is a popular notion encountered in the literature according to which the universities during the post-war period were supposedly transformed from élite to mass institutions. From this description, which has been applied by sociologists, educators, journalists, and government officials to characterize the nature of this 'revolution' in higher education, we are to conclude that the universities are no longer finishing schools for the well-born but learning centres for the majority of university-aged youth – the 'mass.' This is not, strictly speaking, an accurate characterization of the nature of the changes which happened in higher education.

The university has always been and continues to be an institution of privilege, a preserve of the middle class. The upper and middle strata have always been vastly overrepresented as a proportion of the student body at the select private and public post-secondary institutions. Even in the United States, where 46.43 per cent of Americans eighteen to twenty-one years of age were enrolled in institutions of higher learning in 1968, students from the privileged classes constituted at least half the student body at the best state and public schools. (The fact that these select schools were the primary centres of the student revolt in the sixties is not a coincidence.) The shift from élite to mass university did not in fact occur across the board. However, a shift did take place within the middle class. An increasing proportion of middle class youth attended university in the sixties. As expert observers pointed out, university attendance for the middle class was quickly becoming a necessity. At the same time, the role of the university as a gate-keeper of social mobility grew in importance and scope.

For the mass of students streaming through the gates of the academy in the sixties, however, future élite employment was not on its mind. These students didn't worry about it because they had accepted the promise so completely. After all, they were housed in an institution for the social élite. But, within the university and within the growing sphere of mediate production in society, the intellectual élite was indeed being massified. It was this massification process which the theoreticians of the New Left seized upon as evidence of the proletarianization of educated youth and of the development of a 'new' working class which would serve as the vanguard of the coming socialist revolution.[19]

How is it that the new 'masses' of the middle class came to storm the gates of academe? First, the rapid consolidation of the system of capital production spurred the pace of technological development. Along with the demand made upon science in particular for an increase in the productivity of labour (in the inverted form of the productivity of capital) came the want of the system for primary and secondary support personnel: managers, maintenance workers, trouble-shooters, translators, technicians, psychologists, lawyers, and diplomats, to specify only a few. It was the growth in the skill and qualification of labour, the further division and specialization of the same, the increase in labour's productivity, which set the world revolution in education in motion.

But this is by no means the whole story. It has been shown that only about 15 per cent of the rise in educational level in the United States between 1940 and 1960 was due to shifts within the occupational structure, that is, from those jobs which require less to those requiring more training (Folger and Nam 1964:19–33). Another study completed in the seventies has ascertained that only 25 per cent of the rise in educational attainment during the sixties could be attributed to such occupational shifts (Rodriguez 1978:55–67). In other words, most of the increase in educational attainment was due to the increasing level of education within occupations which had not significantly changed in their technical imperatives. The increasing supply of educated labour created a greater 'demand' for it. But mediately the growth of the international capital system forced the further corporatization, bureaucratization, monopolization, concentration, and centralization of economic life. The effect of the movement of capital, its internal consolidation on the one hand and its multinationalization on the other, had been the capture of large sections of the formerly 'independent' middle class within its net.

The rapid decline of the self-employed in the two decades after the war and the rise of the corporate public and private man have been consequences of this development. In the sixties the university represented the only secure means of maintaining class position or of advancing up the social ladder for large numbers of middle class youth. Gone for most were the days when the family business or father's profession could devolve upon son or daughter. For most, the entrepreneurial spirit had vanished under emerging market conditions. 'Working one's way up' no longer indicated the celebrated climb from newspaper boy to industrial magnate.[20] Rather, 'The data support the general conclusion that by the 1950's the American middle stratum used the public education system as a "fail safe" mechanism through which they successfully managed to assume, at a minimum, the status maintenance of their children, and more [*sic*] maximally, further intergenerational upward mobility' (Lockhart 1970).

The consciousness of the recent changes in the character of economic conditions for the middle class, along with the memory of the depression (college graduates in white collar occupations did not fare as badly as other workers then) (Jencks and Riesman 1977:108), led to the elimination of practically all future roads for middle class children but that of the university. Higher education became invested with a kind of transcendental quality; the university became a 'City of God' where miracles occurred and the spirit was regenerated. Keats describes the aura surrounding the university in the following way:

When a high school student leaves home for college today, he thinks he is about to enter heaven. Everyone has told him that college entrance is the chief goal of adolescent life, that once admitted he will be safe for ever and ever. True, some students experience a pleasant thrill of fear as they set off, but all carry with them the exhilarating notion that they are about to encounter some massive experience that will affect their lives for the better. A few months later, the more thoughtful of them will have concluded that going to college and acquiring an education are not necessarily synonymous, and that if college is heaven, then heaven could certainly stand a few radical improvements. (1965:42)

For the average middle class youth in the United States and Canada (to a lesser degree in the FRG, but developing in this direction nonetheless) during the fifties and early sixties, university attendance was simply accepted as part of life's plan. For many, failure to enter the university was tantamount to personal failure:

When few students went on to college, there was no disgrace in not doing so; moreover, except for the professions, it was not so clear that occupational success was closely linked to academic achievement. The Horatio Alger myth, and the American folklore celebrating the success of the self-made (and self-educated) man, served to define school achievement as only one among several legitimate avenues to success. But the rationalization of industry, and the increased importance of higher education for advancement beyond the lowest levels of the occupational structure, make educational achievement objectively more important for later success; the increased numbers of college-going students make this importance visible to high school students. (Trow 1977:112; cf Jencks and Riesman 1977:41)

To these changes affecting the middle class were added the national and patriotic concerns born of the division within the world system of capital and brought to light by Russian scientific achievements of the mid-fifties. Clark Kerr summed up the matter in the following words: 'Intellect has also become an instrument of national purpose, a component part of the "military-industrial complex." Our Western city of intellect finds its counterpart or counterparts in the East. In the war of ideological worlds, a great deal depends upon this instrument' (1963:124).

Consequences for the university

The explosion in higher education in the sixties has been well documented. Not only did enrolments soar, but an entire 'knowledge industry,' to use Clark Kerr's words, was created in post-secondary education.

In Canada, capital expenditure on universities increased from $15 million in 1951 to $88 million in 1960 to $340 million in 1968. Between the years 1956–7 and 1967–8, the annual operating expenses of the universities increased by 814.6 per cent, from $68,531,000 to $626,788,000. At the same time the gross 'productivity' of the universities also increased dramatically. In the academic year 1956–7 12,428 undergraduate degrees were awarded, whereas in the academic year 1967–8 41,250 undergraduate degrees were conferred, an increase of 331.9 per cent. The number of graduate degrees achieved increased even more dramatically, from 1574 in 1956–7 to 8311 in 1967–8, an increase of 428.3 per cent.

In the United States, the total current expenditure for public institutions of higher education jumped from $742.1 million at the end of World War II to $6.9 billion in 1965. The book value of the physical plant increased from $13.6 billion in 1960 to $27 billion in 1966. The total number of degrees (undergraduate and graduate) conferred increased from 376,973 in the academic year 1955–6 to 750,000 in 1966–7, a jump of nearly 100 per cent. University teachers were highly prized during the sixties and increased markedly in number. In the academic year 1959–60 381,000 faculty were employed by institutions of higher learning. By the year 1969–70, their number had increased to 825,000. During the same period the salaries of the professoriate rose significantly.[21] The average annual faculty salary (all ranks) increased from $6015 in 1957–8 to $11,745 in 1969–70.

Although German higher education was given its biggest boost only after the election of the SPD-FDP coalition in 1969, significant growth had been registered during the sixties. Expenditures for all *Hochschulen* increased from 210.8 million marks in 1950 to 877.0 million marks in 1959 to 2,058 million marks in 1964. In the academic year 1960–1 26,445 degrees (all levels) were conferred, whereas in 1969–70 47,892 degrees were awarded. In 1960 there were 10,231 academic positions (all ranks), but by 1964 they had increased to 25,671, a jump of over 150 per cent.

The availability of federal money for research, which in the United States dates from the early days of World War II, increased steadily during the fifties. At the same time the professor became society's acknowledged expert, a consultant, especially to government, and his sphere of activity broadened considerably. Of course many of the humanists reacted negatively to this fresh involvement in worldly affairs, and the split between the 'two cultures' (Snow 1960) appeared in the fifties as a crack within the academy; it was to be forced wide open during the confrontations of the sixties.

In looking at the changes in higher education in our three countries, we find that the pattern which emerges in each case is remarkably similar to the others. Between 1960 and 1969 the number of students enrolled in post-secondary institutions in the United States rose from 3,582,726 to 7,299,000. Whereas in 1960 34.99 per cent of the total number of Americans aged eighteen to twenty-four were enrolled in such institutions, 46.43 per cent of that age group were enrolled by 1969. In Canada, there were 163,143 post-secondary students in 1960, but by 1970 this population reached 475,548. The percentage of Canadians aged eighteen to twenty-four attending post-secondary schools rose from 9.7 per cent to 18 per cent. The FRG had 202,321 post-secondary students enrolled during the academic year 1959–60, and this represented about 4 per cent of the population of the country eighteen to twenty-four years old. By 1970 386,224 students were enrolled in these institutions, constituting about 8 per cent of that age group.[22]

Consequences for the students

This new generation, 'bred in at least modest comfort, housed now in the universities' (SDS 1964), was indeed looking uncomfortably to the world it was going to inherit. It was the sons and, to an increasing extent, the daughters of the broad middle class who entered the universities during the early and mid-sixties. The students themselves and their sympathetic observers painted a picture of mass regimentation, depersonalization, bureaucratization, and rationalization of academic life. A slogan of the Free Speech Movement in 1964, written on an IBM card, read: 'UC student. Do not bend, fold, or mutilate.' Towards the end of the decade the phrase (and the pamphlet) 'Student as Nigger' (Farber 1970) became popular in student circles. Similar sentiments were expressed both in Canada and in the FRG. This feeling of oppression was so strong that it was still making itself felt in the late seventies. At the tenth anniversary meeting of the Columbia University occupation and strike, a former participant involved in the actions told an audience of credulous undergraduates that 'Columbia was hell.'

In the literature produced by the students and their sympathizers, we find a good deal of discussion concerning student alienation, overcrowding, distant professors, irrelevant courses, the anachronistic character of the ivory tower, and the unfeeling administration and academic bureaucracy. And yet the theory of student alienation as a source of student activism is too myopic. Students, after all, lead a relatively privileged existence, for they are freed from participating in the labour of society for the duration of their studies. Unless the student or his family is independently wealthy, some thought must be given to future employment. But it was precisely this university-job nexus against which student anger was directed in the sixties. Occupational considerations were supposedly irrelevant to the 'tune in, turn on, and drop out' generation. In fact, the student revolt itself was a reaction to a world which made such demands upon the free spirit of its youth. Education was to be a pure learning experience, unsullied by contact with philistine matters such as earning a living. There was a characteristic quality of timelessness in the consciousness of the New Left. One Canadian activist of the sixties mentioned that the realization that the movement had come to an end was signified in his mind by the opening up of a future horizon.

The alienation of the student was primarily an 'anticipatory alienation'[23] and is to be understood as one process which stretched from secondary school through university to professional life. The large classes were the forerunners (and forewarners) of the large firms, the university administration the prototype of the bureaucratic company or ministry.

The students who entered the tertiary educational sector, especially those who attended the 'better schools,' were often indulged materially by their families. They were part of a generation which did not have to worry about the basic wants; they were nourished in the lap of relative luxury. As members of this relatively privileged group, students accepted the values of justice and civil equality as easily and as obviously as they accepted and expected the material comforts of life. Unlike the depression and war generations, which understood the formal character of liberal, democratic values, the new student generation believed in the substantiality of these values, not least because these values had a kind of self-evident substantiality for middle class youth.

In addition, the students of the sixties were held in high esteem by their families and communities. Their parents sought to give them everything denied to previous generations of youth. One of the former student leaders in Ontario expresses this when he says: 'We were valued, and the valedictorian classes were still the leaders of tomorrow ... and ... we were prized by our parents, prized by society that we made it to university.' And there was a promise made to this generation, of which its members were extremely conscious, at least in the abstract. They were literally promised 'the world.' Positions of wealth, power, and prestige but also those of relevance, humanitarian purpose, and social beneficence were to be theirs.[24] But the ticket to the future was not free; there was a price to be paid. University attendance was the way, the diploma or degree the door. Yet the students were discovering that many of the future positions in society which had been promised to them were losing their exclusivity and those occupying them lacked the authority necessary to translate ideas into policy.[25]

Although the baby boom generation was conscious at an early age of its mass character, the first serious taste of this massification was had at the university. Students who had been expecting a first class passage on a luxury liner soon discovered that they were second class passengers on a tramp steamer.[26] The promise which had been made to them had not been kept. A Canadian activist of the sixties refers to this betrayal in this way: 'You know, society promises this, that, and the other thing; by the time you're at university, you're able to start to appreciate the fact, that, in fact, those promises were bankrupt. And you get angry.'[27]

The promise was twofold. On the one hand, the students were promised entry to the old intellectual élite[28] through the credentials obtained from the university. On the other hand, they were promised that the values of liberal democracy would be realized. In other words, the students were told they would be part of a powerful élite which could get to work doing socially relevant deeds. Educated youth experienced the breaking of this promise to them as the breaking of the promise to the whole of society. A former influential Canadian student editor summarizes this general theme as follows:

I think it was a matter of expectations not being met that produced a lot of frustration in the middle classes and lower-upper class, and this to some extent, I guess, grew out of my own experiences, but it applies to many of the people who had gone through high school, gone through public school, growing up in their houses expecting that the lollipop of the world was going to be theirs. And they so totally expected that ... The people who seemed to have control of both the bombs and the lollipops just were not listening, or weren't responding in any sort of concrete way.

The disappointment and frustration expressed by the students were directly related to the experience arising out of the process of massification, the devaluation of the university degree (and its concomitant indispensability), and to the relative deterioration in the conditions of intellectual labour in society. The children of privilege were being herded into the universities, but the universities which welcomed them were rapidly becoming changed institutions. Although the middle class demanded (and received) an expanded system of higher education for its children, the children had to pay a price which appeared to many of them to be too high. These new intellectuals who were pouring out of the universities, degree in hand, were in full revolt against those who had not kept the promise. The older, established intellectual élite simply did not understand the nature of the changes which were occurring. Conservatives who proceeded from the 'idea' of the university to a critique of its reality were never able to fathom the social depths of the convulsions which engulfed the ivory tower. They did not know that the real university was being shaped by real social forces.[29] Liberals such as Clark Kerr were perspicacious enough to sense the inevitability of the changes which were coming (Lipset and Wolin 1965:37; Mehnert 1977:26). But they were powerless to control them; nor did they appreciate the nature of the social determinants which forced the changes which led to the student revolt (Mehnert 1977:31). The student radicals were more perceptive. Seeing that the social base of the ivory tower had been eroded in fact (even before the students raised their fists in revolt), they fought to bring the university into line with its new content. The radical difference between the old and new university and intellectual élite (the 'pure' and the 'massified') is expressed by one of the former radicals who was active in Canada in the early sixties: 'It just didn't feel to us like we, like why we were in school and what we were aiming for was holistic and had integrity and was going to fulfil its promise. I'd been told by people who were students in the fifties that they still very much believed the promises of the post-war years ... We certainly didn't feel, the people I knew didn't feel the profound sense that we were part of the same country that the powerful were part of.'

Again and again the former activists articulated their discontent with the university and society: the people who had the say were not listening to them; they were kept from making decisions by the people who had control over both the 'bombs and the lollipops'; the authorities had failed to solve society's problems and the students had the solution but not the power to effect it. If it is true that people's thoughts and feelings are in some way expressions of their own experiences, then it is legitimate to conclude that the student activists were responding both to the transformation of the universities from traditional, status-conscious institutions into modern multiversities, sensitive to the wants of industry and the military, and to the universities' own increasingly important role as gate-keepers of middle class mobility and security.

Thus the student revolt of the sixties is to be understood as occurring not in spite of history, but because of it. Its material roots have been uncovered.

PART TWO: HISTORY

SUPPORT
OUR BOYS

IN VIETNAM

NO MORE DRAFT

NEW
MOBILIZATION
85
Calder

WOMENS LIBERATION

LOOK
WHAT MR. CHARLIE
HAS DONE TO YOUR
MIND

3

A short history of the student revolt

Bearing witness and moral protest

Although students in the United States had involved themselves directly in demonstrations against the House Un-American Activities Committee and against capital punishment (the Caryl Chessman execution) early in 1960 (Bacciocco 1974), the pre-history of the student revolt in each of the three countries lies with the peace campaigns of the late fifties. Although relatively little has been written on the relationship between the 'ban-the-bomb' movement and the rise of student activism in the sixties, the influence of these peace groups on the early New Left activists had been enormous (Metzenberg 1978; Vickers 1975). The moral imperatives of pacifism and direct action tactics, the antitheoretical simplicity of 'antipolitics,' the self-certainty of right action which had attained the fixity of a quasi-religious conviction made an indelible impression upon a small but growing section of the affluent student bodies at the universities in Canada, the FRG, and the United States.

In the mid-fifties the FRG hosted mass demonstrations against the introduction of nuclear weapons on German soil after the Americans had indicated that they were interested in equipping their NATO allies with a tactical nuclear capability. In 1956, the Kampfbund gegen Atomschäden was founded with the support of intellectuals from across the country. In 1958 the influential Kampf dem Atomtod (KdA) was activated and encouraged by the support of the SPD, the Freie Demokratische Partei (FDP), and the Deutsche Gewerkschaftsbund (DGB), even though severe electoral losses suffered by the Social Democrats the following year forced them to dampen their enthusiasm for nuclear disarmament. (Without the support of the SPD, the campaign collapsed.) But the tide would not be turned. Following the example set by the Easter March for Peace organized by the British Campaign for Nuclear Disarmament (CND), the remains of the KDA along with sundry pacifist, religious, and youth organizations planned and executed their first Easter march in 1960. Each year the march grew in size, achieving its greatest success in 1968. This Ostermarschbewegung was a coalition which held together during most of the decade, through a number of organizational metamorphoses (Kampagne für Abrüstung, Kampagne für Abrüstung and Demokratie). In large measure it was supported by German university students and it consistently increased its support within this constituency throughout the decade (Otto 1977).

In the United States a similar manifestation of sentiment against the arms race was making an appearance. Various pacifist groups such as the War Resisters League, the Fellowship of Reconciliation, and the American Friends Service Committee had become active in the forefront of this struggle. Some of their members, inspired by the philosophy of non-violence preached by Mahatma Gandhi promoted and took part in acts of civil disobedience to further the cause. In 1957 the Committee for a SANE Nuclear Policy (SANE) was formed by leading liberal intellectuals and political figures. The student SANE group was strong and influential in New York City, where it attracted university students many of whom were reared in a left-wing environment. It was, however, a Chicago-based group, the Student Peace Union (SPU), which came to exercise a kind of hegemony over the university-centered peace organizations.

Canadian students were also being mobilized around the peace issue. Intellectuals, scientists, liberals, and socialists had formed the Committee for the Control of Radiation Hazards, which in turn led to the founding of the Canadian Campaign for Nuclear Disarmament in 1959. In that same year the first chapters of CUCND were formed in Montreal and Toronto, and chapters were soon started at other universities. In Montreal the influential journal *Our Generation Against Nuclear War* was founded by the CUCND branch there. It soon enjoyed an international reputation and won the respect of the 'adult' movement. Through the journal Canadian students controlled a formidable instrument for influencing the theory, strategy, and tactics of the movement internationally.

The participation of university students in these 'adult' movements was extremely limited. The vast majority of students were untouched by the peace campaign. And yet, the principles and the ethos which were to support the university rebellion of the middle and late sixties were first developed within the framework of the 'ban-the-bomb' movement. At the centre of the proto-New Left world view was the supremacy of the common welfare over partial interests, of humanity over politics, in short, of good over evil. Furthermore, each individual participant was charged not only with the moral responsibility for the well-being of the human race but with the duty to engage in protest in order to effect those changes demanded by moral law. In this sense the protest of the late fifties and early sixties differed from the protest of earlier socialist movements which appealed to material, class-specific interests. It would be wrong to suggest that the 'peaceniks' were involved in the movement only to save themselves from nuclear annihilation. Rather, the movement assumed the proportions of a crusade which was to teach people to 'speak truth to power.' To be sure, students who were active in socialist organizations as well as in the anti-bomb campaign may have had an appreciation of the real economic and political questions involved in the issues. Yet it was clearly the moral, individualist appeal, the activism, the unadulterated humanism which began to fire the soul of the younger generation. Characteristically, youth accepted the professed goals of liberalism; it was the apparent disjunction between the rhetoric of liberalism and the reality of the society of capital which the early New Left recognized as its own concern. Society was not living up to its 'promise,' to the promise which it was thought to have made to the generation of the New Left.[1]

We have already seen that the former German student activists acutely experienced the disjunction between American political rhetoric and the 'racist' and 'imperialist' (civil rights and Vietnam) reality because of the central role which the United States played in Germany after 1945. Former student activists in America and Canada indicated that they experienced this disjunction directly. One former Canadian student radical active during the early and middle sixties analysed the situation then as follows: 'Most of the people in the New Left that I knew, they were sort of middle-class kids who'd been brought up to believe in decency, and they'd been brought up to believe in equality, and they'd been brought up to believe in all these ideas. They began to find that these ideas were being violated all around them, and this was wrong. And, being good Protestants, they proceeded to go out and do something about it.'

This sentiment is echoed by another former Canadian activist: 'The

contradictions between how we were told it worked and how we saw it
work were really quite profound. And the contradiction between our
experience of how it worked and how we were told it should work was
exactly what made us political.'

The following words of a former American activist are representative
of those of her fellows:

I have a sense from talking with other sds people that my personal experience is
shared a lot. For me it was growing up with middle-class liberal parents, and
with a whole bunch of liberal ideals about how the world ought to be, and that
included people being equal and not fucking over people. Then I got out in the
real world with high school, junior high, and started realizing that there was a
real world, and it wasn't what my parents said it was, or ought to be. And for a
number of years I kind of just was really shook up with that.

Another American spoke of the impact which Third World movements had upon those students who had experienced this disjunction
between their nation's ideals and the reality of their country: 'And then
there were liberation movements happening around the world, after the
Second World War. And all of those things affected white students in a
heavy way; and again it had to do with watching other people assert and
define themselves. It had to do with the blowing apart of the myth of
what America was.'

The development of the New Left ran a different course in each of the
three countries. Although the campaigns for nuclear disarmament
played an important role in the rise of student activism in the sixties in
all three, it did not play the same role in each. Only in Canada did the
New Left directly and unequivocally grow out of the movement against
the bomb led by the CND/CUCND.[2] In the United States it developed out of
an alliance forged between radical pacifism and civil rights in a number
of different but overlapping organizations such as the SPU, the Student
Nonviolent Coordinating Committee (SNCC), and last but not least, the
SDS, the organization which after 1965 (rightly or wrongly) came to
stand for the entire movement. In Germany the new radicalism was
shaped at the universities by the SDS, the student organization of the SPD
until it was expelled by the latter in 1960.[3] Not unexpectedly, the
German students were closer to the socialist tradition than their
counterparts in Canada or the United States.

In the United States, the ban-the-bomb movement was killed off by
the Cuban missile crisis on the one hand and replaced by the civil rights

movement as the focus of struggle on and off the campuses on the other. The CUCND never recovered from the loss of the 'nuclear election' which saw the defeat of the ruling Progressive Conservative government (which to that point had refused to import nuclear warheads for BOMARC missiles stationed in Canada) by the Liberal Party headed by Nobel Peace Prize winner Lester B. Pearson, who eventually bowed to American pressure and accepted the atomic warheads. Unlike the situation in Canada and the United States, the German peace movement grew steadily through the decade, separately from but parallel to the SDS. Together, and in union with other such organizations, they constituted the core of the Ausserparlamentarische Opposition (APO) – the extraparliamentary opposition.[4]

The bridge between the American peace movement and civil rights had already been made in the fifties. The Congress for Racial Equality (CORE) and the Southern Christian Leadership Conference (SCLC) were inspired in part by the theories of non-violence espoused and above all practised by pacifist groups. But it was the civil rights struggle which went to the heart of the moral conscience of the white, middle class university generation of America.[5] From 1 February 1960, with the heroic beginning of the sit-ins and freedom rides, through the voter registration drives and community organizing projects, culminating in the Mississippi Freedom Summer of 1964, civil rights activities had become the political focus for tens of thousands of university students. Civil rights was the 'ideal' cause of the New Left. Not only was it a principle which was enshrined in the US Constitution and in the formally espoused public traditions of the country, especially as they were received after World War II, but it was a concept anchored in natural law and morality which for that generation had attained the fixity of a popular prejudice. Second, it was a clear-cut issue. There was right on the one side, wrong on the other. Third, there was something which each individual could do to register a protest and work for change. Finally, it provided the means of expression for a generation of university students to assert itself (vicariously at first, to be sure) in accordance with its own character, formed under new and different conditions.[6]

If the initial period of growth of the student movement (1960–4) in Canada developed within the single-issue mould of nuclear disarmament, and in the United States primarily through peace campaigns and involvement in civil rights actions, the German students were discovering (or inventing) the 'new' politics in their own way. The key to the student revolt of the sixties in Germany lies with the developments at the FU in West Berlin. Formed in response to student protests against restrictions imposed by officials of the old Humboldt University in the Soviet-occupied sector of the city, the FU was known as a 'community of teachers and learners' throughout the FRG, for students were accorded the right to be involved in decisions affecting the operation of the university. This 'Berlin model' was perceived as one of great liberality. Along with those young men of conscriptable age who sought to avoid military service legally by moving to Berlin, the FU attracted students who preferred the openness of its innovative structure. In the fifties and early sixties the students at the FU were militantly anticommunist, and they were continually engaged in heated political debate with well-schooled students from the GDR (that is, until August 1961). If German conservatives are right about the fact that the 'Marxism' of the SDS was imported from the East, then it is true only in the sense that the students at the FU were forced to familiarize themselves with the classical texts cited by the East German students in order to refute them.[7]

Between 1960 and 1964 the German student population as a whole and the students at the FU in particular experienced a series of shocks. For one, the students came face to face with Germany's recent past, many of them for the first time, as an outbreak of swastika smearings spread across the country in 1960. An SDS display portraying the complicity of a number of practising lawyers and judges active in civil life during the Nazi regime led many students to question the extent of the denazification of the country after the war. The construction of a wall around West Berlin in August 1961, which sealed off the western sector from the GDR, was looked upon by many students as an act of betrayal, not by the Russians and East Germans, who were obviously the 'enemy,' but by the Americans, and even the Adenauer government in Bonn. But it was the 'truth' about the real situation of the students at the FU which set them against the status quo. They were given the right to make political decisions when those decisions were in general agreement with state policy (for example, protesting against the GDR), but were forbidden to engage in political action critical of government policy or that of the allied protective powers.[8]

The stirrings of the new student generation in the first half of the 'radical' decade in all three countries were 'radical' in their expression but most definitely not revolutionary in their aims. The essence of the early New Left critique has already been characterized as the recurrent and central concern with the disjunction between the values held by society and the nature of that social reality.[9] It is not the case that the early student radicals were opponents of the ideals of the social order; they were in fact among their most ardent supporters. The demand made upon the democratic order was no more than for the realization of the principles of democracy. Concretely, they were calling society to task for breaking the promise they believed it had made to them. Understanding this promise and the significance of its remaining unfulfilled in the eyes of the student generation is a necessary element in the analysis of the student revolt.

Radical politics 1964–7

The next period in the development of the student movement is ushered in with the Berkeley Free Speech Movement (FSM) in the fall of 1964 and ends with the murder of Benno Ohnesorg in an alley behind the German Opera in West Berlin on 2 June 1967. During this period the student movement attained its mass character. In the early years the activism of the small minority did not make a great impact upon the vast majority of students. However, this transformation period witnessed the development of a sentiment of solidarity among the younger generation in general, and students in particular.

The Berkeley FSM represented both the beginning of an international attack upon the traditional structure and values of the university in the Western world and a protest against those changes which were in motion. It was an attempt to defend and advance the cause of 'democracy,' but at the same time an effort to make the university relevant to the wants of society, or rather of society reformed according to the liberal values cherished by the students.[10] There was a consciousness of the 'oppressiveness' of the system, the 'irrationality' of bureaucratic rationality, the philistine control of the market over knowledge and art. The university had been pulled from the clouds. The ivory tower had been scaled by the baby boom generation, and there was no return from there. But the university which was emerging both in theory and in reality was just as unacceptable to the new student generation as the 'semifeudal' élitist university had been.[11] Caught in the change between the two 'realities' of the university, traditionalist and futuristic, the students were propelled into a revolt against history.

We have seen that the political form of student activism in the sixties was rooted in the pacifist organizations of the fifties and in the growing civil rights struggle of the same period in the United States. But with the growth of the student movement the cultural influences which were exerted upon it and which it in turn exerted upon its surroundings, in particular upon the university, became more and more a topic of popular interest and a centre of public attention. In every country students adopted a style of dress, a sexual code, private jargon, in general a 'life-style,' which not only differed from those of 'straight' society (indeed from the very earliest days of the European universities students were distinguished from the rest of society in such ways) but in addition could not help but provoke the older generation (especially the older 'working class' members of it). The students proclaimed as their cultural heroes, during the first phase of the movement, members of the literary and artistic avant-garde of the fifties. To be sure, a sizeable number of these 'beatnik' intellectuals and 'angry young men' became involved in peace and civil rights actions and constituted part of the first wave of Vietnam War protesters. The CND was continually defending itself against charges that it was a centre of attraction for bohemians, non-conformists, and immoral and licentious misfits of every description.[12] (This charge supplemented the primordial one of pro-communism.)

During the latter half of the decade the Vietnam protesters were portrayed in the popular press as hippies, freaks, drug addicts, and outside agitators. The spread of the counter-culture was not confined to the university, although the campuses soon became a visible stronghold of it, as one might have suspected. In all three countries it was a development which occurred in the big cities: Toronto and Montreal, New York and San Francisco, Berlin and Munich. As the modern manifestation of bohemia, it sought 'authenticity' and a freedom of self-expression which was unconfined by the conventionalities of 'bourgeois' society. The counter-culture counterposed its own values to the values of society: *l'art pour l'art* as opposed to art as a matter of commerce; beauty and truth as opposed to self-interest and bourgeois practicality; free sexuality as opposed to bourgeois hypocrisy; authenticity as opposed to philistinism.[13] But whereas bohemia in the past had shut itself away from the larger society and had located itself in those areas of the cities in which the outcasts of society, the ne'er-do-wells of the lumpenproletariat, were housed, the new bohemia reached out to middle class youth and seized hold of it even in the middle of suburbia. Just as Luther had turned the world into a monastery (Weber 1958), so did the counter-culture turn the world of middle class youth into bohemia. Bohemia had come out of the closet. So pervasive was the evidence of a cultural revolution of youth in the sixties that contemporary observers such as Theodore Roszak (1969) and Charles Reich (1970) thought of it as the most significant force in modern history.

In North America the political and cultural forms of revolt grew separately but symbiotically. At first the cultural revolt was confined to music, art, and literature, but it quickly went over to styles of dress, language, and sexual morality. It was to a large extent influenced by Negro-American culture, which had been 'discovered' by white middle class students during their involvement with the civil rights struggle. In the FRG it first developed in Munich among a small group of artists associated with the Situationist International and it later spread to West Berlin, where it formed a tendency within SDS known as the Kommunebewegung (Commune Movement; Böckelmann and Nagel 1976; Fichter and Lönnendoncker 1977). But even in Germany the cultural revolt was not confined to any one organization but diffused throughout society. It was at first carried by middle class youth before it penetrated the general consciousness through the popular media. Yet in all these countries the counter-culture became a storm centre which the student movement could not weather. The rise of 'Old Left' style vanguard parties and proto-parties was characterized by a rejection of the counter-culture, even though the majority of such groups, following the then current 'Chinese model,' believed in the importance of cultural revolution.

The transformation of the student movement from a small, moralistic, altruistic grouping of concerned youth into ideological, militant, anticapitalist, anti-imperialist concentrations was accomplished during the years 1965–7. There were three general conditions which apparently undergirded the metamorphosis of the movement during the transition years: the defeat of the liberal civil rights movement by the inertia of tradition in white society and by the revolt of black separatist radicals (and the subsequent expulsion of white youth from the ranks of the formerly integrated movement); the escalation of the war in Vietnam; and the rise of student syndicalism and the growth of the student power movement.

The civil rights movement in the United States exerted a powerful influence upon students in Canada and Germany. In Canada the members of SUPA, under the sway of the Toronto branch, adopted the rhetoric of the civil rights struggle and the strategy of community organizing established by the American SDS under its Economic Research and Action Project (ERAP). The Canadians had read and later distributed such SDS pamphlets as *The Port Huron Statement, America and the New Era*, and *An Interracial Movement of the Poor?* SUPA was plugged into the REP distributing system and in fact most of the literature which it sold at its literature tables originated in the United States. At the same time personal contacts between the two national organizations were friendly but limited. One leading SDS figure spent a considerable amount of time working in the SUPA office in Toronto, and at least two SUPA activists spent time with the SDS in the United States. But in spite of the American 'domination' of the movement, the judgement advanced by Jim Laxer (1969, 1970), a marginal New Left leader who in the seventies was to lead the 'left wing' of the New Democratic Party in an unsuccessful bid for the party leadership (Resnick 1977), that the Canadian movement was to a great extent an American import is surely an exaggeration. In fact, as we have already seen, the activities of the Canadians and Americans in community organizing, in civil rights, and in 'helping the poor to help themselves' were based upon similar conditions which confronted middle class youth in both countries. The failure of the projects in both countries is related to much larger social and economic forces which doomed the attempt before it started.[14]

The German students, too, were keenly aware of the efforts of their American counterparts on behalf of underprivileged and dispossessed groups.[15] On account of the denazification and re-education programs conducted under the auspices of the occupying forces in the late forties, German youth were made painfully aware of the differences between the 'totalitarianism' of their parents and the 'democracy' of the United States. Students in West Germany could not but be interested in the apparently hypocritical actions of the Americans with respect to the questions of human rights and civil equality. It is not unfair to say that the disjunction experienced by the American students concerning the rhetoric and reality of 'corporate liberalism' was felt by German students not about their own but about American society. A former leader of the German SDS expresses the concerns of his fellows when he says: 'Totalitarianism means: concentration camps, killing people, aggression against nations, gassing Jews. Democracy means: the guarantee against all this happening. And Vietnam showed us that things weren't this simple. A democratically constituted society such as the American had within itself vehement racial conflicts and it threw itself into an imperialist colonial war in South-east Asia which equalled the deeds of the German Reich under Hitler.'

The end of the civil rights movement and the advent of 'black power' signalled the first great defeat of the white student movement in the United States. In every interview I conducted with former American student activists who had been active before 1965, the shock, confusion, and pain surrounding their expulsion from SNCC and other civil rights groups was unambiguously and emotionally expressed. And the blow was all the more telling since the expulsion corresponded with the decline of ERAP, the only cushion which populism had in the white movement. At the same time fresh blood was pouring into the organization (that is, after April 1965). It was during this period that the formal break with the League for Industrial Democracy (LID), the 'parent' group of SDS, occurred. More ominously, the Progressive Labor Party (PLP) began to infiltrate the ranks of SDS (the PLP was constituted in April 1965 by leaders of the Progressive Labor Movement, which had been founded by a group of young people who had been expelled from the Communist Party USA for their adherence to the Chinese line; Jacobs and Landau 1966:43–8; Newfield 1977:109–24; Sale 1974).

The decline of civil rights as an area of focus for the student movement created a vacuum at the centre of it. However, the rising crescendo of American involvement in the war in Vietnam was accompanied by a growing protest movement against that involvement throughout the world. During this period of the transformation of the student movement (1965–7) the centre of the antiwar movement was located in the universities. Only at the end of this phase of the movement did the leadership of the antiwar forces begin to shift towards the liberal establishment.

There is no question that the politicization of hundreds of thousands of university students (perhaps millions globally) occurred over the issue of the Vietnam war. A former member of the secretariat of CUS commented upon the importance of the war as follows: 'If there had not been a war in Vietnam, I don't think you would have had a student movement with the characteristics and quality it had. I don't think that you would have had a group of people who moved from protest and peaceful and law-abiding assembly to some kind of existential, personal, whatever name you want to give it, refusal to go along with the way that society was going.'

The war was an issue which was substantial, at least in the United States, and symbolic everywhere. Young Americans were being drafted to serve in a war whose aims were not clear to them and whose assumption (that is, the containment of communism) was being questioned in practice by the penetration of the 'Iron Curtain' by the multinationals and the corresponding growth in a *de facto détente* (Goldman 1975; Levinson n d). With the escalation of the war, the '2s' deferment held by American students was losing its effectiveness in warding off conscription.[16] Here, then, was an issue which united the altruism of the movement with the egoistic concerns of the mass of male students. To the abstract mental and spiritual oppression of the 'system' the war added the concrete fear of military conscription and the physical danger of combat. This new threat to male students, it should be emphasized, was not new to the poor white and poor black youth. The antiwar movement gained momentum only when white middle class youth became directly concerned. Since most of them were in post-secondary schools, the natural centre of antiwar activities, at least at first, was located there.[17]

Opposition to the war at Canadian and German universities was different in character from that in the United States. The Canadians sought to establish the connection between Canadian corporations and institutions and the American war effort and to protest against this 'complicity.' The Germans were able to stress the similarities between their own past and the American present without great difficulty. When the good burghers of Berlin, including the social democratic workers of that city, answered the march of the leftist students against the war with a mammoth rally in support of the American effort in South-east Asia, the students were forced into a position of having to attack the 'bourgeois' Springer newspapers for spreading false information and misleading the masses. In all three countries, however, the war provided the background for the development of the 'anti-imperialist' analysis which expressed the ideological turn of leading elements within the student movement away from the liberal goals which they previously espoused to an immanent 'scientific' critique of capitalist society. At this time Marxism in various guises began to command the attention of wider circles within the student movement, although the Germans, for historical reasons, had always been conscious of the influence and importance of Marxism, especially in its new philosophical garb.[18]

'Revolution' and fragmentation 1967–70

The student movement in all three countries was faced with a basic problem which it was never able to overcome: the isolation of the university. The history of the New Left is the chronicle of the pendulum-like movement out of the campus and back to the campus. Yet each time a swing had been completed, the ante was raised and the next outward movement began. One line of development, for example, could be characterized by the following: free speech on campus → antiwar demonstrations → the fight against imperialist ideas in the classroom. The successive defeats and partial victories experienced by the students in society and the general antipathy of the working population continually forced the movement back to the campus. But each time, upon its return, the political struggle became invested with more and more importance until campus politics became in the eyes of those students the centre of the world-historical struggle (Mehnert 1977:218).

Originally this form of campus politics grew out of the concerns of student syndicalism, which was developed in Germany in the early sixties by SDS and the Verband Deutscher Studentenschaften (VDS), in Canada by the Union générale des étudiants du Québec (UGEQ) and then by the CUS in the middle of the decade, and somewhat belatedly by the National Student Association (NSA) and SDS in the United States around 1967. Student syndicalism had been concerned primarily with the material conditions of student life, especially with the schemes of financial assistance offered by the state in support of students.[19] But the issue of university structure and control was also raised in the sixties, and student syndicalism became a force for student power at all levels of the university – department, faculty, administration. The university was understood as an institution governed by the corporate élite (America and Canada) or by officers of the state (Germany) in the interest of the ruling class. And it was only the power of the students which stood between the agents of the ruling class and the virginity of the university.

Nineteen sixty-eight is the year which is remembered as the year of the student radical, the year of the barricades: the Tet offensive, the bombing of North Vietnam, the uprising at Columbia University, the 'Prague Spring,' the May revolt in France, the Russian (and Warsaw Pact) invasion of Czechoslovakia, the 'Czechago' Convention of the Democratic Party, the assassination attempt on Rudi Dutschke. It was also the year of the movement personalities: Mark Rudd, Danny the Red, Abby Hoffman, Jerry Rubin.[20] The counter-culture exploded and sent its spores into every corner of the world – they were borne not by the wind but by international commerce. American hippies slept with

Dutch provos in the squares of Amsterdam. But above all 1968 is remembered for violence, threatened and actual, which marked the last phase of the student movement. For many of the 'old guard' who did not survive the transformation from liberalism to anti-imperialism, the new turn towards violence was incomprehensible, perplexing, and disquieting. (In Germany, the 'generational' differences within the movement did not appear to be as great as in North America.)

Although 1968 has been portrayed in the media as the zenith of the student movement, the fact of the matter is that it was in a serious decline by then. Its inability to make any impact either upon the centres of power or upon any actual 'revolutionary agent' in society at large (those in the movement will recall the endless debates about the revolutionary subject) led to the social construction of a fantastic reality which was contested by various factions within the movement. Generally, the various radical student groupings in each country could be characterized in two ways. First, the antiauthoritarian groups were the true heirs of the early spirit of the movement. They tended to be drawn into youth politics, the counter-culture; they adhered to some variant of the theory of the new working class; they favoured liberal sexuality and generally distrusted rigid organizational forms. They also tended to be pacifistic in orientation, although not all such groups shared this view. Second, there were the vanguard parties, proto-parties, and tendencies vying with one another for a larger share of a diminishing market. In Canada the vanguardists tended to be the newer recruits of the student movement.[21] In the United States SDS split into three organized factions, all of them vanguardist, even though most of the rank-and-file members were only marginally involved in these esoteric and abstract debates which raged between the factions at the national conventions and on the campuses. The members for the most part were still loyal to the youth politics and counter-culture of the New Left, and they were thus estranged from the quarrels at the top. In Germany the antiauthoritarians who remained became part of the so-called *Basisgruppen*, which organized a movement out of the universities into the factories to learn from and to help organize the proletariat. For many it was their last foray into society from the ivory tower. Others joined in the attempts to found parties or proto-parties (Kukuck 1974; Langguth 1976), most of which were influenced by ideological Maoism, and some of which were emphatically Stalinist. Still others were picked up by the pro-Soviet Deutsche Kommunistische Partei (DKP).[22] Some few identified with local 'anarchist' groups, and a much smaller number came under the influence of the Rote Armee Fraktion (RAF), the so-called Baader-Meinhof Gang. At the national level, the Sozialistisches Büro (SB) was formed in April 1969 out of the remains of the Kampagne für Abrüstung und Demokratie, and it sought to provide a focus for those who were not affiliated with a party and who did not wish to be affiliated with a party. Some of the antiauthoritarian students went over to the SB.

It is difficult to assign a date to the end of the student movement. Some have argued that it was dying in 1968 and that the events of May were really its death throes. Others have suggested that the movement continued to have an impact upon the student generation into the early seventies, long after its organizational centres had been dissolved. There are points to be made for both extremes and for even finer distinctions which have been drawn in different countries. One should only recall here that SDS began visibly to crack open at the 1968 national convention in East Lansing, Michigan, and that it effectively blew itself apart at the Chicago convention of 1969. In Canada SUPA, which had gone into receivership in 1967, was being liquidated by a shadowy New Left Committee which was established precisely for this purpose. In this year the action shifted to CUS and CUP, both of which by that time had been 'captured' by New Left leadership people. However, a grassroots backlash occurred on the campuses, and by 1969 many schools held referenda on continuing membership in CUS. Local campus radical groups at this time began to question the top-down character of CUS' 'radical' politics, and many refused to support the national organization during the referenda campaigns. In Germany the SDS, racked with dissension and conflict, formally disbanded on 1 March 1970 at a 'convention' in Frankfurt. Not one representative from West Berlin was present. For the German student movement, at least, the following adage proved to be true: As West Berlin goes, so goes the country.

PART THREE: ANALYSIS

4

The esoteric history of the student revolt

The empirical, analytical, and theoretical literature on the student revolt of the sixties is so vast and heterogeneous in orientation that recent reviews of it have developed different categorial schemes for organizing their presentations. Michael Useem (1975) has ordered explanatory theories of social movements in general under three categories: structural-functional, social-psychological, and political-economic. David Westby (1976) has derived a somewhat different categorial system for organizing theories of the student movement in the sixties: psychological, functionalist-mass pluralist, and left-institutional. In a recent review of the literature Levin and Spiegel have discerned three phases of research on the student revolt, organizing this literature according to broad chronological, rather than purely logical, categories:

Representative samples from the literature, which is simply too vast to review in total, may convey the changing interest among researchers and writers: an initial preoccupation with the question of who the students were, then a predominating interest in the issues, in what the students were really protesting about; eventually, a greater and probably more sophisticated interest in questions of process and response, and finally a search for what it meant and what it may portend. (1979:24)

They also suggest that the literature can be dichotomized in the following way: 'those charging pathology in the students ... and those charging pathology in the environment, to which the students were reacting' (1979:23–4).[1]

In the German context, Margareth Kukuck (1974) has reviewed the various left-wing theories about the student movement. She classifies them as: an expression of the frictions resulting from the real subsumption of science under capital (Kanzow and Roth 1971; Roth 1970:37–45); a petty bourgeois defensive movement (Schmierer 1969:5–14; 1970:29–36); a petty bourgeois democratic movement (Bauss 1974:11–20; Buscher and Heinemann 1974:3–10; Lehndorff 1974:6–46; Priewe 1974:52–62; Schnibben 1974:45–53); a movement of the certified (*diplomierten*) petty bourgeoisie (Keller and Vahrenkamp 1974:38–43, 47–52).

A comprehensive review of the literature will not be attempted in this work. But certain theoretical approaches deserve to be considered here in so far as they have a bearing upon our analysis.

The industrialization of higher education

Michael Miles (1971, 1977) sees the industrialization of higher education[2] as the key to the development of the student movement in the United States. Elite students reacted with shock to this industrialization process, and the struggle for student power was their form of protest against it. In addition, future career prospects were uncertain as a growing 'proletarianization' of the new educated middle class was becoming evident to the élite students. But if this is true why did these élite students not act overtly in defence of their privilege against the possibility of 'proletarianization'? Why did the shock of experiencing the reality of industrialized education lead not to the reaffirmation of élite status but to the radical-democratic demands of student power and later to the revolutionary visions of Marxism or Marxism-Leninism? Furthermore, why did the movement disintegrate at a time in which economic prospects were worsening for the students when the 'proletarianization' of the new middle class was, if anything, accelerating?[3] Miles is indeed right in pointing to the loss of privilege suffered by the students both at the university and in their future careers. But he has not understood that the loss of privilege was relative and not absolute. We are not dealing with an élite which was threatened with 'proletarianization' but with the changing character of the educated élite itself. If Miles had begun his analysis with changing economic conditions, the transformation of middle class reproduction,[4] and the shifting social role of the university and proceeded from there to show how the political, cultural, and ideological conflict of the sixties developed as a result (in his book the ideological dimension is treated first), he might have been able to fathom the movement's truly ambivalent character.

If Miles confounded the changing character of privilege with 'proletarianization,' Christopher Lasch (1978), in a provocative work, has described the relative diminution of privilege in the sixties. In the schools, for example, the attempt to democratize education has led to the erosion of standards and 'has ended by stupefying the privileged themselves' (127).[5] Those educated in the humanities and social sciences have become increasingly marginalized 'as part of the operation of social control.' And now we are faced with the strange situation in which a debased university education is rapidly becoming a 'privilege' of the affluent.

Furthermore, Lasch demonstrates that, on issues of peace and educational reform, certain elements within the New Left advanced an élitist assertion of privilege, in the form of antiprivilege. For example, student exemption from military service, guaranteed by the Selective Service Act of 1951, ensured a privileged position for socially advantaged youth at the expense of poor and 'unassimilated' minority youth: 'The system of academic deferment, when combined with educational reforms designed to recruit a scientific and technical elite, created a national system of manpower selection in which minorities and the poor provided recruits for a vast peacetime army, while the middle class, eager to escape military service, attended college in unprecedented numbers' (Lasch 1978:139–40).

Or, if we consider the progressivist attack upon education led by New Leftists and their allies, it is easy to see that it ran counter to the wishes of many black and minority parents who were seeking basic, career-oriented education for their children: 'The attempt to revive basic education, on the part of black parents and other minorities, cut across the grain of educational experimentation – the open classroom, the school without walls, the attempt to promote spontaneity, to undermine the authoritarianism rampant in the classroom, etc' (Lasch 1978:143). And even the core demands of student power in the sixties can be viewed as cries for special consideration: 'The demand for more "relevant" courses often boiled down to a desire for an intellectually undemanding curriculum in which students could win academic credits for political activism, self-expression, transcendental meditation, encounter therapy, and the study and practice of witchcraft' (Lasch 1978:148–9).

It is indeed unfortunate, even though Lasch did not set out to analyse the rise and fall of student activism, that he did not bring his insight to bear upon his treatment of the movement. When he does concern himself with the New Left, he portrays it arising out of a 'fatal conjunction of historical changes' which are abstract and subjective, and detached from their socio-historical context. For Lasch the motor force appears to be that of 'social conscience,' 'moral rhetoric,' and the 'collapse of moral and intellectual legitimacy.'

The New Left and the new class

In the seventies and early eighties much has been written about the 'new class' by neo-conservatives and neo-Marxists alike.[6] Whereas the latter have been trying to find a place for intellectuals in the socialist movement, the neo-conservatives view the neo-Marxists as conceited radicals and bearers of an ideology of statism. The theory of the 'new class' has also become the foundation for a number of attempts to explain the rise and fall of the student movement in the sixties.

Irving Kristol (1979:15), for example, explicitly identifies the New Left as the front line of a new class which has moved into specific areas of professional life: 'This "new class" consists of scientists, lawyers, city planners, social workers, educators, criminologists, sociologists, public health doctors, etc – a substantial number of whom find their careers in the expanding public sector rather than the private.' Members of this new class are highly trained and generally well-paid professionals and as a class have the most 'radical' political perspective of any group in society. For Kristol, mass higher education was responsible for trans-forming Old Left élitism into the basis of a mass élitist movement:

The earlier movement had been 'elitist' in fact as well as in intention, ie it was sufficiently small so that, even while influential, it could hardly contemplate the possibility of actually exercising 'power.' Mass higher education has con-verted this movement into something like a mass movement proper, capable of driving a President from office (1968) and nominating its own candidate (1972). The intentions remain 'elitist,' of course; but the movement now encompasses some millions of people. These are the people whom liberal capitalism had sent to college in order to help manage its affluent, highly technological, mildly paternalistic, 'post-industrial' society. (1979:15)

Neo-Marxists have also seen the New Left as a manifestation of the new class, but, unlike the neo-conservatives, they see this class being exploited by capital, dehumanized and alienated in the capitalist production process. For the neo-conservatives, the new 'intellectuals' constitute an élite class, and their leftist ideology is seen as self-serving, extolling the public sector while decrying private enterprise.[7] During the sixties and early seventies many neo-Marxists defended the new working-class theory according to which the new educated 'masses' constitute a proletarian grouping; thus their leftist ideology is seen to be an accurate reflection of their proletarianization.

One of the most recent and controversial neo-Marxist 'new class' theories to be applied to the analysis of the New Left is found in Barbara and John Ehrenreich's celebrated essay 'The Professional-Managerial Class' (1978). They define the PMC 'as consisting of salaried mental workers who do not own the means of production and whose major function in the social division of labor may be described broadly as the reproduction of capitalist culture and capitalist class relations' (1978:12). In this form, it is the new working class transmogrified. The fifties and sixties saw the rapid growth of the PMC and, as its fortunes were on the rise, it felt strong enough to challenge the capitalist class, to regain the autonomy it had relinquished to the capitalists (Ehrenreich and Ehrenreich 1978:31). The New Left student movement was part of this PMC counter-attack. However, at the end of the sixties, largely as a result of the threat to PMC interest posed by the black movement for community control, the PMC back-pedalled on its radicalism. The New Left, true to itself, broke with its own class: 'In identifying with the community control movement, the young PMC radicals were taking a position which ran counter to their own objective class interests' (Ehrenreich and Ehrenreich 1978:36). Concretely, this was given expression in the 'radicals-in-the-professions' movement of the early seventies which sought to demystify the practice of medicine, law, psychiatry, and teaching. 'The rule of the experts would be abolished – by the young experts' (Ehrenreich and Ehrenreich 1978:39). But with the downturn of the economy PMC and state repression was able to break the back of this anti-PMC, antistate radicalism through the accrediting and regulatory agencies which enjoyed a monopoly in the professions. The 'New Communist Movement' – a collective term for the various Marxist-Leninist groups and parties which mushroomed upon the corpse of the New Left – repudiated the anti-PMC theory and practice of the radicals-in-the-professions and returned to a view 'which was superficially not very different from that of the earlier generation of PMC radicals.' Thus the movement back to PMC élitism was also effected by means of Leninist vanguardism.

In spite of the Marxist form in which they frame their argument, the Ehrenreichs have not made much of an advance upon the moralism of the early New Left. We have seen how the movement arose ostensibly as a protest against the disjunction between the values and reality of liberal society. The New Left during its formative period attempted to force the realization of the values generally professed by the official political culture but not realized in fact. The Ehrenreichs recognize this when they draw a direct connection between the radicals-in-the-professions movement of the early seventies and 'the militantly egalitarian SDS and SNCC tradition of "participatory democracy"' (1978:39). But major questions still have to be answered. Why does a social grouping come to act against its own class interests? Why does the protest of part of a relatively privileged class assume the form of a movement against privilege? What interest lies behind the moralism and altruism of such a movement?

The Ehrenreichs have claimed that the PMC radicalism of the sixties was indeed an expression of its material interest – autonomy in the ordering of the cultural and ideological affairs of society (although precisely *how* the peace and civil rights movement in the sixties related to this is not specified by the authors). But what is the material interest of the radical students (and professionals) who broke with the PMC? The answer is – there isn't any. It was ultimately a moral crisis, a crisis of legitimacy which fuelled the moralism of the New Left: 'The moral legitimacy of the university, the older generation of the PMC, and the entire American system were thrown into question' (Ehrenreich and Ehrenreich 1978:34). Their argument boils down to this: the New Left radicals were morally superior to the members of the PMC, who were compromised by their class interests. The Ehrenreichs do make reference to the ambivalence of the New Left (which they typically define in terms of the ambiguity of PMC *consciousness*) as a 'mixture of elitism and anti-capitalist militance.' But what they failed to see in stressing the opposition between élitism and anticapitalism was the intrinsic relation between the two: they failed to see that anticapitalism was precisely the form of the New Left's élitist self-assertion.

The suggestion should not be made that the New Left consciously masked its élitism by means of a radical-democratic ideology. The New Left experience was authentic. But the very authenticity of the New Left was predicated upon its inherent ambivalence; the substance of the movement was élitist, the form radical-democratic.

The Ehrenreichs, as we have seen, considered the rise and fall of the New Left in terms of the vicissitudes of the PMC and its rebellious youth without explaining why the New Left broke with its own class and without seeing that élitism can appear in the guise of its opposite.

Helmut Schelsky (1977), the German sociologist, also viewed the student movement as part of the development of a new class and, as we shall see, understood it to be an élitist movement, asserting its own claim to domination through universalistic and democratic forms.

For Schelsky, class conflict in contemporary society no longer occurs between the owners and managers of the means of production and the working class, but between the class of the producers of meaning (*Sinnproduzenten*) and those dependent on it. This new class of meaning producers originates as a result of the rapid growth in importance of information, communication, science, teaching, and training in modern society. These vitally important functions are monopolized by the new class, which sets forth its claim to social mastery by linking its social and political striving to these new means of domination: 'The fronts of class domination today are not the "possession of the means of production" in the sense of the production of material goods, but rather the "possession of the means of production" in the sense of the production of meaning, of the mastery over the consciousness and norms of a people' (Schelsky 1977:282).

It is important to note that this new class does not base its claim to power on technocratic grounds alone. True, it is made up of the masters of technique. But in addition to possessing the instrumental skills of 'mental production,' it monopolizes the power of defining 'ultimate values' for society and for the individual. This is why Schelsky claims that the new class preaches a 'social religion' which is a powerful instrument in asserting its authority. The new class producers of meaning are the bearers of a secular doctrine of salvation.

According to Schelsky, the transformation of the schools and universities is crucial to the constitution of the new class (1977:154). Before the student rebellion of the sixties the two functions of the university – moral education and professional training – existed in a 'stabilized tension' with one another. But with the massification of higher education in our 'scientific civilization,' the mass training function was detached from the process of cultivation of ethical sensibilities; the latter then fell by the wayside. Or rather the ethical-normative function of the university, which ultimately rested with the clerics of 'other-worldly' religions, was taken over by new class social scientists from within the university. The 'other-worldly' morality of the classical university was replaced by the morality of engagement within the world, that is, by a secular religion: 'The postulates of love of the Christian doctrine of salvation directed at the individual and the concrete group or community underwent a transformation into the abstract realm of a demand for salvation in "the here and now" for an abstract humanity' (Schelsky 1977:113).

This abstract religious movement, with the New Left cutting edge, was a means by which the new class could assert its priestly domination of society. (The student masses were attracted to it because it was tied to good professional positions; it was thus an easy road to social mobility.) Having secured the university by usurping the ethical-normative function, or rather by reshaping it as social and political engagement, the new class used the university as a base to launch a religious 'crusade' against other social institutions over which it sought to extend its dominion.[8]

According to Schelsky, all of this is undertaken in the name of freedom, equality, democracy, and humanity but serves the class ambitions of the conveyors of meaning. They attack the political authority while they scurry to find positions within it (217); they argue on behalf of 'communication free of domination' while using language to serve their own power purposes (323); they seek autonomy for themselves not for protection from power, but to assert their power over others (331); they arrogantly imitate the ways of the working class (language, dress, etc) as a caricature of it in order to dominate it (334–5); they sermonize to the masses about political and economic oppression and alienation in order to advance their own claim to societal leadership (492); they preach about a 'legitimation crisis' while 'guardianship' becomes the legitimating principle of their own claim to domination (497); they expose the privilege of others while clamouring for their own privileges (495); and they seek all the advantages of the system without wanting to pay the price (258; cf Scheuch 1968).

Schelsky believes that students are the ideal missionaries of the new class, for they are free of the attachments, responsibilities, and commitments which those involved in the process of social production (mediate and immediate) have to bear. They can afford to take great risks, to act on utopian visions, for they have little to lose (304). But the students, who lead a relatively privileged existence, cannot confront the authorities with their own grievances which, *sub specie humanitatis*, are trivial. Instead, they advance their cause by means of a 'borrowed misery':

In place of neighbourly Christian love, remote social love is posited, abstract humanism which experiences death on the Huang Ho or in Vietnam more powerfully than the death of the unknown neighbour dying in solitude in the same apartment building ... one can have no sympathy for those who use the misery of the war-plagued Vietnamese as a demonstration of their own claims to religious domination [*Heilsherrschaftsansprüche*] and who care not a jot about their fate as persons; one can have no sympathy for those who, as ideological revolutionaries of South American, Arabian, or African provenance regularly demonstrate with their German confederates in the German universities and market-places against the structure of domination in their own countries and then have no greater ambition than to secure a permanent position with an assured income in German universities or other German institutions. The majority of these demonstrators of 'borrowed misery' in any event come from those strata of our population which know of want and misery only from books or newspapers.

Schelsky has provided a service in showing the intrinsic relation between privilege and antiprivilege, élitism and democracy within the movement of the sixties. At the same time, however, he has made 'meaning' into an immediately active factor in human history, independent of the process of labour and social production.[9] (He seems to suggest that one could separate the 'pure' meaning from meaningful relations.)[10] Furthermore, Schelsky may be right in seeing the Frankfurt School as a new grouping of Young Hegelians, but his hypostatization of meaning lays him open to the same charge. As Marx and Engels pointed out with respect to their Young Hegelian opponents:

In order to put aside the mystical appearance of this 'self-determining concept itself' it is changed into a person – 'self-consciousness' – or, in order to appear truly materialistic, into a series of persons, who represent 'the concept' in history, into the 'thinkers,' the 'philosophers,' the ideologists who are now understood again as the makers of history, as 'the council of guardians,' as the rulers. (Man = the 'thinking human spirit') (Marx and Engels 1969:49)

The difference between Schelsky and the Frankfurt School is not one of substance but one of moral tone, for Schelsky is the opponent of the 'producers of meaning' (the 'thinkers' etc) whereas Adorno, Horkheimer, and Habermas, among others, are their advocates. Schelsky's fate is that of Balaam of old who praised Israel the more, the harder he tried to curse it.[11]

In a recent work Alvin Gouldner has also posited the rise of a new class, a class which is founded upon a common culture of critical discourse (CCD).[12] His basic argument concerning the new class is very similar to Schelsky's, especially concerning the ambivalence of its elements:

The paradox of the New Class is that it is both emancipatory *and* elitist ... The new discourse (CCD) is the grounding for a critique of established forms of domination and provides an escape from tradition, but it also bears the seeds of a new domination ... The new class sets itself above others, holding that its speech is better than theirs; that the examined life (*their* examination) is better than the unexamined life. (1979:85)

But Gouldner's explicit treatment of the New Left in this work does not focus upon the vicissitudes of the new class in general, but upon the university experiences of the children of new class parents. Professors' salaries rose and the demands of research served to reduce the contact between students and faculty. Teaching assistants were overworked and, together with the growing number of graduate students who were doubling as researchers and seminar leaders, began to constitute an academic proletariat. Professors in the humanities did not share in the salary and research boom enjoyed by their colleagues in the social sciences, and their ensuing resentment at this relative deprivation filtered down to their students. The bureaucratization of the university led to fewer personal ties and to a homogenization of the student body, which was more conducive to conflict. New class students who shared in the CCD were also upset with the 'decline of discourse' in the multiversity which they experienced 'as part of the denial of full adult participation.' Expansion of the universities led to both a breakdown of authority on the campus and 'intensified student alienation' (Gouldner 1979:70–3). Gouldner has recapitulated Miles' argument about the industrialization of higher education as the key to the rise of the New Left.

Mediate production, the middle class, and the student revolt

As we have seen, recent theories of the student revolt in the sixties have implicitly and explicitly described the rise of student activism in terms of the development of a new class, in a variety of ways. The theories of the 'new working class,' 'new middle class,' 'professional-managerial class,' 'class of conveyors of meaning,' and the 'class of cultural capitalists' have sought to explain the New Left according to the tenets of their respective views of the class basis of the New Left. The student activism of the sixties was indeed related to the changes in the conditions of reproduction of middle class mobility and maintenance. The term 'middle class,' however, does not refer to a social class in the strict sense but is a rather vague collective designation for those who, by whatever means, occupy the middle position in society with respect to such matters as income, education, and occupation. The 'new class' theorists of the right and of the left have demonstrated a sensitivity to the fact that over the course of the last few decades some profound changes have occurred which affect the way in which this nebulous middle class (or a goodly portion of it) is constituted. They differ among themselves, of course, in the way they explain and assess these changes.

Traditionally Marxists have defined classes in terms of the relations to the means of production (that is, ownership or control, exclusion from ownership or control).[13] Accordingly, in bourgeois society the two classes which stand at the centre of the motor of history are the bourgeoisie (the capitalist class) and the proletariat (the working class). Although other classes do exist in this society, and even though they may play an important role in the class struggles, the historical battle waged between the bourgeoisie and the proletariat is the pivot around which all else ultimately revolves.

Within neo-Marxism competing class theories have been advanced. The confusion about social class has sometimes been attributed to the fact that Marx supposedly only incompletely and unsystematically dealt with social class at the very end of volume 3 of *Capital*.[14] Indeed, the Marxists' preoccupation with class is an expression of the fundamental, if not absolute, position which 'class' holds for them.

Although the formal opposition of the mediate and immediate producers reaches back to the distant past, the rapid growth of the class of mediate producers after World War II has been unprecedented in human history. As we have seen, it was supported by governments, the 'military-industrial complex,' and the middle class, for their own reasons and interests. The euphoria over the advancement of learning, science, and technology was evinced in the popularity of the theory of human capital, the rapid growth of the multiversity, and the confidence of the middle class in higher education. But with the very success of the multiversity as a credentializing institution came the unavoidable consequence: the massification of the educated élite, as described above.

It is, of course, true that the mediate producers, even if they have generally been materially privileged, are substantially part of the class of social labour. Yet the student movement as a movement of potential mediate producers was neither a movement of the class of social labour nor part of such a movement. It was a movement which was genuinely set against the existing forms of privilege. Thus, it should be understood as an expression of the substantial assertion of privilege in the form of its opposite.

The ambivalence of the student movement was only in part that of potential mediate producers. Rather it was rooted in the changing character of privilege facing middle class youth and repotentialized by the relations of student life in the sixties. The theories of class and revolution which emerged directly out of the New Left (youth as class, urban guerrilla terrorism, Marxist-Leninist vanguardism, marginal revolutionaries) are the theoretical expressions of this ambivalent reality.

There is, strictly speaking, no new class, working, middle or other. But the expansion of mediate production during the post-war period brought in its wake a shift in the relation of mediate to immediate production, whereby the former provided a means to relative social privilege for the children of those already relatively privileged. The university was at the centre of this change.[15]

Much has been made of the fact that the student movement was composed of those in the arts and social science faculties, students of theoretical as opposed to practical or professional disciplines, and those with vague career goals (Allerbeck 1973:182; Lipset 1976:87–8; O'Brien 1971b:17; Reid and Reid 1969:3; Westby 1976:114–22; Brzezinski 1968:222 argues that the New Left was led by those who would have no role to play in the coming technological-electronic society). But it was precisely these students who were most subjected to the massification process and the relative loss of privilege. At the same time, there is reason to believe that students in the theoretical, non-professional faculties and disciplines tend to come from relatively more privileged backgrounds on the whole than students in the applied disciplines and professional schools (Lipset 1976:87–8).

The neo-conservatives are thus right in seeing the 'new class' as a socially privileged group, but they are wrong in calling this group a class *sensu stricto*.[16] The theorists of the new working class were right in calling attention to the growth in the number of university-trained intellectual labourers and the differences in the content of their training and the conditions of their eventual employment. At the same time they were wrong in seeing in this 'new working class' the vanguard of the proletarian revolution. This disagreement about the character of the new intellectuals is itself an expression of the ambivalence of the position of the intellectuals in society. The neo-conservatives are the tried and true friends of the private sphere, having made the interest of private capital their own interest, which they tout as the public interest. The neo-Marxists, on the other hand, are the sworn enemies of the status quo, of the market, of capital, and of the state. But the revolt of the left-intellectual is a self-serving act which has as little to do with the transformation to socialism as the revolt of the bohemian artists and poets. It is condemned to be a one-sided response to general social conditions whose central motor lies elsewhere.

Social movement theory applied to the student movement has, for the most part, been concerned with formal and categorial aspects, according the substance a secondary role, if any. The movement is not approached in its specificity, in terms of the actual historical context in which it is situated and out of which it develops; rather, a system of dichotomous categories (for example, violent and non-violent, centralized and diffuse, democratic and authoritarian) is established and the student movement is fed through this categorial meatgrinder. For example, 'structural strain' (Smelser 1962; Westby 1976; Wood 1974; Useem 1975) may be applied analytically not only to the study of social movements but to the phenomena studied by physics, biology, and engineering as well (Marx 1972d:212–13). And the mere existence of generational conflict across time and place gives us little information concerning the specificity of actual historical conflicts.[17]

There are those who will no doubt object to the imputation of a hidden or unconscious social determination of the student revolt of the sixties. They will ask us to take the students at their word: peace and civil rights were the goals, just as the belief in universal human freedom and justice was the true basis of the movement. Without entering into a long theoretical digression, we can raise certain questions. To begin with, why was it this student generation that made these causes of peace, freedom, and social justice its own, not only in theory, but in practice as well? Why did the German university students of the late Weimar Republic actively support the Nazi Party *en masse*? Why did large numbers of British students help break the back of the General Strike of 1926? Why did European students rush to don uniforms and participate in the general slaughter on the battlefields of World War I? To reply that students in the sixties were wiser or more intelligent or had learned their lesson from history is to idealize the capacities of this student generation. Second, the ideological struggles which human beings carry on are expressions of the conditions and relations of their lives in a specific, historically determinate way. The appearance that history is made by the struggle of and for ideas, religious beliefs, and political principles is itself an expression of the real struggles within a particular society.[18] The universal values of human equality and freedom have only arisen in their present form in modern civil society; in both form and content they have made their appearance late in human history (Marx 1972b:73–4; 1973:239–50). Intellectuals who inhabit the world of ideas, a world severed by the division of labour in society from the world of everyday life, can easily assume the mantle of spokesmen for the universal interest of human kind.[19] The New Left was in the first instance not an ideological movement advancing universal ideals; rather, the changing conditions of life of the student generation of the sixties (and the responses to those changing conditions) were expressed in the form of an ideological movement advancing universal ideals.

The present work has its theoretical presuppositions, of course. Matters of form are not separated from substance. The subjective and objective as well as the theoretical and practical moments are developed in their internal relation, not treated as externally related variables. Moreover, ideological matters are not the starting-point of the analysis. Rather, the starting-point is the actual relations of life; then it is shown how they are given ideological expression.[20]

We have been following the changing situation of post-war middle class youth, the changing economic relations of middle class life, and the concomitant changes in the university. In addition, we have considered the essential characteristics of the student movement, which we derived from an admittedly all-too-brief inspection of its historical development. For the most part the objective and subjective sides have been treated in isolation from one another; the subjective cannot be reduced to the objective, for the human order is both subjective and objective. In practice the two cannot exist in separation from one another. The statements made by former student activists are at once expressions of the subjective life of movement members a decade after the decline of the movement itself and, at the same time, a part of the objective record of the legacy of that movement.

Consciousness is not a general quality, either in the human brain or in the mind; consciousness is in the human order, in the world of historically transitory (that is, historically specific) social individuals – in civil society, class-individuals.[21] Here the views and opinions of a group of former student activists are presented as the subjective expression of, and response to, the collective biography of the student movement, and to the generation of youth which supported it. It is true that the activist students, especially during the latter half of the decade, thought about themselves and their role in history in a way which was, apparently, not consonant with what they were or what they were capable of doing. Yet, we have seen why they presented themselves as that which they were not, why privilege paraded around in the guise of its opposite.[22]

Moralism and material conditions

The student movement of the sixties ostensibly began as a critique of the social and political reality of 'liberal, corporate capitalism' from the point of view of liberal democratic (that is, bourgeois) ideals. It continually held up to the older generation the values which it preached but did not practise. The nature of the student critique was not founded at first upon any consideration of *Realpolitik*, upon concrete economic or political analysis, but upon a wholly moral basis. During this early phase of the movement the active students sought to be the protectors of the weak, the defenders of the poor, the great righters of wrongs, in short, the knights errant of the modern age. One of the Canadian participants likened them to Christian penitents who travelled the countryside washing the feet of the poor and downtrodden.

A former leader of SUPA recalls: 'There had been a substantial religious basis to that. That's one thing one does well to recall every once in a while ... Things like the Student Christian Movement, like the Quakers' speaking truth to power, you see. Smith, I think, believed to a degree he could speak truth to bureaucrats, reform the institutions, and then the world would, in fact, be different.'

This moral orientation to the problems of the world determined, to a large degree, the character of New Left organizing and the kind of relationship established between the student activists and their 'clients.' In the words of this SUPA leader:

I think a woman like Betty B. basically felt that the world was pretty hideous, and society was pretty hideous, and one had to do something about that, and you really started to work wherever you could create movement. In fact, I think I can remember her once saying that to me. I remember once arguing with her, I think, about, yes, it was her, about Indians in the Neestow project, and so on, and I said: 'You know,' and I was thinking about the obvious point, 'it doesn't make the least bit of difference what Indians do, they're outside of everything.' 'Yes, that may be true, but at least you can generate some movement there.' There was a kind of sense of, just get something started and something good may come from it.

Another feature of the movement was the strong generational solidarity. This was expressed in such slogans as 'Never trust anyone over thirty' and in the lyrics of Bob Dylan, Phil Ochs, and other troubadours of the New Left and youth culture. There was a new openness to experimentation. Everything handed down from the past was mistrusted, as it appeared to be somehow tainted. A chasm opened up between the world of the middle class youth of the sixties and the world of their parents. This chasm appeared to widen over the course of the decade.

In addition to the moral character of the initial student activism and the intense generational solidarity which was present, it was noted that the student movement itself was extrmely ambivalent both in form and in content.[23] Later in the decade it swung from one extreme to the other – from pacifism, non-violence, and libertarian openness to terror, violence, and authoritarian rigidity. From an apparently altruistic perspective and orientation during the years 1960–4 it moved, during the middle years of the decade, to an apparent egoism which became a central feature of its political moorings. During the period of decline, the moralism of the movement expressed itself both altruistically and egoistically, manifesting an inherent ambivalence.

But to say that the character of the movement was both moral and ambivalent does not exhaust the matter, for the goals and aims of the movement were abstract, and its programs and statements excessively theoretical, paradoxically in an anti-intellectual way.[24]

The moralism, ambivalence, and abstraction of the New Left were not unrelated.[25] The moralist is an outsider; he looks upon the real movement of history, upon real historical struggles, from without. The ideals of his moral code are continually mocked by social reality. His appeals to the powers that be, made on moral grounds, come from a position which is external to the immoral situation. These appeals from without must remain ineffective in the long run in order for the moralist to survive. It is the failure of morality to effect fundamental change which constantly recreates the moralist as moralist. As a moralist he knows no real constraint and no real power. Altruism is moralism in and for itself; egoism is moralism in itself, for us. The altruist is by nature religious. As such he is a slave to others, ultimately to *the* Other, or God.

The egoist emerges as his opposite, as the one who will brook no externality, who comes to see all constraint as self-imposed, who can only become an atheist by first becoming God (Engels 1973:11). Both the altruist and the egoist stand in an abstract relation to the world, which they consider from a position 'external' to it.[26]

The moral character of student activism has led supporters and critics of the movement alike to search for its origins in moral, spiritual, or psychological terms. In this way they have taken the form for the substance, hypostatizing the former and mysticizing the latter by de-historicizing it. In one psychological account (Feuer 1969) the youth revolt is understood not in its specificity, but as an instance of the eternal psychodynamic conflict between the generations. In other accounts the character of the New Left is explained by the nature of parental practices of child rearing without a concrete link being drawn between these practices and social history. The moralist who criticizes the youth rebellion does so on the basis of a perceived moral degeneracy manifested in the movement (destroying the moral fibre of society). The moralist who supports the students understands youthful protest as a justified expression of outrage at the disjunction between social reality and socially accepted moral ends.

Many of the activists themselves shared the moralist's view of the movement. It is neither an unflattering portrayal nor a terribly inaccurate one. The students who risked their lives in the service of just causes were, to be sure, highly moral individuals. But the point which this book tries to maintain throughout does not preclude the existence of morality, morals, or moral individuals. It only suggests that moral thoughts and actions do not arise *sui generis*. They are circumscribed by social and historical conditions of which they are the expression. Morality is thus a secondary historical factor, never primary (Krader 1972:329). Here it can be active only mediately.

We have already seen that the student revolt of the sixties was understandably an expression of the real life situation of a large stratum of middle class youth facing radically changed prospects at the university and later in society.[27] The disappointment with the university was directly linked with an anticipatory disillusionment with future prospects. The present and future were tied together in the two dimensions chiliasm (Mannheim 1936:211–19, 236–9) and its opposite, nihilism, both of which were equally pervasive in the New Left. The former affirms the higher reality of the future by seeking to make it part of the present just as the latter affirms the future by attempting to destroy the present.

Elitism, populism, and radicalism

In spite of the fact that the New Left understood itself as a universalistic social movement – during the early years as a moralistic, altruistic, and humanistic one, during the later years increasingly as part of a revolutionary, world-historical one – the fuel which propelled it was the breaking of the specific promise to the youth of the broad middle strata. If one understands the nature of that promise and the significance of its remaining unfulfilled, then the puzzle of the 'radicalism' of relatively privileged youth can be solved without too much effort.

The student protest movement of the sixties sought to redress its specific grievances by means of agitation on behalf of a variety of causes far more compelling than its own. (In fact the New Left understood its own cause only as part of these much larger causes.) Even though the early New Left grew out of the soil of peace and civil rights issues, whereas important elements of the later movement declared themselves to be part of the Third World awakening, the anti-imperialist struggle, or the vanguard of the proletarian revolution, in every case the students were giving expression to their own predicament. As we have seen, the specific problems of the sixties generation of youth which led them to political activism were directly related to the changing character of middle class intergenerational mobility, of the 'intellectual élite' of mediate producers, and of the university itself.

A former Canadian activist, now a professor of sociology at a major Canadian university, describes the impact of that broken promise upon the youth of the sixties in these words: 'The kinds of principles that they taught me were ones that you could make your own way, that, as long as you were hard-working and honest, things would work your way. And when that was exposed both for me and for them, it became an incredible exposure of the system ... You were being told that education was the way you were going to get there, and it was very difficult.'

For many, the student movement itself filled the vacuum left by the empty promise. A former American New Leftist, now a teacher in New York City, tells how the movement made up for the deception:

I guess my own perspective on the student movement was that it really had to do with certain contradictions that were developing in terms of college education and the economy. I also went through the realization that the dream which people had been promised either at the beginning of college or else by their parents was not too much of a reality ... I think there was a feeling of finally saying: 'We don't believe what you are saying any more.' And I think it came around warped. You know, 'If you get good grades in school you get good jobs,' and I think that people began to feel bad. That was also bullshit, because it was not going to change anything. And I guess for a couple of years that was a very refreshing kind of feeling to be able to get out and say something; to know you were supported by a fair number of people.

One of the former leaders of the German SDS uncritically brings together the 'idealistic' and the 'egoistic' elements of the New Left in this thought:

The answer to it is bound up with the re-education here in the Federal Republic of Germany set up by the Americans, by means of which very many children in primary school were equipped with very high ideals. A very great disappointment spread among these pupils and later among them as students owing to the American war in Vietnam. This was bound together with an already visible uncertainty concerning the future status of students in the work force. At the same time, the universities were considerably expanded and they became real mass universities.

In fact the connection between the war in Vietnam, civil rights, community organizing, and student power becomes clear if we focus upon the substance of student concerns in the sixties. Given the changes in the social and economic reproduction of the middle class which have been outlined above, university attendance for middle class youth was becoming increasingly compulsory in the post-war era. Youth was promised entrance into the societal élite upon completion of university education. In a sense the promise was kept. University graduates of the sixties did gain entry to the rapidly expanding intellectual élite of mediate producers. But the character of privilege itself had been changing; the élite, as I have indicated, had been 'massified.' As Toqueville might have put it: middle class youth had been promised watches when very few people owned watches. These original watches were ornately decorated and of high quality. However, when the watches had to be mass produced in order to make good on the promise, the significance of owning a watch (and the quality of the watches themselves) declined considerably.

Former activists in all three countries indicated that it was precisely the crucial role of the university in this process of massification which lay at the root of student protest. The reason for the adoption of non-student causes by the students in the sixties is to be sought in the character of student life and the relations of the student in and to society.

First, students as students are unable to effect social change without the support of other major groups in society. As a former member of the German SDS relates: 'Students are outside of production. They have no real power. And the groups or classes in society who have the real power were not directly involved in all that.'

Second, the struggle for humanistic causes such as civil rights, nuclear disarmament, community organizing, and so on is a direct way of highlighting the failure of the current élite (that is, the leaders of the society who made the promise to the students) in both domestic and foreign policy. The following statement of a former CUP activist exposes the abstract relation which the students had to the issues which they raised and reveals the wish to replace the current élite with the egalitarian-minded student élite:

I think these people came, in a somewhat abstract way, to sit back and read about world poverty. And you can see it in the ban-the-bomb movement. I mean, who the hell in the ban-the-bomb movement had ever had anything to do with a bomb? ... I mean, there was no relationship to it. You were sitting back, you were reading the newspaper, you were saying that these things were awful and that they could be corrected. The bomb could be banned, world poverty could be responded to ... You were constantly looking at India in particular and how, if it wasn't for corrupt government officials and stupid American politics, the Indians could be fed ... These people were demanding that the bomb be banned, that the lollipops be shared around the world. And they just weren't getting any response. The people who seemed to have control of both the bombs and the lollipops just were not listening, or weren't responding in any sort of concrete way. I think that produced a frustration which moved sort of to a second stage where your same people, still secure in their own position, now start demanding, well, all right; if the people in power are not going to come to these obviously sensible conclusions that the power be shared, so that the people [namely the students] who have those obviously sensible solutions can start to implement them ... that is how I see much of the birth of the student and youth radicals in the sixties.[28]

Third, by identifying with Black Power groups, the Viet Cong, Castro's Cuba, and so on the students were able to participate vicariously in revolutionary actions (the Viet Cong, for example, were doing precisely what the students wanted to do – revolt against a corrupt élite, against a system which doesn't keep its promises) and to register a moralistic protest (the American bully versus the 'little guy' – Cuba, Vietnam, or whatever). This heavy accent upon moralism was supposed to establish the superiority of the student élite to the existing societal élite.

We have already seen that the war in Vietnam called forth a deeply rooted student opposition in Germany to American foreign policy. In addition to providing a focus for the expression of specifically student discontent, it also offered the students a channel for expressing a heavily veiled form of German nationalism. (The nationalistic thrust of the German left in general has become more and more apparent in the late seventies and early eighties; see Pohrt 1981.)

The American activists in the sixties also identified with the struggle against us domestic and foreign policy. As one former sps member said, 'People wouldn't take it anymore. The blacks wouldn't take it; the Vietnamese wouldn't take it. They started fighting back and other people started supporting them.' Another American who was clearly puzzled by this identification with foreign groups made the following observation: 'Yeh, people will go and see *The Battle of Algiers* five and six times, sitting in the dark trying to take notes and figuring what was the lesson in that for us, and Lord knows ...' And yet a third American reflected on the militancy of the black movement in relation to his own radicalism: 'To be for blacks in the South in that period was to be pre-conscious ... the situation in your own class ... let's put it this way: when I saw black people revolting and fighting back, something about what they were doing, it struck a chord in me. I wanted to fight back too and I wasn't black, but I already knew something was wrong.' Finally, a former student at the City College of New York recalls the 'wonderful feeling' he had about a visit by Fidel Castro to New York:

I remember how excited I was. I was in college during the revolution in Cuba, and how excited I was, and my friends were. And I think part of it was the fact that here was this group of people running around the mountains of Cuba that had successfully fought repression and now were going to run their own country. And the fact that they could spit in the eye of everybody else.

I remember Fidel was supposed to come up to City College, he came to Columbia ... to talk to ... and I remember showing up Saturday morning, 8 or 9 o'clock in the morning and he didn't show and I was furious. But it was okay that he didn't show. It was okay because it was more important that he spoke to other people than to speak to a bunch of students up at City. I felt that way, that he had a message, that right was on his side. But it was such a terrific feeling ... July 26, there was a whole bunch of us running through City College, and I don't know if it was all political. It was the fact that here was these bunch of mountain guys – and they were able to really spit in the eye of the United States and capitalism and repression, and machine guns and tanks and planes and all that stuff and get away with it. And I had this wonderful feeling about it. I still do.

If one accepts the point that what people think and feel is inextricably bound up with who they are and what experiences they have, then the strong attachment to the revolt of the underdog, the revolt of the oppressed, on the part of the students can only be understood in terms of the experiences of the students themselves. Few of the former activists interviewed grasped this connection. A former officer in the National Office of the American SDS in the early sixties has not seen that in identifying with militant minorities the students were giving expression to their own plight in a way which was open to them:

I think people, myself included, who could have had very good jobs – I had worked for ITT – felt that there was some dissatisfaction with being even successful under capitalism, and that a lot of my friends dealt with the black movement, Chicano movement, and so on in terms of finding ways to make their lives more real. But by identifying with that they failed to understand why they themselves were dissatisfied. So what happened in the late sixties was that while there were thousands, millions, of students dissatisfied with their lives, the only identification was with the Vietnamese, with the blacks, and there was very little overt concern about why they were dissatisfied with their own, with my life *per se*.

If what we have said about the devaluation of élite jobs is true, then the dissatisfaction which this student and his friends felt about the 'very good jobs' can be seen in a new light. The 'very good jobs' were still good, that is, privileged, positions, but not as good as they once had been. The students did not articulate this directly; rather they built their movement and counter-institutions around the 'reality' of others – blacks, the poor, the Vietnamese, the Cubans, and ultimately the proletariat. In the end the student movement came to act as a substitute for the 'promise' which in their eyes was never realized.

It is interesting to note that many of the former activists in the late seventies had, in a general way, understood that the rise of the New Left was connected with the changes in the character of the élite of mediate producers. The shifting fortunes of middle class youth in the sixties were described in the following way by a former leader of the German SDS: 'I do believe that the position of the intelligentsia in the fabric of the social classes and strata is no longer the old one or is tendentially changed. Not that they are becoming proletarians. But they are becoming a kind of elevated wage-labourer, at least the majority of them ... But the professional is a kind of wage-dependant who can always imagine that he is particularly privileged.' At the same time, a process of social levelling has occurred: 'In the big city, ride in the subway. You don't know if you have a professor, a skilled worker (if he has gloves on you know nothing more about him), a white collar worker, or a grocer in front of you ... Fifty years ago it was possible without difficulty [to see the differences] simply in clothing, in every aspect of their appearance.'

Another former SDS activist in Germany directly linked the process of élite massification to the specific issues raised by the student movement:

Thus, students are no longer becoming a functional élite in the welfare state as Habermas still said they were, but rather a bit of normal professional life was coming their way ... And for me it is not coincidental that all the protests within the university started with the question of freedom of opinion ... The suspicion clearly arose among the students that we are no longer the functional élite of the people; we are rather a stratum which is perhaps better off materially, which has better job prospects, which still has better chances of fulfilment in its work, but where one has the premonition that all this is threatened with failure ... Thus, when you notice that you have to have your course of study finished in a determinate time, when you notice that you are sitting in a seminar ... with a hundred others and not twenty, where there is no opportunity for discussion, then it dawns upon you that what you learn in your courses and what you are able to do when you graduate are not the same.

Here we have a clear description of the sense of massification which was experienced by the university students of the sixties. We can also see why this affected middle and upper class students more than lower and working class students, at least in North America: an élite job of diminished privilege is still a brighter prospect for lower class youth than it is for youth of the upper and middle class. The lower class student wants a good job, which a university degree did in fact guarantee in the sixties. The higher class student wanted the power to put 'the course material' into practice in his 'immediate social activity.' The university degree did not guarantee that this would come to pass.

When we look at the New Left assessment of this future 'immediate social activity,' that is, the future professional life facing the students, we find a complaint that the practice of a profession does not operate according to rational criteria but is rather determined by extra-professional forces – economic, political, juridical, and bureaucratic – which are controlled by non-professionals. The call for a rationally functioning professional practice is at bottom a call for the autonomy of the professional. This is clearly expressed by one former SDS leader in Germany;

But the most important point is certainly that the academically trained notice, or a fraction of them notice, that they don't have rational professions ... I don't mean money now, rather the work itself, a sensible job. Thus, for example, a doctor in the hospital notices that he only fumbles about with symptoms, that he must labour under the rules of the hospital which force him to act in such a way that he is never really able to cure the patients ... When he has become experienced in his profession [he will see that] he is unable to fulfil himself [in it]. Wherever intellectuals work, they are buffeted about by crisis conditions in this society.

In a similar vein, one of the American respondents sees the rise of the New Left student movement in the sixties as a protest against the 'monopolization' of the professions by the big corporations: 'It was the left wing version of protest against the monopolization of formally petty bourgeois fields – engineering. If you're an engineer today you work for a big corporation instead of your own company ... and all sorts of other things – journalism – the whole thing. Even lawyers mostly, today, work for insurance companies. So the monopolies were taking over our class and turning us into workers ... and we kicked because we didn't like it.' He goes on to indicate that the élitist reasons behind the rise of the American SDS (which he didn't realize at the time) are to be found in the social situation of the intellectuals in the sixties:

I've heard the SDS described as the aristocracy of the left ... That aristocracy was saying: 'Don't wipe out our class.' I think you get a similar tendency in Latin America among people who are highly educated, and there's nowhere for them to work or grow. In Mexico most of your professors and government thinkers are leftist because they're petty bourgeoisie in a society that really has no place for educated people ... compared to the industrialists they have nothing, compared to the businessman they have nothing. It's this kind of protest. I hate to say it, but that's not what I thought it was about when I started. When I started I thought it was much more moral – I saw it in more moral abstract terms. I thought I was more sensitive than other people, and that may be true. I don't think that has to be true to do what we did ... sds often thought it was morally superior. God, that was half the game; that's why we tore each other up. (Cf Kelman 1970:121–2, 193)

It is clear from what he says that the university bore the brunt of the student anger over the process of élite massification, that is, over the breaking of the 'promise': 'Now during the period when the petty bourgeoisie was having a good time, my father's generation was poor; university was a place where propertied people sent their sons and daughters for social finishing, to have a good time, and to get smatterings of liberal education. By the time we went to university, it was a damned trade school for the big corporations. That bothered us.'

A former student leader in Canada evaluates the impact of the changing character of the university on his generation in this lengthy but enlightening statement:

Sociologically you can talk about that category of people who move in there with strong conventional motivations about professions, about mobility; we went in there and got told we were going to be the captains of industry ... and you looked around the University of Waterloo, and you said, 'You know, there ain't gonna be no captains of industry come out of this place; they go to the Harvard Business School. They don't come out of the University of Waterloo.' Now from that very conventional motivation we had been told by our parents, our guidance counsellors, so you knew we would study hard enough to get through our grade 13 exams, that we were going to be fucking important. You know, we were going to be the leaders of society. And we got to Waterloo and suddenly this didn't look like where the leaders got trained. It was more like where the privates got trained – this looked like boot camp; it didn't look like, you know – it felt like boot camp, okay? And I mean in retrospect this struck me as very important that we really thought we were shit hot. I mean we counted, okay? And what we thought and what we felt and what we did was really important to the future of the society. It was really ... all the guidance counsellors and John Kennedy's speeches and all that stuff; we're going to march forward into the sunset ... On that very conservative traditional motivation we marched forward into the political fray ... If it was the shits we were going to make something of it, okay? In retrospect it really does seem somewhat naïve and socially arrogant and a kind of élitism that was built into it; but we really mattered and what we thought really mattered. And certainly when I look around at the students now in university they don't think they matter, they don't think what they think matters, they don't think what they do matters; they'll be happy to survive.

Here we have a clear statement of the underlying anger which fuelled the student revolt in the sixties. The growing importance of the university for the youth of the middle class and the concomitant massification of the institution set the stage for the rise of student activism. Having been denied access to the 'old' intellectual élite (since it no longer existed), the students created an 'anti-élite,'[29] an élite of egalitarians which would make its own rules. It would save society from those problems which the older élite had not been able to solve.[30] This student Messianism was the product of 'an abstract élite consciousness.' Through their politics the students were to fulfil the original promise made to them. Throughout the decade they moved to and fro, from the university to society and back again.

Students in the sixties were buffeted by forces over which they had little control and about which they had little understanding. The movement to abolish the distinction between school and society could not have been made without abolishing the university as we know it; ultimately it would have necessitated the overcoming of the division between mediate and immediate production in society, a utopian condition at present. At the same time the training and qualification of labour would have had to be integrated into the process of social production (Goodman 1964; Illich 1976). But even if this were to happen trainees would by definition still be excluded from full membership in the class of social labour in practice. The student, the trainee, will always be part of the process of social reproduction but not fully part of the process of social production. The tension between the two is internalized and constitutes one source of his social ambivalence.

But if the student movement could not revolutionize society in its various sorties from the campus, it could attempt to turn the politics of the campus, by means of a fantastic substitution, into the politics of society. Thus the university became not only a mini-state replete with parties in power and parties in opposition but a mini-world where superpowers confronted one another. As Gitlin has observed,

To those who contend in the internecine battles of the Left, the stakes often seem global. They fight for control over a known object, an organization of manageable extent and vast significance, whose shadow seems to eclipse the rest of the world. Ferocious in their myopia, the contenders are often oblivious to the concrete political implications of their actions – the impacts their factional differences have on the policies of political adversaries. (1980:92)

There were two ways in which the university could 'absorb' society. The first was by means of a gross exaggeration of the centrality and importance of the university (and especially of the student constituency) in the social and political dynamic; the second was a complete denial of the reality of the university, the affirmation of a fantastic revolutionary agent or subject in society, the abolition of the division of training and production, mediate and immediate production, of social production and reproduction, in thought. The first way was taken by the youth and new working class politics, the second by Marxism-Leninism and/or Third World politics. The different factions of the student movement were in agreement that the problem was their isolation on the campus; they differed only in the fantasy concerning the means which was supposedly to overcome the problem.

But both these positions – the self-exaggeration of the student constituency and its self-denial – expressed in different ways the fundamental ambivalence and helplessness of the student population. Self-exaggeration makes a virtue of student helplessness and isolation; self-denial, a vice. The one puffed itself up and with bravado substituted itself, a tiny marginal part, for the much larger social whole; the other willingly denied and debased itself in order to set itself at the head of an imaginary whole. In addition there were tendencies in each country which were even more ambivalent, being self-effacing and self-inflating at the same time. These were the greatest expressions of the impotence of abstract moralism in the form of egoism: terror (Hegel 1974:431–41; Marx and Engels 1971:266–80).

The war in Vietnam

The student movement was transformed during the years 1964–7 by the escalation of the war in Vietnam. Certainly the war dominated the formal and organizational aspects of movement life during the late sixties. Some former activists, like this ex-campus radical in Southern Ontario, believed that student frustration over the failure to end the war led to the fragmentation of the movement as a whole:

I think that one of the things that really depressed a lot of people was the Vietnam War. Like, I don't think that particularly stimulated political development. I think it put a damper on it and led to a lot of people going up to the ML groups, to nut groups. Because when you talk about the moral thing, starting out at the beginning of the sixties, a lot of liberal people came into the movement, and our inability to do anything about the war pushed them into adopting crazy positions.

The same sentiment is expressed by one of the former SDS leaders in New York:

The Vietnam War, as it became more and more dominant, you know, sort of completely eroded the base of action as being located in this country. In spite of everything that people said about the army, the draft, and those being significant instruments of domestic repression, the fact of the matter was that it was the war itself, the image of the war and the plight of the Vietnamese people. I think it really motivated people. I think people went crazy behind it. They couldn't deal with their inability to really stop the war machines and that escalated the rhetoric and escalated the level of opposition beyond the point where there was any kind of popular base to support it. And it drove people away from any kind of more integrated perspective of our society and what kinds of forces were working within it and how you could really change it. So I feel like, paradoxically, the war which helped build SDS and the whole group was also its undoing.

In the United States SDS had already engaged US foreign policy over its nuclear commitment, the blockade of Cuba, and American support for fascist dictators. The appearance of Oglesby and Shaull's *Containment and Change* (1967) signalled a heightened awareness in the student movement of America's economic penetration and exploitation of underdeveloped areas. In Germany, SDS had already fought battles against the French involvement in the Algerian war. The Canadians were quick to pick up on 'US imperialism' as an issue, especially in relation to American domination of Canadian industry. Throughout the development of the New Left in Canada a kind of Canadian nationalism diffused through the movement and in fact survived the demise of student activism. That Canada did not fit the image of an exploited country was somewhat of a puzzle at the time. Endless arguments took place concerning the nature of Canada's role in the world – was it an exploiter or one of the exploited?

The New Left had discovered the classical texts on imperialism, and the theory seemed to be confirmed by the actions of the United States in Indochina. In fact the language of anti-imperialism was the vehicle for conveying student sentiment concerning the war in Vietnam. True to its character, however, the real basis of condemnation of US policy was moral: a little guy was being attacked by a big bully. The war was unjust. Nobody wants to be on the side of Goliath in his struggle with David. A former Canadian activist reports:

I could say without exaggeration that the war in Vietnam changed my life irrevocably; it'll never be the same, and in some sense I can even remember the day that this happened – there was a picture of ... the Americans had been chasing the Viet Cong around ... for a couple of years and I'd never seen a picture of a Viet Cong ... in fact I barely even knew where the country was. And one day in all the newspapers, there was a picture. The Americans had with all their military might finally managed to capture a member of the Viet Cong who was described in the newspaper picture, in the caption, as fourteen years old. The astonishing thing about this picture was that the guy must have been no more than five foot two tall and he was being held upright by two US marines who were at least six two, and they dwarfed this poor guy; and there they were, equipped in the latest of every possible piece of equipment, and there was this guy who had, point of the story, had a rusty twenty-two ... some impossible piece of homemade equipment. And that picture, you could use it as an allegory for the whole war. Here was a group of people who were ... God knows, underequipped, taking on a group of overfed, overequipped characters; that in one sense was absolutely insane. And on the other hand I said to myself: what in heaven's name have these great huge well-fed characters got to do with the poor little guy? And for me that picture ... turned me from saying this is a crazy war, this is a stupid war, this is wrong; that picture turned me to the point where I wanted those other little guys to win.

The mainstream of the antiwar movement never abandoned the moral critique, and it remained throughout the decade a central motif of the antiwar message. But the New Left moved increasingly away from this overt form of moral criticism as it embraced the theory of anti-imperialism in a variety of different and sometimes conflicting ways. The theory of imperialism which the New Left had advanced to explain the war in Vietnam (for example, the defence of the interests of big capital, the multi-nationals, Wall Street) could not explain the real character of the war. On the other hand, the theory of anti-imperialism did give expression to the interest of the students but not *as* the interest of the students; rather the sectional student interest was blended in with the cause of downtrodden humanity.

A former regional organizer for the American SDS saw that the war provided the students with an issue around which a framework could be built which would allow the students to discover their corporate role in history. This concern with their historical role (which in fact was one of political and social impotence, from the point of view of the major issues such as the war) led to the search for a general theory of history (which was of necessity abstract and ahistorical):

My feeling of what changed is that the impact of the war and the draft, and the development of the student movement as such, which was unlike the student movement as adjunct to the civil rights movement, gave people a sense of themselves as a coherent social stratum for a time. And that sense was certainly very varied from place to place ... And as some people began to experience that, they needed some framework for understanding who the hell they were in the historical process. There's an old recipe book that's full of nice, neat formulas about all of that, which is put together by Uncle Karl. And so it is natural that people turn to the classic texts to begin to find some sort of historical social framework for understanding their experience.

In the United States the foremost concern of liberal, middle class, male college students at the time was the possibility of being drafted for military service in Vietnam. Since this particular war could not be sold to the middle class youth ideologically (Mehnert 1977:35–6), a large number of them put self-preservation above the law. But the war was a much broader vehicle which youth and students in many countries were able to seize upon to convey their own grievances. In general, it was a convenient weapon in the war between the generations, the material-social roots of which we have had occasion to examine in part. Youth politics was able to point to the alienation of students in the 'education industry' and to the oppression and exploitation of youth in the military. The Canadians were able to fire their slings and arrows of outrageous fortune at the Yankee giant at last, apparently not out of envy of American wealth, power, and opportunities (especially for the educated classes) but on moral and humanitarian grounds. At the same time they challenged their own government by attempting to rewrite its foreign policy practically, in the streets, with the 'people.'

The German students could not help but revel in the moral equivalent of war which they declared against the Americans, who, after all, were an occupying foreign power in their midst.[31] In addition it was the

Americans with their notions of democracy and equality who had beaten their fathers in a war and had attempted to re-educate them in their own image. As we have seen, German students, former members of SDS, spoke of the deep ambivalence of their feelings about the Americans.[32]

Carl Oglesby (1977) has recently informed the public that he first began to question the thesis of monolithic imperialism in 1968. But it wasn't until the mid-seventies that he attempted to publicize his new thoughts on the matter. Basing his work on the earlier efforts of Caroll Quigley (1966), Oglesby outlined the thesis that the war in Vietnam, after 1967, was conducted with the full support of only the maverick wing of the American ruling class – the 'Cowboys' (located in the 'southern rim' and western states) – over the growing protests of the eastern Establishment – the 'Yankees,' to employ Oglesby's terminology. The eastern Establishment had an original interest in the war in terms of tin and tungsten extraction and, in a geo-political sense, in securing South-east Asia for the Western bloc. Kennedy's interest, according to Oglesby, was in a limited involvement to 'stabilize' the area. But the empire of the 'Cowboys,' founded on aerospace, chemical, petroleum, aviation, natural gas, munitions, and nuclear industries, had a direct interest in an expanded military operation. In addition, the southern and western oil interests wanted to keep a finger on the oil deposits in the South China Sea. The eastern capitalists were quite willing to follow suit in support of the war until American economic stability began to be threatened by a further prosecution of the war effort. Kirkpatrick Sale supports this view as well:

It was because of this prolongation that the first serious cracks began to show themselves in the wall of support which the business community and its followers had erected before 1968. Both Northeastern and Southern Rim capitalists, of course, wanted to keep Southeast Asia open for the American empire, and both, therefore, hoped to pacify Vietnam. But there were certain costs that the Yankee community wanted to avoid, and as the balance of payments grew steadily worse, as inflation kept mounting, as the social dislocations at home became even sharper, and as the futility of the operation grew more apparent, more and deeper cracks appeared, more Wall Street businessmen joined the ranks of the polite dissenters. (Sale 1975:266–7)

John M. Lee (1978), business and finance editor of the *New York Times*, zeroed in on the disastrous economic effects the war had produced by 1968. He traced the roots of the current crisis in the economy and in the international monetary system to the forces set in motion back then:

It was March 1968. The Tet offensive had not only penetrated the American Embassy compound in Saigon but given lie to Administration claims that the war was being won ... It was also a year of breakdown and change in the world financial system, as political turmoil added to the problems of huge foreign deficits and weak national currencies for Britain and the United States. A decade later the fallout from devaluations, revaluations and shifting rules of the game still imperils world prosperity ... In retrospect, the gold rush cracked the keystone of the world financial system, and the weakened structure collapsed three years later ... But when, in an atmosphere poisoned by Vietnam, American policies were viewed with doubt or distrust, gold could be demanded for greenbacks ... Currency speculators turned on the dollar with a vengeance, and Washington furnished increased amounts of gold to the London market out of its own reserves ... On Sunday, March 10 [1968] the normally tight-lipped group [of central bankers] issued a 70 word communiqué affirming that it would continue to sell gold to speculators rather than risk the monetary upheavals from breaking the gold-dollar link and thereby devaluing the dollar.

But that same Sunday, the lead story in *The New York Times* was headlined: 'Westmoreland Requests 206,000 More Men.' The force in Vietnam was already 510,000. Inflation already threatened at home because of President Johnson's deceptive delay before seeking, just a few months earlier, a tax surcharge to finance the war. Increased spending in Southeast Asia would increase the deficit abroad. The perception of these developments fuelled financial fears. As political opposition and economic concern spread around the world, the demand for American gold in London reached overwhelming proportions. The United States was being bled of metal that might eventually be needed for military purposes as well as economic influence and power.

It was a tumultuous week. Senator Eugene J. McCarthy won 40 percent of the vote against President Johnson in the New Hampshire Democratic primary. Robert F. Kennedy said he was ready to run for President. The gold pool was losing well over $100 million a day (with Washington footing 59 percent of the bill) and on Thursday, March 14, the demand neared $400 million.

That night, Queen Elizabeth was awakened to sign a proclamation closing the gold markets.

The Americans tried to get the international financial community to accept a new reserve asset which would be a kind of paper gold and would eventually come to replace the metal as the global form of liquidity. Over the objections of the French, who demanded that the Americans pay their foreign debts in gold, the Western nations accepted the Special Drawing Rights, or sDRs, as a form of international debt payment. Theoretically, this would have allowed the Americans to continue to prosecute the war further without the immediate disastrous economic consequences. As Lee (1978) reports:

A street opposition also emerged from the pro-Viet Cong and anti-American attitudes in Stockholm at that time. In Sweden, every public action is tested for its political engagement, and sophisticated students protested the meeting at the secluded Foresta Hotel waving placards that read, 'sDRs Mean Genocide.' The charge was that monetary reform would enable Americans to keep killing Vietnamese. Radical youths rocked the car of Henry Fowler, Secretary of the Treasury, who had rested one toothpick against another to build political agreement for this new venture.

For these reasons, the centre of the critique of American foreign policy with respect to the situation in Vietnam shifted from the New Left student organizations to sections of the political and economic élite in 1968. Yet the student opposition to the war during the years 1965–8 proved to be prophetic and in the end congruent with the interests of the eastern Establishment. The student left of the sixties was consistently prophetic about events, and in many ways it stood in the vanguard, not of the working class revolution, to be sure, but of the most powerful and progressive elements of the representatives of capital.

This 'progressive élitism' of the movement is explained in the following way by a former American sDS leader:

I think one of the reasons that the earliest part of the movement in America was largely composed of privileged people was because, just like every generation kind of instinctively knows what they have to do to perpetuate their class interests, this particular group of people knew. First of all, there had to be integration in the South and in the North. Second of all, there couldn't be a war in Vietnam. In other words, they had to be radicals. This is a complicated thought, but in order to preserve their sort of class position, the things that they wanted to do, all that – when it didn't happen, when that failed, they got radicalized.

There were two areas in which the students displayed a remarkable

perspicacity: the changing character of the university and the development of East-West *détente*.

Accomplishments of the student movement

In all countries it was the student movement which provided the
'muscle' necessary to bring the structure of the university into line with
its new content, its new social role and function. If we examine the
pamphlets and manifestos, brochures and leaflets of SDS in Germany and
the United States, of SUPA and CUS in Canada, we can, with little
difficulty, separate the kernel from the husk. The rational proposals
aimed at doing away with the fetters with which the old élite university
bound the new middle class 'mass' institution found their way into
official university and governmental reports and commissions, and
many of them were adopted in part or whole.

It should be emphasized that the students themselves perceived their
actions in an entirely different light. They were soldiers in an army sent
to secure the university, but they were never quite sure for whom they
were fighting or what their objectives were. They were angry (as good
soldiers should be) on account of the broken promise, as we have seen.
But they were part of a living contradiction; their tragedy was based on
the fact that this contradiction, being fuelled from without, had no
possibility of internal resolution.

In North America clever administrators were able to seize the
opportunity to help erode the power of the departments by strengthen-
ing the faculties, which were more closely tied to the central authority of
the university. In all countries the junior faculty to a very great extent
made common cause with the student rebels to break senior professorial
control of departmental decision making.[33] At the same time academic
standards began to deteriorate. The students and the faculty are not to
be held solely responsible, Allan Bloom's suggestion (1969:115) not-
withstanding, since the 'craze for change' which had as its goal 'nothing
but change itself' was an expression of real social forces which impinged
upon the university in the sixties. The students, to be sure, were equally
blind to these forces which were at work behind the scenes. Looking at
that period from the present, it must appear to them now as having been
the work of the 'cunning of reason' itself.

In addition to the changes which the student movement brought to
the university it was the first non-communist 'political' voice to be
raised in opposition to the cold war politics in the Dulles, Adenauer,

C.D. Howe era. It thus became the harbinger of the politics of *détente*. In the United States it developed through a critique of US imperialism. In Canada it was expressed as a nationalism opposed to American ownership of Canadian industry, American penetration in the areas of culture and the arts, and, of course, American professors at Canadian universities. In Germany, SDS had clashed with the SPD over the question of establishing contact with youth groups in the German Democratic Republic (GDR). This issue played a prominent role in the internal politics of the organization as early as 1955–6. By 1958 SDS was demanding official recognition of the borders between East and West Germany and immediate negotiations between Bonn and Pankow (the seat of the government of the GDR) to formalize and regulate relations between the two German states. The SPD whip in the federal parliament responded to these proposals with anger:

It is impossible to play into communist hands any more than was done at Frankfurt [the conference of delegates of the SDS in 1958 met in Frankfurt]. This shows that communist infiltration in our ranks is achieving its goal, and it shouldn't be allowed to become even greater than it is. A defence must be mounted at the outset. I am of the opinion that the socialist students who do not wish to allow themselves to be saddled as the Trojan ass for Pankow should separate themselves from SDS. It is necessary to draw a clear line of separation. (Brein 1979:347)

The vehemence of the attacks directed by the SPD against SDS (they were to continue on and off for the next two years and ended with the exclusion of SDS from the SPD) is understandable if we consider that SDS had become the 'farm club' of the party and trade union élite of the FRG. When it became clear that SDS had gone inexorably beyond the ever-watchful eye of the party leadership, an attempt was made to create a new student organization more to the party's liking. That this attempt failed highlights not the extent or success of communist infiltration but the real changes effected within the younger student generation, to which the party apparatus was blind.

It wasn't until the late sixties that the SPD accepted the notion of *Ostpolitik*. By this time the financial and industrial centres of the FRG had recognized the lucrative aspects of an East-West 'dialogue,' and Willy Brandt's electoral strategy was to tap into this source of support. By the end of the decade the program of SDS in this matter had become state policy.[34]

In the United States the tension which existed between SDS and its parent organization, LID, had its origins in the SDS commitment to internal democracy, which LID viewed as a softness towards communists. Nonetheless, by the end of the sixties not only had the American government initiated *détente* with the Soviet Union (and somewhat later with the People's Republic of China), but it was actually a Republican president, a communist-baiter and witch-hunter, who instituted this new policy.

Of course the formula for *Ostpolitik* and *détente* was originally written neither in German nor in English, but in Italian. Stalin's corpse was barely cold when the first contract was signed between the Kremlin and Fiat. The French were not slow to follow. The lure of a pool of skilled labour with no right to strike was too tempting for a weak and besieged Italian capitalist class. By 1968 the lucrative market of Eastern Europe could no longer be denied to US and German investors. The communist states, on their side, desperately needed 'hard' currency to buy grain and technology, and, in addition, they required the services of advisers and managers to help revamp a chaotic economic infrastructure. As Yenta, the matchmaker in the Broadway adaptation of Sholem Aleichem's *Tevye der Milchiker*, remarks upon bringing together the blind girl and the homely youth: 'It's a match made in heaven!'

The war in Vietnam itself was no hindrance to the process of *détente*. It was, however, a great obstacle to oil exploration in the South China Sea. As long as hostilities continued, oil could not be retrieved. But it took several years for the 'Yankees' of Wall Street to convince the 'Cowboys' that capital packed more of a wallop than a whole fleet of B52s. Similarly, a 'free,' 'socialist' Angola was more to the liking of the multinationals, which now no longer have to work through sick and corrupt Portuguese colonials. American foreign policy shifted. Midwestern shopkeepers and southern farmers may still salute the flag which presidents Johnson and Nixon ran up the pole to get the 'boys' to defend the American way of life in the rice paddies of South-east Asia, but the multinationals shrug their corporate shoulders and marvel at the 'rawness' and naïvety of the countryfolk and small townspeople.

5

The end of the student movement

Sociology is a science of hindsight. Few sociologists predicted the rise (or fall) of the New Left in the sixties with any accuracy. The sociologist arrives with the philosopher at his side *post festum* when the owl of Minerva takes flight. Literary works by and about former movement members (see, for example, Davidson 1977) have awakened memories of love and hate, pleasure and pain, sound and fury, but they cannot provide an analysis of the play of forces which tossed the movement to and fro, dashing it finally on the shoals of history. There have been writers who participated in revolutionary upheavals and were able to analyse their actions after the storm had subsided. But the New Left, it seems, has been unable to come to grips with its own ambivalence and historical helplessness. Instead it has cultivated its own myth, not unlike the rather flattering nostalgic portrayals of the mass media.

Sectarianism

The end of the movement organizationally was brought about by the sectarianism and fragmentation of the last years of the sixties. Each faction considered itself to be the leading force, or agent of the leading force, in the historical struggle, even though the understanding of this struggle differed from group to group. One party declared itself to be the vanguard of the proletariat; another, the representative of Third World liberation forces; a third, the centre of the youth revolution. Most of the 'troops' (as one major student leader in Canada used to call the mass of sympathetic non-leadership students) were left cold by the antics of the leadership and simply dropped out of the organization. The struggles at the top had little to do with the actual proletariat or the Third World, save as caricatures of them. The fragmentation was the result of the unravelling of those ambivalent moments upon which the movement had been founded. The unique mixture of élitism and radical democracy which characterized the New Left during its early and middle periods gave way to the explicitly élitist assertions of some groups, the hyperdemocratic pretensions of others.[1] All the debates, conflicts, and feuds over the question of revolutionary agency which characterized the late New Left represented a last attempt by the core activists to graft themselves onto the substantial process of history.

The end of the boom

The real question concerning the end of the student movement, however, is not how it happened, but why it happened when it did. The first part of the answer is economic. The recession of 1968–9 in North America signalled the end of the post-war economic recovery and the end of the explosive growth in higher education.[2] In both Canada and the United States the spectre of graduate underemployment and unemployment began to haunt the universities; at first weakly felt on campus, it has grown to become the greatest fear students have today.

The Carnegie Commission on Higher Education has contrasted the employment situation for university graduates between 1950 and 1968 and 1968 and 1973 as follows:

1950–1968 Demand for the college-educated kept up with or ran somewhat ahead of supply, which itself expanded greatly, and the long-run narrowing of wage and salary differentials ceased. Demand was buoyed up by these factors:
A rising GNP, more of which went into expenditures on services and the professions where college-educated persons are particularly employed.
An explosive increase of R&D funds and of aerospace employment that called, in particular, for more scientists and engineers.
An explosive increase in primary and then secondary and then tertiary school enrollments, requiring more teachers.
A greater increase in college graduates, as we moved into mass higher education, was met by an equally advancing market for their services – a most favourable period for the college graduate.
1968–1973 The favorable demand developments of the prior period stopped being so favorable, but the outflow of college graduates continued to increase:
A recession took place.

Research and development funds were cut back, and so were the funds for the aerospace industry.
School enrollments and teaching positions began levelling off. (1973:6)[3]

In Canada E.B. Harvey sees the chronic situation of unemployment and underemployment of university graduates beginning in 1968.[4] Twice as many graduate students cite 'no suitable employment available' as the reason for going to graduate school in 1968 than they did in 1960 (Harvey 1974:133). The number of graduates who experienced some unemployment doubles for both sexes from 1960 to 1968 (149), and the number of jobs applied for greatly exceeded the number of job offers extended (142). For males of high socio-economic status, job dissatisfaction increased during this period as well (166). Finally, the upward social mobility which had been the universal promise of higher education could no longer be counted upon as a matter of course: 'The percentage of respondents obtaining higher prestige jobs after graduation is significantly lower in 1968 than in 1960. In other words, the amount of father-son intergenerational upward social mobility via university has declined in the past eight years' (166–7). The debasement of the university degree is directly related to the decreasing marketability of the degree holder. This prompts Harvey to suggest that 'the university no longer plays as significant a role as it has in the past as a "feeder" to higher socio-economic status in society' (10).

We are now confronted with a puzzling situation: the student movement begins to come apart at the seams precisely when the employment outlook for the first generation of 'baby boom' college graduates begins to darken.[5] In other words, when the material grounds for protest become most apparent, the movement begins to collapse. The puzzle is soon solved, however, if we keep in mind the character of student protest in the sixties. It was born of an expanding tertiary level educational establishment which provided devalued credentials and access to debased élite employment, but élite employment nonetheless. In 1968 the first signals were detectable, warning of the possibility of there being no élite jobs for graduates (this in fact is what 'underemployment' means in this context) and the distant possibility of there being no jobs whatsoever. It was this hint, not of élite massification, for that had already occurred, but of the possibility of real 'proletarianization,' that began to have an impact upon the 'troops,' those who were marginally committed to the New Left. (The effect upon the hardcore counter-cultural rebels and politically oriented activists was negligible.) In terms of the continuing viability of a mass student movement, the economic situation served to split the mass of organizable students away from the committed leadership people, thereby causing the isolation of the latter.

The impact which the changing job market for university graduates had upon the mass of activist students is given expression in the following explanation offered by a former radical from New York:

I think that people got a little worried about their next job. It was really easy to be an activist in the 60s. I was a social worker through a good portion of the 60s ... I also knew that if you got arrested, it probably would help you more than it would hinder you because there were a lot of jobs around. Everybody was into some kind of crazy behaviour, and it was reinforced. I think that there was a feeling that you could continue to push things and you would get more. And I think that because of it, probably a very small part of it, because of an economic slowdown, I have this feeling that people began to say, 'Holy shit, maybe we'd better begin to accept what we have and stop pushing; maybe that's really a dangerous thing.'

The situation in Germany was sufficiently different to warrant specific comment. Although there was a considerable expansion of higher education in the sixties in that country, the real take-off point did not occur until the election of the SPD-FDP coalition in 1969. The recession which affected the economy of North America in 1968–9 had no parallel in Germany, and the relatively small proportion of university-aged youth actually attending a university suggested that the expansion of higher education was in order, especially given the growing importance of the university for the German middle class (which was a growing SPD constituency). But not even prosperous Germany was spared the spectre of harder times for its *Hochschulabsolventen*. As Tessaring and Werner observe: 'Since the beginning of the expansion of education there have been fears that the supply of academically trained professionals would overtake society's need for academically trained personnel in the near future, at least in some disciplines' (1975:56).[6] The biggest problem was faced by students in the teachers' colleges, since the declining birthrate signalled a falling demand for new teachers. And by 1970 about 40 per cent of all graduates of institutions of higher learning were members of the teaching profession. The effect of this upon the hardcore activists in Germany was nil, but as in North America it served to alienate the leadership and their committed followers from the general student body over which they had exerted a considerable influence to that point.

Co-optation

One of the greatest fears shared by movement organizers in the mid- and late sixties was that of being co-opted. Allowing oneself or causing one's group to be co-opted was the equivalent of committing a mortal sin in the New Left. Co-optation was a process whereby someone or something radical or revolutionary was made to work for the system. In practical terms, anything undertaken by the authorities which served to alienate the mass of students from the radical core was referred to as an instrument of co-optation by the activists. (There were, to be sure, student leaders who wished for nothing more than to be co-opted, although, given the spirit of the times, they could only rationalize this to their colleagues in such terms as 'using the system against itself'.) In fact, the 'system,' especially the university system, did respond, slowly but surely, to student pressure. Most *in loco parentis* regulations had been abolished by the end of the sixties. Some student power demands were met, especially those concerning student representation on university committees. In the United States many élite schools established special study programs of direct interest to black and Hispanic students. The curriculum changed everywhere, both in form – fewer required courses, less rigorous examinations, fewer credits required for a degree – and in content – more esoteric courses, courses with an anti-system bias, and so on. There were even some notable attempts by administration and faculty at élite institutions to facilitate protest against the war in Vietnam. And finally, the response to 'crisis situations' was becoming more sophisticated on the part of the university and the civil authorities.

A former activist at the University of Wisconsin-Madison outlines the growing sophistication of administration responses to student protest in the sixties as follows:

I think it involves partly the absorption of the protest by college administrators; I mean, not that there's a conspiracy, but simply by trial and error the administrators learn to keep the lid on. And I've always been struck by the sorts of things that erupted in the fifties on college campuses – panty raids and water fights – and there were ways that these could be dealt with. For example, after a water fight at the University of Wisconsin – I think in '58 – the next fall, all the wastebaskets in the dormitories had holes in the bottom, so you could put waste paper in them but you couldn't put water in them. And with panty raids the administrators learned that the important thing was to mingle with the crowd and recognize people, call them by name, break down the anonymity of the crowd. In the sixties the crowd was too big to deal with in that way, but a lot of the petty, more infuriating regulations were simply disappearing. Compulsory ROTC [Reserve Officers Training Corps] was pretty much gone. A lot of the course requirements were much less rigid. Dormitories, well, you're even starting to get co-ed dormitories, although those would have been in the early 70s.

There was also a perceptible change in Western foreign policy at this time. True, the war in Vietnam was being prosecuted with a greater intensity than ever. But at the same time the winds of *détente* were blowing. Deep trade links were being established between East and West. SDS and CUCND-SUPA calls for international rapprochement and co-operation were becoming state policy by the end of the sixties. Canadian University Students Overseas (CUSO) and the Peace Corps recruited young idealists and radicals to work with the poor in underdeveloped countries, just as the Company of Young Canadians (CYC) and Volunteers in Service to America (VISTA) provided state funds for community organizing at home.

These changes, which served to isolate the radicals on and off the campus, spoke to the vast majority of students in a meaningful way. The job picture was now different, the university was an institution transformed, and monolithic anticommunism had been softened. Many former student activists in Germany attribute the decline of the New Left to the election of the SPD-FDP coalition in 1969. But the greatest change in terms of the daily comportment of youth, especially at the universities, concerned the meteoric rise of the youth culture.

The counter-culture

The soil which nurtured the New Left and from which it drew most of its recruits was the counter-culture of youth. The early New Left shared the ethos of the bohemia of the fifties and early sixties to a great degree, although the latter was decisively apolitical and reclusive. (The early activists shared the beatnik and existentialist concern with authenticity, alienation, and individual freedom, but unlike the beats they were trying to change society, not opt out of it.) The New Left, especially through its involvement in the civil rights struggles, gave the counter-culture its activist, proselytizing character. If the hippies brought forth the symbol of the flower, it was the New Left which added the substantive 'power' to it.

The symbols of the cultural revolt of middle class youth were taken from earlier bohemian forms: poetry and unconventional music as a means of free self-expression, a simple jargon free of pretension, supposedly capable of expressing 'authentic' sentiments, casual habits of dress and hygiene, sexual openness and experimentation, racial tolerance, and pacifism. During the early sixties, this style of life may have been an expression of idiosyncratic normalcy for the relatively few souls who made up the new bohemia. But after 1966, after the commercialization of the hippies, the flower children, the drug cult, it was for the vast majority a mere style, a form, at best an ephemeral diversion, whose content was all too willingly provided by the industries of the 'peace and love' capitalism.[7] In short, the global counter-culture of youth became the stepchild of capital, by legal means (record companies, clothing manufacturers, and the like) and illegal means (drug pushers), even though the impulse was a genuine expression of the yearnings of middle class youth.

As a revolutionary social force, the counter-culture was doomed to fail before it began. As a revolt of privilege – privilege of exemption from labour, of freedom from want – it had no real input into the potential, substantial forces of social liberation; it was repelled by the crude materialism and philistinism of those who 'chose' to labour for their daily bread. It wanted to short-circuit history by an act of will and to propel itself thus *tout-à-coup* from the realm of necessity into the realm of freedom. By declaring the 'metabolic interaction with nature' irrelevant, it sought to soar above natural necessity. It is, of course, just as senseless to criticize the counter-culture rebels on theoretical grounds as it is to lecture a hungry man for stealing food. The essence of the cultural revolt was practical; it arose out of the specific conditions of life of that generation. And it did have an enormous impact upon the forms of social intercourse, not only among youth, but across the face of society.

The rise of the mass youth culture in 1966–7 not only drove a wedge between the core political activists and the rest of the student body; it fostered a split within the leadership as well. The counter-culture exerted an influence over the New Left which reinforced an already existing tendency within the movement, a tendency which can be grasped through concepts such as personalism, immediacy, authenticity, and sensibility. Instrumentality, in all its forms, was thus eschewed. If elements of the 'Old Left' had made organization into a fetish, elements of the New Left raised the principle of antiorganization to the same absolute and thus ahistorical level. At the same time it should not be forgotten that still other New Left elements were repotentializing the organizational formulae of the Old Left. In other words, the fragmentation of the New Left occurred not only around the question of what kind of organization, but around the logically prior question of whether any organization at all. As the ambivalent strains of the New Left began to unwind, the counter-culture reinforced one of the movement's polar tendencies, that of hyper-democracy, just as Marxism-Leninism fed off the movement's intrinsic élitism in an explicit way. But why did the ambivalent poles of the movement break apart and seek their own incarnations during the late sixties?

Victory and defeat

Throughout the sixties, the New Left student movement won or helped win a number of victories at the university and in society. These included changes in dress codes, dormitory regulations, student representation, and the like, the recognition of the right of free speech on campus, the registration of a black electorate in the United States, the passage of civil rights legislation, an increase in the awareness of the wants and rights of minorities and women, a sensitivity to environmental problems, the general acceptance of the legitimacy of many counter-cultural values, and the growth of a mass antiwar movement in the United States.

Yet, when asked to express their views on the successes and/or failures of the movement, the former student activists in the three countries showed considerable lack of agreement. At one extreme were those who believed that the New Left had won a complete victory. A former member of the cus secretariat advances this view and at the same time expresses his astonishment that some former activists feel that the movement suffered a total defeat: 'Well, I'll give you, in your own terms, a question that intrigues me. Why, faced with an absolute victory – and God knows absolute victories rarely come along – faced with an absolute victory, why did so many people feel they'd lost? Moral virtue, arguing the right cause ten years before anybody else would argue it. Going on day after day, and all of a sudden for some reason there's a bunch of idiots that want to say, "Christ, we didn't do anything!"; it absolutely astonishes me.'

Indeed, there are a sizeable number of former movement members in all three countries who did feel that they had suffered a total or near total defeat. As an early SDS activist in the United States sadly remarked: 'It bothers me to say it, but there isn't this larger legacy. Somehow it was so easily wiped out. It really has been since there was this mass amnesia of the sixties or else its perversion. The word *revolution* is used to sell everything. It's really strange.'

Still others, such as this former SDS leader in Berlin, feel that the movement had failed, but that the struggle itself had been worthwhile: 'That which we imagined under a democratic educational system ... did not come to be. To this extent, we suffered a defeat. The larger social matters which we seized hold of – actually, let's take only those campaigns against press manipulation – "Smash Springer." Springer lives and prospers better than ever. Hence, if one asks for the balance of our campaign objectives, so to speak, there is only a negative balance. Or let's say, one could have already known it then. And many of us, more or less, suspected it and knew it.'

Most of those interviewed, however, offered a mixed assessment of the movement's accomplishments. In a positive vein, it was felt that student activism in the sixties was responsible for or contributed significantly to the reform and humanizing of education, a heightened public awareness of ecological and environmental issues, the liberalization of sexual mores and laws, the formation of movements for sexual liberation, the growing sensitivity of government at all levels to the people they govern, the breaking of the hegemony of cold war ideology in the West, the creation of a generation of left-wing intellectuals, of a new socialist literature, of progressive institutions, the change in the media from 'objective reporting' to 'socially engaged reporting,' and a whole host of changes in the personal relations of the sixties generation including choice of career and attitudes towards work, sex, religion, child rearing, and so on. In a negative vein, it was felt that most, if not all, of these changes had been taken over by the 'system,' that the spirit of experimentation and innovation had died, and that the lasting historical effect of the movement had been minimal.

In the movement's own terms it did not achieve its major objectives. It did not succeed in forming an alliance with the poor and downtrodden, either in the black ghettos or in the white slums. In the United States, the civil rights work which the student activists selflessly undertook led to the creation of a black political constituency which gave its loyalty not to the white students but to a new generation of middle class black political leaders. The passing of civil rights legislation did little to eliminate the social and economic plight of the poor blacks. The peace movement in the early sixties was generally a failure. The antiwar movement of the late sixties was no doubt a factor (although not the most important by any means) in the political decision to end the war, but it was the mobilization of non-students, off campus, under the leadership of establishment liberals, which was a much more potent force than the campus-based extremists. Finally, few people today have the power to make the decisions which affect their lives in a meaningful way. If anything, this unmet demand, 'power to the people,' was at the core of the New Left program.

By 1967-8 the first wave of baby boom students had firmly entrenched itself at the university; members of this cohort had taken over the leadership of the student movement. They were looking for a way both to explain their successive defeats in society[8] and to provide a means for them to become an active force in history.[9] 'Defeat' in the realm of peace, civil rights, and community organizing was compounded by the apparent ineffectiveness of the antiwar movement. The war in Vietnam was of material and symbolic interest to students in the United States, of symbolic interest to students everywhere. But, unlike earlier causes which were morally and traditionally impeccable and clear, the war was a many-sided issue full of subtleties and having many skilled defenders, at least until 1968. Before the Tet Offensive, the war had the active or passive support of the majority of the population. The very vagueness of the war as an issue, combined with the political helplessness of the students, created a concern with theory – in particular theory about the war, in general theory of imperialism. Added to this was the desire to explain theoretically the failure of the movement to establish substantial links to other groups in society.

A former leader of SUPA suggests that the turn towards theory began with the perceived failure of the community organizing projects around 1964-5:

At the time what was happening, people felt, was that the projects were failing, or they weren't going anywhere ... There was a perceived failure of the activities that people had been carrying on up to that point. In fact, that perception was coming in fairly early, that perception was certainly there as early as 1964 ...

even the activities around the black question in the United States ... were perceived as being a failure and as being limited, and therefore one wanted to get something else. That required one to come up with some rational explanation as to why the protesting had failed, and to think your way into doing something else. All of that led to push people to the adoption of some theory.

This perception is shared by a former New Leftist in the United States who had been working for civil rights in the North in the mid-sixties. According to her, the turn towards ideology in the movement began with the expulsion of the whites from SNCC in 1965: 'At first the white liberals were very accepted, and, in the summer of '64 we were welcomed ... The welcome then got withdrawn ... I suspect that that was really important, that all of a sudden we were told to go where we belonged. And it was almost having to create a place to belong. "Oh yeh, we're Marxist-Leninist working class vanguard," which all of a sudden made you much more legitimate. And I think that that pressure pushed people to places they wouldn't have gone.'

In Germany, theory was supposed to give the students the answer to the question of how they could continue working politically. As one former leader of SDS put it: 'The student movement then studied Marxist literature and the history of the workers' movement and then tried to find answers from these readings to the question how they could continue doing political work.'

The movement was engaged in a search for a theory which could bring everything together, a theory which could explain failure and provide a formula for victory. Thus it is no surprise to find that several varieties of Marxism attracted New Left attention during this period.

The growing alienation of the leadership from the mass of students and the inability to find a meaningful resonance in society led to a growing pressure on the leaders for answers and action. Subjectively there was a need for immediate explanation of failure which would lead to quick, practical corrective measures. As one of the SUPA leaders remarked: 'People were hungry to know right away. I mean there was pressure on people to respond right away.' Under this pressure, the contradictory strains which had been more or less successfully bound during the early period of the New Left began to separate from one another in this frantic search for 'answers and action.' The result of this was the formation of oppositional fractions, the 'praxis axis' and the 'action faction,' the theorists and the doers, the dogmatists and the spontaneists, the Stalinists and the anarchists, the pacifists and the terrorists. The fetishization and mysticization of both theory and practice had their parallel developments at this time.

There are still missing elements, however, elements which proved to be important in the fragmentation of the movement which have yet to be considered: terrorism and the women's liberation movement.

Force and violence

The failure of the New Left to develop a mass politics and the turning away of even the student constituency from radical appeals led to the further unravelling of the various strands of the movement and to the investiture of pure theory or pure practice with fetishistic powers. As one of the leaders of the early American SDS suggests:

It comes from the same point that I mentioned before, that when you can't create a transition which keeps you in touch, which roots you in a social reality, the conceptual aspects of politics, the abstract aspects become the guiding force, and that's a very false guide. It's a necessary one, but not a sufficient one. And if it becomes dominant, history tells me, looking at movements, it becomes destructive, no matter if it be anarchist-syndicalist or whether it be Marxist. It becomes highly destructive and dangerous in fact. We couldn't make a transition to maintaining a rooted base in social reality, a larger and larger social reality outside the student movement. Yet our politicization, our consciousness keeps rising because the struggle keeps going up. We keep raising the stakes. We keep fighting. We keep dedicating more and getting more force, strength, more victories ... But there's this chasm when you step outside the university which was created; that unroots us and sets us adrift.

As the helplessness, frustration, and alienation grew within the movement, the rhetoric and action of some of the core groups took on a fantastic quality.[10] The inability to master reality led to the creation of a fantastic realm of theory and practice which could be mastered.

The political failure of the New Left and the helplessness and isolation of the students led some to search for an answer through the use of hallucinogenic chemicals. A former leader of CUS says: 'For us, our opiate was the right analysis. Parks and Jones would lead the others looking for the right chemical. Others would say, you know, would need the right analysis or the right ideology. That's what led to the vanguard stuff. We were all looking; it was slipping.' A small minority of others sought the answer in terroristic acts. Terrorism was the highest expression of this fantastic realm, for it matched a futile practice with a wholly abstract theory of history. But if some elements of the New Left were becoming violent, government agencies were employing greater force against selective targets. Demonstrations by moderate students were being handled with greater sophistication than before, but groups of 'hard-core' extremists were being met with greater force than ever by the authorities (Sorel 1950:194).

In all three countries a wide variety of repressive measures were undertaken by state agencies. If we set aside the activities of *agents provocateurs*, who sowed discord and confusion among the leadership and provoked individuals and groups to rash and violent actions, and concentrate upon the public expression of the machinery of repression, we can see in the shooting of Benno Ohnesorg, the massacre and jailing of members of the Black Panther Party, the Kent State shootings, and the invocation of the War Measures Act in Canada a warning to a generation of mildly radicalized liberal youth that the ante had indeed been raised and that it was going to cost them considerably more to stay in the game (Viorst 1979:509, 543; cf Cutler 1973:156–7).

According to a former officer of CUP, this is the significance of the destruction of the computer at Sir George Williams University in Montreal by occupying students, following a police charge in February 1969: 'I don't know what all was taking place, but the ante got upped and I think that worried a lot of people too. And I think Sir George came to ... represent the ante being upped beyond the point at which they were willing to participate in the game.' Consider that these same students were slowly becoming aware of the shift in the employment situation for college graduates. At the same time they were achieving representation on university committees; they could dress as they pleased for classes; in the United States, they could work for a peace candidate; they could visit their boyfriends/girlfriends in the dorms at night. It is no wonder that they became increasingly unwilling to engage the police and military or to be swayed by the empty revolutionary rhetoric of the movement. As a former member of the CUS secretariat observed: 'It was getting to the point where if you wanted to go out and protest about the war you were going to get shot at. And nobody was going to say boo all about it ... You got people saying: "I'm not going to go out in the street demonstration and get shot." You know, perfectly reasonable.'

The pressure upon the activist students was simply becoming unbearable, as this former field-worker for the American SDS suggests:

I think what happened by '70 was, I mean, what you saw in people, if you looked underneath, was an incredible frustration, just an unbelievable frustration. We were living our lives in meetings, and work and fear, and in jail; and people had been killed; and people had died; and the war in Vietnam was still going on harder and heavier than it had been after all these years struggling against it. And the revolution wasn't just around the corner. And nobody gave a shit. Or worse. They hated us. And no form or ideology could take us past through that. No one. And not a stronger understanding of ourselves, our own role, our own history and the context we were in could carry us through that.

At this point the vast mass of students, sick and tired of the rhetoric of a chaotic leadership and of its abstract internecine ideological warfare, felt that the game was simply not worth the candle. Even the illusions of Woodstock were shattered by the violence which erupted at the Altamont rock festival later that year (Mehnert 1977:63, 136; Young 1977:351).

Feminism

Within the leadership of the late New Left, it was the rise of the women's movement which made the business-as-usual process impossible. The meteoric rise of feminism in the late sixties was itself an expression of changes in the gender composition of the labour force and the concomi-tant transformation of domestic relations. It is interesting to note that both the university and the family had, to some extent, been able to withstand the assault of market relations until the sixties. The student and feminist movements were in fact Trojan Horses of the commodity relation in the university and family respectively. To paraphrase the words of Henry Maine, the basis of the formal existence of students and women in society had been shifting from status to contract (Levitt 1979:651).

The student movement, in particular the leadership, was, at least until the mid-sixties, a relatively tightly knit group which functioned on the basis of more or less forthright discussion and open debate. The rise of the women's caucuses, which effectively excluded half the movement from its meetings, made the continuation of this process impossible. According to one of the original Michigan sds people: 'There was a period of time when it was literally impossible to have a political organization that had both men and women in it and not be totally occupied with struggles over sexism, and that simply made it impossible to do political work ... I have no doubt that that struggle and that strife made it difficult or impossible to keep organizations together.'

Supporters of the women's caucuses protested at the time that women in the student movement had been relegated to more or less secretarial positions, tending the copying machines and preparing the coffee, while the men engaged in serious debate and made all the decisions. There is a kernel of truth in this. The males were generally more concerned with the larger issues, with theoretical and strategic questions.

Interestingly, it was not the most submissive and least articulate women who led the attack against the 'male chauvinist' leadership. Rather, the 'revolt of the women,' as some have called it, within the New Left in North America (feminism did not achieve the same degree of prominence in Germany during the sixties) was led by the most politically experienced, articulate women, in many cases in league with junior male leaders. A prominent Canadian student leader in the sixties explains the matter frankly as follows:

You get these up-front, very experienced, socially very experienced, personally very experienced, politically [very experienced] women saying: 'Women must caucus together so they can get their act together,' sort of thing, which, to my mind, was really phony. Because you've got women doing that speaking who have every verbal skill, political skill, and a background of political practice, you know, equal to most and exceeding some of the male leadership. Maybe they had been kept out and that was some discrimination or something. But they led that off as an excuse, I think, and started their own external movement that split the movement, done in the name of and the image of this grouping of women who were inexperienced, couldn't speak in meetings, were intimidated, and all the bullshit, when, in fact, the only ones who ever spoke were these women who were thoroughly politicized, thoroughly competent to act, organize, write, speak, or any other goddam thing.

In general, the women were much more involved with the daily affairs of the movement, with the tactics and immediate responses to situations.[11] It is no accident that the women's caucuses arose precisely at the time when the turn towards theory was in full swing. The women's movement not only provided a political vehicle for articulate female leaders; it also re-established the primacy of the immediate response, the practical moment, the here and now. It reasserted the early New Left emphasis upon explicitly moral action to effect social change.[12] What was supposed to change, however, was not, in the first instance, society; it was the relations and attitudes within the radical groups themselves (cf Young 1977:360, 371–2).

The rise of feminism within the New Left was directly related to the reasons for the movement's collapse – the successive defeats in society and the alienation of the leadership from the mass of students. The male allies of the women's caucuses were, to a large degree, younger recruits in the secondary leadership who had not been through the early peace and civil rights struggles. They felt the want, not of theoretical reflection, but of practical action.[13] With the loss of the practical initiative of the New Left in civil rights, antiwar protest, and the transformation of the university, feminism became the matter *par excellence* of the New Left.

Consequences

As the sixties advanced, the grandness of the New Left political goals grew in direct proportion to the increasing helplessness and isolation of the students. With the full demographic force of the largest youth generation in history behind them, the advance guard of the baby boom asserted a global political claim. This is given expression in the following recollection of a former Canadian student leader: 'It was probably at the CUS seminar at London [Ontario] when somebody actually got up and said: "Look, reforming the university isn't good enough; we have to reform the whole world."'

When the actual weakness of the student movement became apparent (of course, it should not be forgotten that this weakness was in part a result of its limited successes), the activist core proceeded to emphasize its fantastic strength by different means. As a former National Secretary of the American SDS views it: 'The way I see the demise is the failure of the student movement to grasp the specificity of its own social, historical moment and to find effective organic links beyond the campus. And in that failure it attempts to find either mechanical links to the blue collar proletariat, or melodramatic links to the Third World.'

That part of the student movement which denied its student character sought to overcome its real weakness by means of a fantastic identification with some much more powerful constituency. The former SDS national secretary explains: 'Thus enters the problem that they began to accept all of the formulations of the mid-nineteenth century in a very mechanical way, as applicable to describing the reality of advanced capitalism. And since the good book said the workers were ... for real, a lot of people decided the students were for shit and they should go out and organize the workers; and mass confusion resulted.'

With the desertion of the mass student base at the end of the decade and the 'upping of the ante,' as we have seen, reality gave way more and more to political fantasy. 'Proletarian' parties were formed which were differentiated from one another on wholly abstract ideological grounds. All of them, however, shared one characteristic: the notable lack of a 'proletarian' membership. At first some of these parties were able to evoke a certain degree of enthusiasm from those who believed they had at last found an entrée into real history. However, the sharp rebuke which these groups suffered at the hands of the very constituency which they sought to lead caused great disillusionment. Those parties which did manage to survive did so as sectarian groups whose members were held together by a kind of religious attachment. One of the former leaders of the German SDS describes the reception experienced by the student vanguard parties at the hands of the real proletariat: 'The proletariat doesn't love you at all; rather they say: "Oh God, are they weird? They have the opportunity to study and now they're here in the factory twisting screws into tin. I think that's a riot!" Thus, the law of the proletariat which they wanted to reach, they did not reach. The proletarians said then, mostly very correctly: "God. Who knows how long it will last? At some point in time they will be our superiors once again." It very often happened that way too.'

Another former German SDS leader echoes this view that the student turn towards the proletariat was essentially a manifestation of an élitist self-assertion: 'The student movement encountered rejection among many sections of the population, especially among the workers, because in many points, really, this mentality of the sons of the ruling class, so to speak, and also certain claims to domination were symbolized by it.'

But just as one part of the student movement was developing its own version of a *Proletkult*, other groupings were lining up with the oppressed peoples of the Third World and with the exploited minorities within the heartland of imperialism. In its extreme formulation, the ideological viewpoint of these groups portrayed the white, industrial proletariat of the 'advanced' countries (especially of North America) as hopelessly racist and in collusion with the capitalist class. If some groups sought to overcome the helplessness and isolation of the student condition by means of a fantasy about an actually revolutionary proletariat, the Third Worldists in their fantasy took leave of their respective countries altogether. As a former leader of the early SDS in America says:

I said at the time last summer [at the SDS reunion, summer 1977] that it wasn't that we had abandoned the blacks; it was most of the organization ... abandoned this country as a whole in terms of any kind of change here. It really became Third World/antiwar, and we saw ourselves as sort of the extension of the Third World movement here rather than as an indigenous movement. That was always the big conflict with the 'prairie power' folk, at least among the 'prairie power' folk, who were the most indigenous types you could find, trying to fit into this cookie mould, you know. Were they Chinese? Were they Vietnamese? What were they?

Yet, in spite of the radical democratic rhetoric and the near worship of the Third World people, there was an élitist self-assertion by the students here as well, as one of the second generation of SDS leadership people in the United States recalled: 'It was an incredible sense of power and of being different, not being like them. It was arrogant too. That's another thing, arrogance. I was better, we were better, we were better than everybody else. And what a fine feeling it is to be better than everybody else.'

In spite of the appearance of these numerous 'proletarian' parties, Third World support groups, urban guerrilla cells, and so on, the mass of formerly sympathetic, generally liberal students had become thoroughly disenchanted with the leadership of all factions. As the ideological rhetoric grew increasingly remote from the real world, fewer and fewer students would listen (in spite of their persistent apprehension about the war – after 1967 they preferred to follow liberals such as Eugene McCarthy and Robert Kennedy). A former member of the CUS secretariat recalls the irrelevance of the ideology of the late New Left as follows:

I mean, you had Stalinists and Leninists and all the rest. They all had nothing to do with what was going on. A huge web of words that absolutely had nothing to do with what was going on, not a thing. Arguing about this and that, and if you stopped and took a vote ... I mean they had twelve people who were in on whatever the vocabulary was at that time. I think Oglesby's description of that process was absolutely perfect: vanguarditis. You know, its connection with the flu is absolutely perfect. I mean it hit fewer and fewer people leaving fewer and fewer people, and in some sense it's a perfect reflection on North American society ... You have a theory that has absolutely nothing to do with the society.

Throughout the sixties the New Left students had always been able to return to their 'natural' base, the university, after having suffered defeat in the society beyond. However, at the end of the decade the student movement could no longer hold its momentum on the campus, as this former SUPA leader elaborates: 'We had to go back into the universities. That was where the natural base was. And if we were to grow, it would be in the universities. This didn't happen. One of the obvious reasons it didn't happen was that more and more people who were professional New Leftists were no longer based in universities. They graduated, they dropped out, they'd whatever ... And it was impossible to get back into the universities in any substantial way.'

But there is more to this story. The 'political generation' of students in the sixties was only the vanguard of a larger baby boom cohort. The relatively apolitical students, especially those in North America, who followed their activist co-generationists into the academy learned a lesson from the experiences of their forerunners. They saw the futility of antiwar protest, the end of the lucrative job market for university graduates, the Kent State killings, the declaration of the War Measures Act, the eruption of left terrorism and its consequences, and so on. At the same time, there had been partial victories, and enough of them to allow one to live at least in a state of peaceful coexistence with the system. Satisfied with partial victories in the face of a host of negative incentives for continuing with or joining the New Left, the post-1950 baby boomers began to turn away from the movement.

Paradoxically, it was the series of partial victories which the New Left won which was responsible for cutting it off from society at large and from its mass student base. It was robbed of the little substantiality which it formerly possessed, and it was left with an empty shell of rhetoric which imploded owing to a lack of meaningful content. The last struggle of the movement with itself was a struggle over words and phrases full of sound and fury, but signifying nothing.

One former CUS field-secretary referred to the isolation of the students in the following terms:

These were mainly students, mainly young people. What in heaven's name was the rest of society doing? What the rest of society was doing was going to work every morning and paying off a mortgage. And I'd say without cynicism, it's a perfectly reasonable occupation; and the rest of society, the bulk of people that were going to work and paying the bills – perhaps starting working in the depression or in the Second World War or in the fifties – that was the bulk of the working population. They had a particular set of attitudes about this, that, and everything. And you have to ask yourself ... what in heaven's name could this movement of young people accomplish? What – ignore the war for a second –

what in heaven's name could it say to them? And the answer at that point, if one's realistic, is, not a hell of a lot.

Pointing to the irrelevance of the student movement to the larger society he continues: 'They couldn't get the point that there was a whole society that was continuing in spite of all the notions, all the categories, and all the predictions of their theory. And it was a theory that ... it was a vocabulary borrowed and like a bad band-aid stuck on something.'

There is more to be said about the nature of the theory which appeared to the person speaking above to be a 'bad band-aid.' For the present, however, we shall be interested in the assessment of the failure of the student movement made by the former activists themselves. Time and again they expressed the ambivalent character of the movement, the seemingly irresolvable contradictions, and the isolation of the students from the general life of society. A former SDS organizer from New York suggested: 'You can't have any kind of movement, because what we're about is, we have to negate who we are and become sort of a pure expression; and everything we've been about has not been mass constituent politics, but sort of a pure act of rebellion ... and that was the dominant politics of SDS when it ended ... it was always a part of SDS and it's one way of dealing with class ambivalence, class tension.'

One former leader of the Revolutionary Youth Movement (RYM) II faction of SDS suggested that, even though the fractionalization of SDS was not inevitable, there was indeed a 'problem in being a substitution for the [working] class.' On the one hand SDS would say the students were everything, while on the other hand they would say that the students were nothing. An independent SDS leader who was present at the Chicago convention in 1969 made a similar observation: 'We were totally isolated from them [the membership of SDS] and they were isolated from our base. We flip-flopped constantly and it – just a capriciousness to everything we were doing. It's deadly, and we were destroyed.'

The German students voiced the same kind of views as their North American counterparts concerning the dissolution of the student movement. One student leader in Berlin had the following analysis to make:

Students are outside of production; they have no real power, and the groups or classes in society who have the real power – they weren't directly involved in all that went on. And so all the desires and ideas and all that, that which one had believed, all of a sudden collapsed. One had to find other solutions – then came the fractionalization within the student movement and the founding of the κ-groups [the various communist parties] of organizations which asserted that they were the vanguard of the proletariat, without having any relation to the proletariat.

A former leader of SDS, now a professor of philosophy in Bremen, saw the source of the dissolution in the isolation of the students: 'The students began to act crazy when they considered where the real powers were supposed to come from with which the changes which they recognized as necessary could be carried out.' A former student leader in Hamburg, now a journalist in that city, echoes the sentiment: 'But precisely this sub-cultural dimension was one which basically allowed no contact with the population. Because these sub-cultural experiences, which were, perhaps, the most essential for politicization, occurred on a wavelength where perhaps segments of working youth were reached, but otherwise, nobody.'

Finally, a music teacher in Frankfurt with a doctorate in philosophy presents the following critique of the student movement in discussing the reasons for its collapse: 'Actually the students revolted because they lost their status; for the same reason the revolt collapsed. The student movement did not collapse because the students made mistakes. They didn't capitulate to a superpowerful enemy, and they were not the victims of the police. Rather, it ended because their task – the destruction of the old university and the preparation of a free area for wilful incursions by the state – was completed. When the curtain drops, the actors leave the stage.'

Previous works on the student movement have been preoccupied with the forms of expression of the movement, ignoring for the most part the content. The authors of these works would have us believe that the student movement had its own independent, internal dynamic; that it was a free response to political and social events; that it entered into profane social history; in short, that it was historically substantial. We are presented with conference resolutions, counter-resolutions, faction fights, slogans, counter-slogans, strategies and counter-strategies, demonstrations, marches, and other actions and are told that this is the substance of history. Here the formal side has been consciously neglected in so far as it was an expression of its content. But the student movement fashioned its own instruments of expression from the experiences of the generation of post-war middle class youth, experiences filled with the symbols and artefacts, hopes, fears and wants, conditions and relations of a prosperous middle class, but at the same time of a middle class which was gradually but inexorably losing its room for manoeuvring.

In this way the New Left can be understood only in terms of these conditions. We can conceive of it allegorically as a modern Western movie. (The baby boom generation was fed a steady diet of such films during its formative years.) The hero and the villain were easily identifiable, and the distinction between good and evil appeared in a palpable form on the silver screen. In the end, good would always triumph over evil. It has been argued that youth was 'brainwashed' by these films, by television, the press, and the schools. But the themes which were presented, ingested, and internalized were ideal expressions of the situation of youth in the society of relative prosperity that existed in the fifties and sixties. The student movement chose its own costumes, sets, and props from the world of politics, but it harnessed them to those themes which were a central part of its own constitution, which were expressions of what it in fact was. The play may be the thing, but it is a drama which portrays the reality of the players as-if. In the last instance, the fantasy is built upon real relations and interests from which it is derived; or rather, specific relations and conditions give rise to fantastic representations which are nothing other than the fantastic representations of the specific relations and conditions requiring them.

PART FOUR: IDEOLOGY

I AM
A HUMAN BEING:
DO NOT FOLD,
SPINDLE OR
MUTILATE

WHERE IS
OSWALD NOW
THAT WE
NEED HIM

10th Anniversary FESTIVAL OF LIFE
Yippie!
CHICAGO Aug 26-27

INDUSTRIAL WORKERS OF THE WORLD
I
W★W

I AM A
BOURGEOIS
LIBERAL
CAREERIST
ELITIST
NEO-HEGELIAN
IDEALIST
PIG

Ż

6

Marxism and the final beatification of the student movement

We have seen that the last phase of the organized student movement was marked by the growing influence of Marxist theory, Marxist rhetoric, and Marxist forms of organization. In Germany the members of SDS were abstractly aware of the great Marxist tradition of the social-democratic and communist movements, but the concern with Marxist theory was not widespread in the SPD during the fifties. The party did not act on the appeals from different quarters within SDS to establish theoretically oriented institutes, programs, and journals. At the universities in the FRG there were, with barely a handful of exceptions, no knowledgeable Marxists to be found (Briem 1979). The basis of the understanding of Marxism within SDS in the fifties was obtained unintentionally as a by-product of the confrontations between SDS and the Freie Deutsche Jugend (FDJ) of the GDR. In order to deal with the stock arguments of the latter, the members of SDS were forced to familiarize themselves with the basic texts of Marx and of Marxism. Not until the mid-sixties did a body of literature exist *en masse* which could support the theoretical want of the students for Marxist texts.

In the United States many of the New Leftists in SDS turned towards Marxism as a defence against the growing influence of PL within their midst. One of the original Michigan SDSers explains the growing influence of Marxism in the ranks of the New Left in the following:

Within SDS there was, well, the Progressive Labor influx; what did this mean? They had a clarity of analysis, of expression, that no one else in SDS could match. They had a coherent line. It was wrong. People felt it was wrong. How do you answer this? If you answered it anarchistically, presumably you were vulnerable to all kinds of dirty allegations, of petty bourgeois, self-indulgent tendencies

... But how do you answer that? ... My answer would have been ... if I had been involved directly in the sds debates, I would have tried to work it out. Not a Marxist answer, but an answer which came out of the experience of the people directly as students – anarchism, or whatever. But the people who tried to answer them answered on Marxist grounds that they thought were the most effective. You could undermine them best if you could show that they weren't even quoting Marx right; they were stupid Marxists.

There had never been a mass tradition of Marxism in North America, and classical works of Western Marxism in English were all but unavailable. Theoretical Marxism trickled into the movement from a variety of disparate sources: the 'humanist' writings of Marx introduced by those such as Erich Fromm (1961, 1962); the critical theory of the Frankfurt School, especially the writings of Herbert Marcuse after 1965; Old Left literature, especially through the Communist Party (cpusa), pl, and the Socialist Workers Party (swp); and the tradition of black and Third World Marxism. In Canada an additional input came from the socialist and separatist movements in Quebec, which had been influenced by currents of contemporary neo-Marxism in France.

The rapid conversion by segments of the New Left (especially of the leadership) to some form of self-professed Marxism is one of the fascinating puzzles of the student movement of the sixties. Many former activists believe that one of the major accomplishments of their movement consists in the establishment within the intellectual world of the legitimacy of Marxism as a vehicle for the expression of thoughts and ideas. They point with pride to the number of journals which survived the organizational collapse of the New Left and they indicate that a substantial number of Marxists, many of whom are veterans of the student movement, are currently employed as faculty members at leading universities. Not only has Marxism become 'respectable' in many disciplines, but in some fields it occupies a leading theoretical position.[1]

The overwhelming agreement among former activists concerning the shift to Marxism in the New Left was founded upon their acceptance of a correspondence theory of truth: Marxism was embraced by the New Left because it was 'true' or 'correct,' a reflection in theory of the truth of history. As a former cus activist suggests:

First, Marxism is correct. Correct in the sense that it's the single most useful analytical tool. If you've got a bunch of people like highly idealistic, moralistic university students who in the beginning to mid-late sixties were trying to sort out what's going on in the world, whether it's nuclear weapons, or whether it's civil rights, or whether it's accessibility to post-secondary education, or whatever ... It's not surprising if they're serious about finding out that they hit upon Marxism.

In addition, many added that it had been 'successful' in Russia, Cuba, China, and Vietnam, although it was not clear if the success of Marxism was supposed to be a function of its truth or its truth a function of its success. To be sure, the theory of Marxism is a powerful intellectual instrument and it does hold an attraction for serious students of society and history. But it is difficult to believe that the student movement was drawn to Marxism for these reasons. On the one hand, the student left prided itself on the emphasis which it placed on practical political and social action. On the other hand, the conversion of New Leftists to Marxism did not occur on an individual basis; Marxism literally swept through student circles in country after country, pulling thousands into its hold and capturing the imagination of an entire movement in the period of its decline. Such a process demands a sociological explanation. But there are further difficulties in understanding the Marxism of the student movement, difficulties which compound the conundrum. Those who are familiar with the history of the socialist movement will know that it was at one time indissolubly linked to the working class, that it was a movement of the dispossessed producers of social wealth. Marxism was part of that history, and the works of Marx constitute a basis for the theory of socialism. Even though a core of intellectuals had acted as the keepers of the holy script, the key texts of Marx were read and studied by the workers themselves.

Samuel Gompers, as a young cigar maker, would read aloud from *Capital* to his fellow workers on the job, while they took up his share of the labour. Sailors took the works of Marx with them to sea. But the works of Marx are no longer part of that living struggle of the working class. Instead, they have found their way to the universities, where they have been appropriated by the numerous schools of Marx-interpretation. The students who have remade Marx in their own image have taken up the moribund tradition of the working class as an unintended caricature of it. The academic Marxism which flourished in the seventies was fed by the 'graduates' of the student movement of the sixties.[2]

The solution to the riddle of middle class Marxism is at once the key to the understanding of the student revolt, for the *Unbehagen* of the sixties generation which found expresion in Marxist theory emanates from the same conditions which gave rise to the student movement. But we have already traced the profane history of the movement and established the specific conditions out of which it developed: the changing character of middle class life and the impact which this had upon the universities and the youth of the middle class. The necessarily ambivalent and tragic character of the student movement is determined by these conditions.

At the end of the sixties we find a curious situation in which one part of the student movement is embracing Marxism because it has nothing to do with students (students are at best petty bourgeois allies of the proletariat) while another part is embracing Marxism because it has everything to do with students (students as proletarians, new working class, and so on). This ambivalence in relation to Marxism was another expression of the ambivalence of the relations of this student generation in society.

In 1967–8, when the movement took a sharp rhetorical turn to the left, the leaders of the student movement, seeing the last connections with social reality slipping away, began to construct a fantastic theory which would secure for the movement not those links to the real world but the real world itself. The student role in one tendency was completely denied in order that the students – the 'Party' – could stand at the head of an imaginary revolutionary force – the 'proletariat' (Mehnert 1977:235). The organizational form which this tendency assumed was borrowed from the Old Left and in most cases, consciously, from the Stalinist past. The zeal and brutality with which the bourgeois devil within each comrade was exorcized by the 'Party' were not powerful enough to drive out the roots of the ambivalence of the student condition.[3] In the United States, the Stalin T-shirts worn by some members of the RYM II faction of SDS were symptomatic of the self-mockery of the comrades. These new 'Old Left'-style groups rejected the counter-culture and its accoutrements. The clean shaven, short-haired men and well-dressed and neatly attired men and women had reached the point of extreme dissociation of mind and body as they played out the ambivalence of the movement within themselves: in body they were the very picture of bourgeois respectability – good children; in mind they were the demonic harbingers of destruction of the basis of that respectability. The Stalinist-Maoist was thus a living contradiction.[4]

The terrorists, members of the Weather Underground in the United States, of the RAF in the FRG, although composed of only a handful of movement members and supported by a few more, were not divided body and soul in the above-mentioned manner. Rather, they projected their bourgeois personae into a totally hostile external world. But one cannot live as pure negativity except by consuming everything which lies in one's path. Having destroyed themselves body and soul, they were forced to destroy themselves as others. Terrorism was the search for the moment of pure freedom in the act of destruction. It represents the greatest alienation of the moral consciousness from the forces of society and history. The moralist asserts the moral position for its own sake. This moral position thus depends upon its ineffectiveness in time and space. The 'abstract' terrorist engages in acts of terrorism for a similar reason: terror is the expression of the complete helplessness of its perpetrators before the real forces of history.

The bearers of the early New Left 'tradition' during the period of decay of the student movement were those who were committed to the general values of the counter-culture and the youth revolution. New Left leaders, trained in the disciplines of sociology, economics, and political science, made use of the tools of those trades in searching out the roots of the generational revolt. Gone was the view that the student revolt was a moral protest against a society whose ideals and actuality were out of joint. The students were no longer seen as 'bourgeois' moralists preaching against the hypocrisy of society and its institutions. The students' struggle was now becoming a class conscious challenge to the capitalist order itself. The students had a class interest which they were promoting. Like the proletariat of old, the students had no ideals to realize (Marx and Engels 1975).

The most ambitious attempt in the sixties from within the New Left in North America to account for the student movement, in terms of changing material conditions, was the popular 'youth-as-class' analysis (Rowntree and Rowntree 1968a, 1968b, 1968c). Using US data, John and Margaret Rowntree demonstrated that the post-war American economy 'had been changing from a goods-producing private economy to a government-supported economy producing war and knowledge' (1968b:8). By the mid-sixties, they argued, at least half the male population between the ages of eighteen and twenty-four years were students, soldiers, or among the ranks of the unemployed. (The ranks of the unemployed, in their view, would have been much larger were it not for the fact that the schools and the military had already absorbed vast numbers of otherwise unemployable youth.) According to their analysis it was the function of the learning and warring institutions to deflect potentially surplus manpower from the labour market. The condition in which these youth in the schools and in the military found themselves was highly exploitative. 'The young are exploited as soldiers, as students, and as unemployed workers.'[5] As unemployed they are robbed of their productive potential; as young soldiers they are underpaid and trained to kill; as students they are forced to produce and reproduce themselves as skilled labour to suit the wants of corporate capital. In short, the New Left was thus a genuinely proletarian response to the proletarianization of youth.

This essay of the Rowntrees (1968a, 1968b, 1968c) was reprinted in a number of different formats, and it was made available to the New Left internationally. It can be seen as the distinctly North American contribution to the general theory of the new working class which had been developed in France. Attempting to explain the increasing militancy among the young and highly trained sections of the working class, the French theorists 'discovered' that a change had indeed taken place in the conditions of labour in the advanced capitalist countries. Skilled technical and scientific labourers, educated in the higher academies and reared to be creative and self-actualizing in the practice of their professions, were entering the authoritarian and stultifying work places of capitalist industrial production, where creativity and self-expression were necessarily suppressed by the predominance of the profit motive and the exigencies of the bureaucratic organization of the enterprises. According to the theory of the new working class, these highly trained, repressed, and thus rebellious sections of the working class would raise the radical demand for control of the process of production and by their bold and revolutionary action would animate the old factory proletariat. Factory occupations in France and Italy and university rebellion around the world were seen as the proof of the theory. Thus, the new working class, growing in size with the influx of university graduates, would come to act as the vanguard of the working class as a whole.

As we have seen, those who became 'new working class' or 'youth as class' Marxists elevated in importance the historical role of youth and students. Unlike those Marxists who glorified the blue-collar workers (seeking in this way to escape the student condition), the new Marxists saw in Marxism a world-view which was meaningful to them as students, which was about their lives. As one former leader of the American SDS put it: 'Don't you see, that Marx was rediscovered, or discovered by many people. And it is in that context that people were looking at the role of the working class. And, people felt, especially in this country I'm talking about – now I want to repeat that – people felt that when they were talking about the working class, they were talking about a reconstituted proletariat. They were in fact part of it ... It was not a completely foreign thing to them.'

According to the theory of the new working class, the educated workers, those who are creative, self-actualizing, and independent, would not allow themselves to continue to be oppressed and exploited by capitalism. In the view of a former CUS activist, students recognize this contradiction:

Marx said it was going to happen when people got together in factories. I mean we weren't exactly in factories, that's quite true, and we weren't productive labour. On the other hand, it was for us, for those of us who became politically involved, and we were confident, we were together, which Marx said would have to happen like a sack of potatoes analogy, that we would have to be in the same place doing the same thing. And he thought industrialization would bring that about. And it seems to me industrialization precisely brought us about. It was also the contradictions created by capitalism. At the same time that they wanted to produce us as people who could run the system, we had to be people who were independent enough to make our own decisions, people who could develop, people who would be educated enough to be able to make their own decisions and operate the system. At the same time, they had to control us. And those two contradictions ... are going to come into conflict. And they came into conflict.

It has been shown above that the 'contradiction' which gave rise to Marxism within the New Left was not between educated labour and the wants of capital, but rather between the promise of élite access for middle class youth and the massification of the élite of university-trained mediate producers. Understood in this way, the following explanation of the New Left turn towards Marxism offered by the CUS activist cited above becomes immediately intelligible: 'Marxism, for us, did not arise out of nowhere. It arose out of our real conditions. It arose out of the contradictions that we faced in our daily lives between the ideas and realities and also between the kinds of opportunities and realities.' In a further statement, she actually tells us that 'proletarian-ization' means becoming 'middle management':

There is a proletarianization of this group going to university. Before, the mass post-secondary education people went to university to learn specific professional skills or to get a civilizing veneer, before they went out to rule. Starting in the sixties, the perception of this was very dim at the beginning to be sure, but, starting in the sixties, it was the factory for people to start doing middle management – from the enrolment figures, from the recruitment on campus, all that kind of very hard data. You get a new kind of university student.

But why did the students choose Marx? For centuries youth and students have adopted extremist positions 'pour épater le bourgeois.' But in the sixties the students were angry about what they perceived to be the 'broken promise,' and they reacted by choosing as an expression of their discontent a political ideology which was, in the context of the cold war, the antithesis of the liberalism which had betrayed them. As a former member of the cus secretariat states: 'What's the opposite of capitalism? The opposite of capitalism is communism. Who writes about capitalism? God knows – Adam Smith. And who writes about communism? Karl Marx. Karl Marx, the bad guy.'

That Karl Marx, like Robin Hood, was a bad-guy hero is clearly evident in the following exchange between a former campus leader and a national student leader in Canada:

JOHN P.: I think to some extent, yes, because of the character of the duration and the depth of the cold war, what was the one thing you know, that was so diametrically [opposed] to the whole thing was Karl Marx. We all knew that name – Karl Marx. I knew that even before we read him.
CAM C.: Especially before I read him. I was afraid of reading it.
JOHN P.: Especially reading it. And I think we even knew that before we went through the intellectual or psychological process of positioning ourselves in diametrical opposition to the society. We knew that ... the bottom line was Karl Marx. I don't even know how I did. Maybe the Catholic grade school system or some goddamn thing, okay? But I knew, you know. I didn't even know what was there in the writing, you know, but I knew ...
CAM C.: He was the guy.
JOHN P.: That was it.
CAM C.: Big bad Karl.
JOHN P.: He was, he was the guy. But if we had to reach for something that was the ultimate 'fuck you' ...
CAM C.: But at the same time, very few of us read him ... and few that read understood.
JOHN P.: Right.

In Germany the name Karl Marx also had this same quality of being a *Bürgerschreck*, a word which brings terror to the middle class. As one of the leaders of the Berlin sds says: 'It also had a provocatory significance, especially in a country such as Germany where Marx had been thoroughly banished, where you could terrorize the middle class just by carrying round a copy of *Capital*. If any citizen saw that you had a book not by Karl May, but by Karl Marx, under your arm, he would be terrified.'

The Marxism of the late New Left was not something artificially foisted upon the movement. Rather, it gave the movement a way of (fantastically) explaining itself to itself and of coping with its isolation and political helplessness. By allowing the most contradictory 'readings' and 'interpretations,' it was the perfect ambivalent theory for the ambivalent reality of the student movement. The students could only be makers of history by taking leave of history, that is, by making history in their heads. As an astute former sds leader in Hamburg observes:

I believe, if one assumes that more was said about Marx than people reading him, and secondly, when one asks – why precisely Marx? One would first have to say to that it is characteristic of every bourgeois movement ... that they deny themselves and that they attempt to be other than they are. Then they try to take leave of history too. To this extent this would perhaps be an explanation for the fact that precisely Marx ... above all when one sees that Marx ... was a symbol for this wholly other world. Precisely then when he wasn't read or when he was read as a total key which explains everything. Then that was an attempt to basically get out of history, not to study society, but to make out of it an abstract concept. Hence, not to search out society, but to have the world in one's head.

In fact, the New Left groups were nowhere able to mount an effective challenge to the power of the Communist and Social Democratic trade unions. Even the great general strike in France, in May 1968, was not able to wrest the rank-and-file away from the leadership of the Confédération générale du travail (cgt) and the Parti communiste français (pcf). The New Leftists, with good reason, yelled betrayal and sell-out, but they failed to understand that history is not made by party leaders and union bureaucrats. The Communist Party of Germany during the formative years of the Weimar Republic made the same error in accusing the revisionist leaders of the spd of leading the masses astray, breaking their raw revolutionary sensibilities, and selling them out to big capital. But it was precisely the revisionist wing of German social democracy which gave expression to the will of the German working class.

Similarly, it was the CGT and the PCF which embodied the will and consciousness of the French proletariat in 1968. In spite of the momentary suspension of the rules of the game, the working class did not fling aside the Communist leadership because the working class was not prepared to rise in revolution. Yet the defeat of the 'revolution' in France was considered by the New Left to have been engineered by political forces from without. Both the sell-out of the French workers in June and the Soviet-backed invasion of Czechoslovakia in August of that same year were condemned in apparently political terms; yet the content of the condemnation was clearly moral. In fact the shift which occurred within the New Left from liberal moralism to 'Marxism' was a shift of form, but not of substance. The same moral impulse which underlay the civil rights struggle of the early sixties sloughed off its liberal husk to emerge newly encased in Marxism. We now trace the developments within the movement which were given expression in the new Marxism.

7

The puzzle of middle class Marxism

Most of the former student radicals who were contacted in connection with this study did not find the question of the Marxism of the New Left terribly perplexing. Of this group, those who did not become Marxists in the late sixties (a distinct minority of those interviewed in all three countries) confessed that they did not understand their fellow activists' fascination with Marxism. Some of the non-Marxists saw it fulfilling a psychological need for identification with a progressive historical force at a time when the movement was being attacked from without and racked with dissension from within. Those who had embraced Marxism or who had come to sympathize with it simply argued that it was correct or successful, in short that it was an accurate, objective view of history and of the historical development of society. The non-Marxists cannot be pressed further, for they are not required to see the inner connection between ideology and class interest to be consistent with their own assumptions. But the majority of those who both addressed themselves to the question and professed an allegiance to Marxism must consider the nature of the relationship between their Marxist world-view and their own social interest. The well-worn saying about the middle class intellectual who joins the proletarian movement – that he has become a traitor to his class – may hold for the isolated defector, but the 'mass' conversion of sizeable numbers of university students clearly demands a sociological explanation.

We have seen that the 'new working class/youth-as-class' analysis was a self-serving one carried out in Marxist guise. Revolutionary activism was the a priori given condition; the analysis was carried out *post festum* to locate a revolutionary agent or subject in history. Once discovered, the analysis of contemporary conditions could be presented as the revolutionary chronicle of the historical agency which, in this stylized account, appears as the very motor of historical development. But this kind of argument can only feed on itself. Once the ephemeral crest of protest has receded, the position had to be discarded or made into an article of faith (that is, projected into some indeterminate future). The history of Marxism is littered with the wreckage of such ideological systems as it is strewn with a varying assortment of sacred texts and 'incontrovertible' theories.

One former member of the German SDS provided a clue to the solution of the puzzle of student Marxism: 'That of all people the students should have held aloft the flag of Marxism does not lie in the particular conditions, for example, of the student movement, but rather is, even if it is a contradiction, one of Marxist theory itself, and as such can be followed from its beginning. The contradiction is based on the fact that Marxist theory is a theory, that is, is limited in so far as it has a determinate medium within which it is composed. That is the deeper explanation.'

It cannot be that the enthusiastic reception of Marxism by many activists students in the late sixties had nothing to do with the particular conditions of the movement. Yet the insight that Marxist theory itself contains its own contradictions and that this has been manifest from its inception is an interesting and important thought. In 1923, Karl Korsch published his *Marxism and Philosophy* (1971a) in which he portrayed the development of Marxist theory in the light of the changes of the relations and conditions of the struggle of the proletariat. It was precisely this theoretical medium, this separation of theory as a realm independent of practical struggles, which was accomplished in the development of Marxism,[1] to which Korsch called attention in this work.

Frank Parkin, in his study of the CND in Britain, characterizes middle class radicalism in the following way:

Given the greater degree of security which professional and white collar employees enjoy, it is perhaps understandable that they should be less inspired than industrial workers to press for deep-seated changes in the entire economic order. By directing the main focus of grievance on to issues of a moral nature, movements based on the middle class are in a sense able to avoid any direct challenge to the legitimacy of the existing social structure, since solutions to problems of this kind do not usually entail serious readjustments to basic institutions ... The approach of the middle class radical movement, unlike its working class counterpart, is to treat each evil *sui generis* and not as reducible to some greater underlying malady which throws into question the legitimacy of the existing order. (1968:54)

This description and explanation of middle class radicalism may apply to the very early period of the New Left, but it does not even consider the possibility, in fact it denies the possibility, of a middle class movement which 'throws into question the legitimacy of the existing order.' Either Parkin's analysis of the character of middle class radicalism is too narrow, or the student movement was not middle class, in which case all the empirical studies would have to be challenged.

Werner Sombart argued that middle class intellectuals who became socialists were individuals who had failed in life's tasks and were attracted to a revolutionary world-view for this reason (Michels 1932:815–16). Hendrik de Man (1928) and Robert Michels (1932) both argued, in opposition to Sombart's thesis, that the resentment of the socialist intellectual is an effect of joining the movement and not the precipitating cause for so doing.[2] George Orwell, in an autobiographical sketch (1958), has portrayed the radicalism of the bourgeois intellectual as a revolutionary response to the brutalizing conditions of capitalist society: 'I felt that I had got to escape not merely from imperialism but from every form of man's dominion over men ... At that time failure seemed to me to be the only virtue. Every suspicion of self-advancement, even to 'succeed' in life to the extent of making a few hundreds a year, seemed to me spiritually ugly, a species of bullying.'

Karl Korsch, eschewing the psychologism of such explanations, examined the social interest behind the ideology of Marxism (1971b:130). He found that Marxism was not the 'revolutionary form of development of proletarian class consciousness and class struggle but rather ... its fetters and limitation, which for the first time presented in bold strokes generally for all to see the ideas and goals of the bourgeois class, which was revolutionary in a bygone historical epoch.'

To ask the question concerning the attraction of Marxism for the student rebels is to ask the question abstractly, separating that which cannot be separated and later joining the two sides by means of an artificial construction. One does not begin with the two independent qualities – the student movement and Marxism. Rather, Marxism is seen as an expression of the student movement during the period of the latter's dissolution. A scientific grasp of the relation between the movement and its expression must begin with an analysis of the movement itself (that is, with the conditions determining its development).

Student identification with and participation in the civil rights struggle and the peace movement occurred because of the failure of domestic and foreign policies, at least in the eyes of the activist students, even though some progress had been made in both areas (for example, the Supreme Court decision of 1954, the election of John F. Kennedy, and so on); the student movement sought to remake state policy on its own. In the words of a former Canadian activist:

I basically now see the New Left as the activities of middle class kids coming out of the liberal arts schools with fairly strong social consciences trying to remake the world and particularly the government, and I think this particularly involves the state – 99 per cent of what the New Left did involved the state. I mean, it was objecting to state policies, state institutions, state activities, criticizing the government in this way and that way ... It's not irrelevant to point out that the initial movement was around military policy, which is the absolute simple prerogative of the state ... And I think what they were doing was creating the state in an image which would allow for themselves occupationally, ideologically; and my suspicion is, one of the reasons it declined was by and large that that effort was successful.

The new student generation was forcing its way into (and being forced into) the institutions of higher learning which had not been able to 'retool' to accommodate the changing wants of education for this future mass intellectual élite. The student movement was thus at once an expression of the problem, a protest against these conditions, and an ill-fated attempt at a solution. The students believed that they were responding to a situation created wholly by others, when in fact they were responding to a situation which they themselves were helping to create. The opening of the university to broad sections of middle class youth (who were then more dependent than ever upon university training and credentials for material and spiritual rewards) led, at the same time, to a drop in the value of these credentials (students were required to work hard for less), the deterioration of conditions within the universities (industrialization of higher education and the so-called alienation of the students), and the lack of a clear and unambiguous path which led from the university to the very centres of social and political power.

The student response was at first tentative, piecemeal, and overtly liberal. It was a calling of authority to task for not living up to its own ideals. The students embraced those social and political ideals in a practical way (direct action) by attacking those instrumental mechanisms which had failed to realize these generally held ideals. It was the agencies of the state – the state institutions and their policies – which were attacked. The New Left critique was theoretical and practical, although it was the practical side which captured the attention of both the students and their opponents. Practically and theoretically students were becoming the new agency of social policy, or so they thought.[3] In one sense this was the expression of a fantasy which grew out of a condition of social frustration associated with changes in education and the intellectual élite. But at the same time it served as a means to destroy in a practical way the 'old' university which was under attack, and it helped to create the conditions which then allowed this new intellectual élite to take its place in society. This has in fact happened in all advanced countries. The state sector expanded rapidly during the course of the sixties, establishing thereby the occupational infrastructure, especially in the service areas, for which the students had been trained in the universities. This development was not purely political, as some astute observers seem to suggest (Collins 1979). It was not merely a response by a capitalism threatened by high levels of unemployment. Rather, the middle classes were demanding these services, and they were willing, as long as they were able, to pay for them. In the latter half of the seventies and early eighties, funding for these programs has been severely cut as the middle class rebelled against the yoke of taxation and vented its fury against one of its own class fractions, encouraged by the press and private sector.

It has been pointed out that the Marxism of the late New Left accompanied the dissolution of the student movement; hence it was not an expression of strength but of weakness.[4] The acceptance of Marxism by broad sections of the student leadership (it is difficult to make any serious claims concerning the rank and file) was (and still is) seen as an explicit rejection of liberal ideology, of the promise of the ideals of liberal corporate capitalism. But in fact it was a rejection of existing reality which failed to measure up to its ideals. Marxism showed the student radicals that liberal capitalism could never live up to its lofty ideals; further it 'scientifically' demonstrated that the ideology of the system was itself responsible for the social evils of capitalism. The new goals of the movement were thus anticapitalist ones. The students would no longer primarily concern themselves with civil equality, freedom of speech, and pacifism, but with anti-imperialist struggles, anticapitalist actions, and human liberation. The latter were not moral exhortations to action; they were being advanced in a practical way by the forces of history itself. In the last instance, it was Marxism as the expression of the logic of history which captured the imagination of the students in the late sixties. The principles of Marxism were seen to be the very principles of the movement of history, and those who armed themselves with them and acted on them in a political way would be part of the vanguard of those progressive forces which were at work. The belief that 'nothing can change the shape of things to come' did not lead to a passivity among the student Marxists any more than the doctrine of predestination did among the followers of Calvin (Weber 1958).

It is, of course, true that not all students who adopted Marxism in the late sixties accepted the iron law of historical necessity blindly. But all of them felt that Marxism was closely in touch with real historical forces and agencies which were at work undermining the capitalist order and which eventually would blow the entire system apart. If they rejected the idea of the Old Left that the factory proletariat would lead this struggle (and not all of them did so by any means), they advanced a 'new' working class thesis or a theory of marginal revolutionaries or a variant of Third Worldism, all attempts to recreate the historical vanguard. Civil rights and peace campaigns were tools of the ruling class which hindered the growth of a 'true' and 'correct' consciousness among the oppressed. In accepting Marxism, the students were merely accepting a view of the world which was 'correct,' which was a faithful mirror in theory of that which was occurring before their eyes. In this way Marxism came to be seen as a theory which is objectively true (that is, whose principles correspond to reality). This understanding of Marxism was not unique to the radical students of the sixties. It was held and defended by no less a figure than Rosa Luxemburg herself in an article in the Social Democratic paper *Vorwärts* in 1905:

If we, therefore, sense a theoretical stagnation in the movement at present, it is not because the theory of Marx from which we ate and drank is not capable of development or has 'outlived' itself, but quite on the contrary because we have already taken the most important spiritual [*geistigen*] weapons which were necessary for our struggle in the foregoing period from Marx's arsenal without making full use of them thereby; not because we have 'surpassed' Marx in the practical struggle, but on the contrary because Marx surpassed *us* as the practical party of struggle in advance in his scientific creation; not because

Marx is no longer sufficient for our wants, but rather because our wants are not yet sufficient for the utilization of Marx's thoughts. (1974:368)

Karl Korsch cites the *Critique of the Gotha Program* to show that even Marx himself 'was not entirely free from this somewhat dogmatic and idealist conception of the relationship of his Marxist theory to later manifestations of the working-class movement' (1971a:101n).

The first phase of the student movement (1960–4) represented the political expression of the demands of the students which were based on the promise which was made to them. The goals of the student movement were the professed goals of society. During this earlier period, the first wave of the post-war baby boom crashed into the universities, and the universities were unable to fulfil the expectations which had been raised by the promise. They could not possibly have done so. The real demands of the student generation were free access to the intellectual and social élite (conceived of in terms of the conditions of the forties and fifties) and the simultaneous democratization (and hence weakening) of that élite which was necessary to accommodate the new giant wave of university-trained people. The fulfilment of one set of demands would mean the automatic frustration of the other. This contradiction lay at the very heart of the student movement and determined its specifically ambivalent character. The first phase of the movement emphasized such goals as democratization and universal accessibility. But with the attainment of a modest degree of success in this area (the new generation had lodged itself in the universities) attention was called to the other pole, to the 'élitist' set of demands which has already been described. But the fulfilment of these demands had now been made impossible by the success of the process of 'democratization,' of the *de facto* destruction of the spirit of the 'élite' university.

The escalation of the war in Vietnam provided the student movement (at least in the United States) with another strong interest of its own (Krader 1971:61), but opposition to the war soon shifted away from the campus, as we have seen. As the focus of the movement began to move from democratization and equality to questions of power – that is, to the demand for real or meaningful élitism (1965–7) – the criticism of the conduct of the war in Vietnam was used by the students in their attack upon power and authority. By 1968 it had become clear that the student movement had lost its control of socially relevant protest in America. It had been 'expelled' from the black power movement (1965–6), it was defeated in the white slums of America, it was being co-opted or pre-empted by the government, and, of course, it was being suppressed and subverted by the agencies of the state. At the same time, *in loco parentis* regulations were being repealed and the ethos of the counter-culture had firmly established itself among the generation of sixties youth. But as real involvement with the issues was being eroded in fact, a turn was made to an ideal involvement, not with issues, but with 'history' in fantasy. The Marxism of the class of budding mediate producers represented an attempt to cast the world in such a way as to assign to this class a powerful and centrally important role in history.[5] We have already seen how the different 'warring' factions of the student movement attempted to do precisely this. Far from being a scientific view of the historical forces at work in society, the Marxism of the student movement, in all its forms, was a covertly moral condemnation of society, overtly presented as a scientific apprehension of an existing state of affairs which assigned to the student intellectuals (in differing ways) a central role in the class struggle. Since the student movement was being thwarted in reality, Marxism provided it with a better counter-reality. But Jürgen Habermas (1968, 1970) and other critics of the student Marxists were wrong in dismissing the new direction of the movement as pathological. If there was madness, there was reason in it. It is easy to point to the fantastic character of the student movement in its later phases. Yet it is necessary to grasp the reality which gave rise to this fantasy in order to appreciate fully the sociological determination of the character of the New Left.

This great wave of new intellectuals had moved into the universities but had yet to establish itself in society. The barriers which were only slowly being dismantled had to be completely brought down before these certified intellectuals could move into the new middle class. Here too, they faced the same contradiction which they confronted upon entering the university. The jobs which were being established for them, especially those created by the state, were moderately paid, bureaucratic sinecures, which were turning the new intellectuals into cogs in the service machinery of the state. That these jobs were being created cannot be doubted. One former Canadian activist made the following observation:

The simple fact of the matter was that the number of university trained people who were spilling out of the schools could not possibly have been absorbed in the economic structures that existed at that time ... they simply did not find the social equivalence, the jobs, the institutions, etc, that matched up with the ideology and the vocational training and the intellectual interests that these people had been given; and they were perfectly right, they didn't exist. Social welfare was a relatively small thing; you had none of the sort of planning functions developed then to anywhere what they are now, and these people really ... they came out of schools with all the solutions in their heads to all sorts of problems for which the social mechanism was lacking; but what they were really doing was demanding that the state create those social mechanisms, which, I would say, by and large, the state has done.

But this can only be half the story. If the great transformation within the state agencies and institutions had been definitive, then we would expect to find a New Left identification with the state. But the evidence points to the contrary. Most of the former radicals in all three countries have remained the greatest critics of the state and state policy. There are even some who service the state bureaucracy by day and talk revolution by night. How do we explain the existence of the bureaucrat who seeks the overthrow of the state?

Robert Michels, who had a great influence on the intellectual and political development of the student rebels of the thirties in the United States, was intensely interested in this relationship between intellectuals and the state:

One distinguishes two categories of intellectuals. The first has succeeded in finding lucrative employment in state and society in a position appropriate to his class, while the second besieges the fortresses in vain, without penetrating them. The one group can be compared to mercenaries who defend the state that employs them by any means out of a sense of duty or of concern over losing their positions and other such selfish motives ... The others are the most sworn enemies of the state, restless elements who inflame every dissatisfaction, who put themselves at the disposal of every insurrection. To appease this second dangerous category of intellectuals the state sees itself, from time to time, forced to open the locks of its bureaucracy and thus to bring a line of malcontents and restless spirits over into the 'conservative' camp ... It has need of this defence all the more urgently since the intellectuals are intellectual warriors and, as a rule, when they are forced to remain in the second category, they are inclined to attack precisely that institution whose protection that state sees as one of its central tasks: private property. (1932:814–15)

Although Michels' observations may have been relevant in his own day, they are contradicted by the existence of a group of intellectuals who have been taken into the bosom of the state like the lamb unto Abraham and yet maintain an intransigent hostility to it. But if we recall the nature of this class of intellectuals, we will understand that the issue was not simply one of employment but of a particular kind of employment, 'creative' employment, 'meaningful' employment, 'human' employment – in its social context, élite employment.[6] This demand could not be fully satisfied. Further, the battle with and within the state had not in fact been definitively won by the student radicals, and the outcome of the clash of social interests within the state has remained volatile and indecisive. Marxism has thus become the ideology of the new intellectuals. Arising within the student movement during the period of its dissolution, it continued to represent a power interest of the same class of intellectuals after they left the university and became the servants of the state and the public sector. For the most part today, Marxism has become a statist ideology opposing the existing state to the 'Marxist' state. In this way it is carried by petty bureaucrats and public employees, social workers, teachers, and university professors. This is the material basis of Marxist ideology which has been featured in scientific and literary journals in the Western World over the last decade.

Very few of the former activists who were consulted during the preparation of this present study indicated that they understood the reasons for their failure. They were ready, even eager, to criticize strategies and tactics, theories and actions, organizational forms and interpersonal relations, but few could even consider the possibility that the politics of the period was one of futility.[7] Not being political was, for many of these people, the same as not existing. This was the assumption which under no circumstances could be put into question.[8]

When the movement had played itself out (1968–70) and the precipice beckoned 'Hic Rhodus, hic saltus,' a few leaped (even to their deaths), but most pulled back from the edge. Those who reached the limits of history withdrew into themselves (through drugs, communes, or religious mysticism) or leaped forward into that dimension which in fantasy exists as politics but in reality as terror. The former who arrived at the end of the line abandoned themselves for a fetish or guru. The latter who reached the same point abandoned the world for themselves and made history by committing suicide. When the principle has been grasped that only the proletariat can sweep away the ghosts of the past and present and that it was not living up to its historically appointed task, the temptation to substitute, to 'act in the name of,' becomes difficult to withstand. But one can no more leap over one's time than one can leap over Rhodes. The question is not why the proletariat does not jump through the hoops held by the radical intellectuals, but why the intellectuals emerge as a leading constituency in socialist movements and as a group are the modern spokesmen of Marxism.

For those who came to the edge and did not find the proletariat waiting to ferry them to the other side, the future meant a search for the 'lost' proletariat. Surprisingly, in Germany it was the Communist Party which pulled many of the formerly antiauthoritarian students into its orbit. The DKP and the SEW were able to conjure up the ghosts of the struggles of the past, to show the students the 'real' course of working class history. They could produce 'real' workers who were party members, generic proletarians who embodied the ideal of the class-conscious worker. But above all, the communists were reasonable, oh so reasonable (Mehnert 1977:362). They showed the students that there was no longer a reason for them to be at war with society; what was required was a broad united front of all oppressed and exploited classes against big capital.

To Maoism in its various forms went the immediate spoils of the student movement, even though it began to lose its hold in the early seventies and was all but crushed with the Nixon-Mao accord. Many of the Maoist groups had the characteristics of the religious sects which also mushroomed on the corpse of the student movement. Chilling accounts of the psychological torments experienced by former members have since been published (*Wir warn die stärkste der Partein* 1977). Yet the student movement always had its foreign models – Cuba, China, Vietnam, Albania. Just as value cannot exist in a free state but must move from body to body, stripping off its narrow and limited earthly form in the universality of movement, revealing its wholly social character only in the expression of indifference to any physical body, so too did the New Left comprehend socialism only in the merry-go-round of socialist states taken in turn as incarnations of the socialist heaven. What is this but the wishful thinking of the rootless intellectual, not about his actual roots, but about the ethereal roots of his one-sided intellectuality?

Karl Korsch saw the modern period as a time of general counter-revolution. All the opposing forces on the political spectrum – bitterly divided as they are on matters of politics, philosophy, law, religion, and ideology – are tacitly allied in so far as they are forces of the substantial bondage of social labour. The student movement, especially in Germany, briefly flirted with Korsch in so far as it was able to use his work to secure its own interests.[9] But if Korsch emphasized the question of revolutionary will and consciousness, of the unity of theory and practice, it was always clear that it was the consciousness and practice of the proletariat with which he was concerned. In the long run, Korsch was of little use to the student movement.[10]

The intellectual development of the student movement and the Marxism which emerged out of it comprises a series of flirtations with any and every theoretical position on the spectrum which is exotic and esoteric. The Marxism of the New Left, or rather of its theoretical legacy, is not a fad, but an ensemble of fads.[11] It is the conspicuous consumption of intellectual pretension, arrogance, and superficiality. It is the literary domain of half-baked Marxist prima donnas and their gullible students, a 'space' of which it can be said, 'Dans le royaume des aveugles le borgne est roi.' It is supported by large publishing houses in many countries, fed by the pens of would-be weekend bohemians, and purchased by school teachers, social workers, graduate students, and professors with a strong penchant for political fantasy. It is the opium of the intellectuals.[12]

8

The New Left 'ideology'

Introduction

Any study of the New Left which accords the ideological and theoretical statements of the various radical groups (especially in the first half of the sixties) the major role in either the growth or the daily functioning of the movement falsifies the historical record. In Canada and the United States, and to a lesser extent in Germany, the appeal of the New Left was practical, its orientation one of action and involvement, its message moralistic. Very few converts to the movement were won by means of a careful presentation and sifting of evidence, through reasoned debate, or by weighty intellectual argument. Those social theorists who were embraced by the activist students – and the media in most cases overstated the degree of influence which they had upon the movement (see Young 1977:343) – had been able to articulate in theoretical terms what the students had been experiencing and demonstrating in practice.

However, in spite of the fact that ideology is no independently moving force capable of generating or sustaining a social movement, it is important to consider ideological matters analytically as expressions of the historically specific conditions and relations out of which social movements are generated. Even the anti-ideological early New Left pioneers formulated statements and manifestos in which they attempted to explain the world and their place in it both to themselves and to the public. In the foregoing chapters the student movement of the sixties has been presented as a result of, response to, and protest against the condition of middle class youth at that time. In this chapter, the ideological aspects of the movement will be considered with the aim of establishing precisely how they gave expression to the concerns of youth in that period.

Sociology and the student movement

The New Left forged its critique of society out of elements which were culled from a variety of intellectual and literary sources. Humanism, anarchism, existentialism, and psychoanalysis provided the input which informed and gave expression to the new radical view of the world.[1] But above all the thinking of the early movement was deeply influenced by the sociological tradition. The attraction of sociological criticism for the New Left was not primarily a result of intellectual congruence but a reflection of the similarity of conditions facing intellectuals in the social sciences and humanities and the educated youth of the sixties.

In North America the writings of C.W. Mills (1956, 1959, 1960a, 1963) filtered sociological theory through a radical prism for SDS and CUCND/ SUPA. In Germany the writings of the critical sociologists of the Frankfurt School provided the conceptual tools for the theorists of SDS. Although the student activists challenged their professors in the classroom and although they attacked the complacency and conservative bias of functionalist sociology, little did they realize that their new radical critique of society had its roots firmly planted in the soil of classical and modern sociological theory.

The sociological critique of society gave expression to the ambivalence of intellectuals in the market-place and to the hostility of mediate producers towards the agents of capital.[2] This is not to suggest that the man of letters or of numbers is either part of a class of 'free-floating intellectuals' whose own interest is closest to the interest of society as a whole or part of a social stratum free of interest altogether. As mediate producers, actual or potential, they are actually or potentially part of the class of social labour as a whole; yet throughout the history of civil society they have for the most part not taken the side of the labouring classes. In modern society mediate production has become an increasingly important part of social production. Yet the criteria of judgement of the value of literary labour have become increasingly those of marketability, fad, and fashion. Radical chic (Wolfe 1970) sold well in the sixties and early seventies. We had the paradoxical situation in which the antimarket and anticapitalist products of intellectual labour found a lucrative market (and thus, by definition, served to enhance the power of capital). This accounts in part for the *Narrenfreiheit* accorded the sociological critics of society.[3] The ambivalence of the radical sociologists originates in the tensions and pretensions of their relations in civil society to the immediate producers, to the class of non-producers, to the class of social labour as a whole, to the state and public sector, to the exigencies of the market, to competition, and to each other. It is precisely these complex relations and the interests arising out of them which power the sociological critique of modern society. That the conditions of the middle class youth of the fifties and sixties and those of the 'critical intellectuals' were similar and in some respects congruent accounts for the affinity of the one group for the other.

The sociological critique of modern society

The great sociological theorists of the nineteenth and early twentieth centuries were concerned with the *differentia specifica* of modern society. Auguste Comte (1973) had written of the law of the three stages according to which the human mind progressed from theological to metaphysical and then to positive or scientific thinking. Corresponding to each of these stages were different principles of social organization. Herbert Spencer (1910) argued that the evolution of society was part of the evolution of nature. Primitive society – organized along military lines and coercive in character – would give way to modern society based upon industrial organization and voluntary co-operation arising out of the division of labour. Emile Durkheim (1960) wrote that the social solidarity which held society together under primitive conditions was different in kind from the social solidarity which is the foundation of modern society. Georg Simmel (1890, 1908) wrote of the differences between the ways in which individuals were organized in archaic and modern societies. The modern condition is characterized by mechanical, abstract, and impersonal relations among individuals.[4] Ferdinand Tönnies (1979) described the difference between *Wesenwille* and *Kürwille*, between essential (or organic) and rational will. The former underlies the ideal types of social action which Max Weber called traditional, affectual, and value-rational; the latter corresponds to purposeful-rational action. The basis of *Gemeinschaft* is the *Wesenwille*, the foundation of *Gesellschaft* is *Kürwille*. *Gemeinschaft* and *Gesellschaft* are different forms of human sociation. Modern society is the *Gesellschaft*.

The historically specific character of modern society called for a historically specific critique of its foundation. In the sociology of Max Weber this project attained its clearest expression. For Weber the achievement of modern society was an ambivalent one. Modern society did not signify 'progress in the consciousness of freedom' alone but rather 'progress in the consciousness of freedom and unfreedom.' If we have created a world of material abundance, we have paid the price: a loss of spiritual values and of the higher meaning of life. With the rationalization of social life, society itself is riven in two: bureaucracy grows alongside of and within democracy; the form and substance of social life are separated and opposed to one another; domination and emancipation become powerful opposites inextricably united in the very fabric of modern society. Weber understood this as the historically specific development of the West, and he devoted much of his research to discovering the cause of this unique situation. But, whatever its causes, the rational organization of society having been accomplished, modern man was ensnared in a trap, or rather an 'iron cage':

The Puritan wanted to work in a calling, we are forced to do so. For when asceticism was carried out of monastic cells into everyday life, and began to dominate worldly morality, it did its part in building the tremendous cosmos of the modern economic order. This order is now bound to the technical and economic conditions of machine production which to-day determine the lives of all individuals who are born into this mechanism, not only those directly concerned with economic acquisition, with irresistible force. Perhaps it will so determine them until the last ton of fossilized coal is burnt. In Baxter's view the care for external goods should only lie on the shoulders of the 'saint like a light cloak, which can be thrown aside at any moment.' But fate decreed that the cloak should become an iron cage.

Since asceticism undertook to remodel the world, material goods have gained an increasing and finally an inexorable power over the lives of men as at no previous period in history. (1958:181)

The 'iron cage' is made up of institutions organized on the basis of the rational principles of utility, efficiency, formality, and impersonality. Historically the rational organization of economic life was created by capitalism – the rational pursuit of profit and for ever renewed profit. The rational organization of the institutions of modern society is the bureaucracy – a hierarchical, meritocratic, impersonal order of administration based on values of efficient and rational application of means to ends. In this view modern man is confronted and dominated by machines, industry, capitalism, and bureaucracy,[5] all of which are seen as embodiments of the principle of rationality which has become an end in itself. Reason in the modern world was thus turned into its opposite (Lukács 1972b; Marcuse 1968).

Weber was certainly not the first modern thinker to develop this theme. The domination of man and the formalization and rationalization of modern social life had been taken up by Rousseau, Hegel, and others. But Weber made this theme a central concern of historical and sociological investigation, and it is his work which has spawned or at least influenced to a considerable degree three-quarters of a century of writing on the problems of modern society. Modern sociological critics, the teachers of the New Left students, have developed these thoughts on the modern condition suggested in the works of Weber.

Modern sociological theory: the source of New Left critique

Certainly one of the most widely held notions in Western sociology is the identity of modern society (the date of origin is placed between 1750 and 1825) with the society of industrial production or, simply, industrial society (Dahrendorf 1959; Drucker 1950; Mayo 1975; Moore 1951; Rostow 1971). According to this view, modern society as the society of industry is determined by the character of industrial relations. Society itself serves the industrial imperative. The political and ideological differences which exist among the industrialized nations, archaically referred to as capitalist or socialist, are pale in comparison with the very similar industrial organization of these nations. One variant of this thesis argues that these political and ideological distinctions will become even less important over time, that a convergence of all industrial nations will occur politically on the basis of the similarity of industrial production.

Another impressive theory concerning modern society, not unrelated to the first, is the perspective of technological determinism shared by many sociologists and social thinkers. This view, popularized by Jacques Ellul (1967) in the fifties and sixties, is in some sense a refinement of the theory of industrial society. The weaker thesis of industrialism claims that the character of society is determined by its industrial base. Nonetheless, industry is generally understood as the modern means to satisfy social wants. In order to sustain these means society is forced to organize, plan, and administer, in certain ways, according to the structural demands of industrial production. The thesis of the technological society takes a further step. Industry may be the means to the end of satisfying social wants, but technique has become an end in itself. Technique is understood not only in the sense of industrial technique but as technical universalism, where every sphere of modern life has been penetrated by the methods of 'technicism.' 'Today technique has taken over the whole of civilization,' claims Ellul (1967:128).

In all forms of human society we find men employing technical operations; however, the technological phenomenon is the purely modern form. Here the standardization, hence impersonalization, of technique has been accomplished. Unlike the primitive who used technique unconsciously, spontaneously, modern man brings 'consciousness and judgement' to bear upon the technical operations (Ellul 1967:20). Efficiency has become an end in itself. The technical phenomenon 'technicized' every aspect of modern life. Efficiency itself has become the goal, and the specialist the arbiter of truth. No area of social life can resist the technical imperative. Our leisure time is just as much dominated by the imperatives of technique as is our necessary labour time. Even our sexual and artistic pursuits are thrown under the rule of technique. And, finally, even the revolt against technocracy has been defused by the latter's power of absorption:

All instincts seem more unbridled today than ever before – sex; passion for nature, the mountains, and the sea; passion for social and political action ... But these phenomena, which express the deepest instinctive human passions, have also become totally innocuous. They question nothing, menace nobody. Behemoth can rest easy; neither Henry Miller's eroticism nor André Breton's surrealism will prevent him from consuming mankind. Such movements are pure formalisms, pure verbalisms ... The great bell in the cathedral tower, formerly rung to call the city's warriors to arms, is sounded to amuse foreign tourists ... these spiritual movements are totally confined within a technical world. (Ellul 1967:416–17)

The technological society is one-dimensional. It is not the society of capitalism in crisis but the society in which capitalism has 'delivered the goods' not only to the bourgeoisie but to the proletariat as well. It is not the society in which 'the working class and employing class have nothing in common,' but rather the society in which the working class and employing class have everything (that is, all values) in common. Herbert Marcuse (1966) referred to the individual in this society as the one-dimensional man, a creature not unrelated to *das Man*, the modern being conjured by his teacher Martin Heidegger.

One-dimensional society is modern society whose movement towards liberation has been arrested; the 'is' has swallowed up the 'ought,' and the true forces of progress have been turned into their opposite. Modern society does not kill the body; it destroys the soul. It is the great marshmallow which catches everything in its sticky, sweet pulp. This society, according to Marcuse, is a repressive whole which has been 'made into a powerful instrument of domination.' But how did this come to be? Socialist theory had always held that capitalism would not and could not fully integrate the labouring class. The law of surplus-value was itself an expression of the intrinsic character of exploitation. Growing class consciousness, it is true, was not merely an automatic reaction to changes in 'objective' conditions; but the historical possibility of the growing consciousness of the radical wants of the proletariat could never be entirely obviated, since the very existence of the proletariat is the existence of the possibility of the growing consciousness of its radical wants and hence of the radical transformation of the social and economic base (Marx 1975:183–7).[6]

This is not the case, according to Marcuse. It is true, we still have capitalism, exploitation, oppression, and inequality. But in the advanced industrial countries even the exploited benefit from the revolution in technology which has developed within the bosom of capitalism. Technological rationality rules the lives of exploiter and exploited; in fact, Marcuse seems to be saying that domination of technique, the elimination of all values but efficiency itself, erases the differences between exploiter and exploited. Everyone is a victim.

This is the pure form of servitude: to exist as an instrument, as a thing. And this mode of existence is not abrogated if the thing is animated and chooses its material and intellectual food, if it does not feel its being-a-thing, if it is a pretty, clean, mobile thing. Conversely, as reification tends to become totalitarian by virtue of its technological form, the organizers and administrators themselves become increasingly dependent on the machinery which they organize and administer. And this mutual dependence is no longer the dialectical relationship between Master and Servant, which has been broken in the struggle for mutual recognition, but rather a vicious circle which encloses both the Master and the Servant. (1966:33)

Marcuse's view of the one-dimensional society incorporates elements of the industrial-convergence theory and much of the thesis of the technological determinists: 'In the face of the totalitarian features of this society, the traditional notion of the "neutrality" of technology can no longer be maintained. Technology as such cannot be isolated from the use to which it is put; the technological society is a system of domination which operates already in the concept and construction of techniques' (1966:xvi).

For Marcuse, then, technology is neither passive nor neutral but an immediately active factor in human history. Technology, the creation of man, has come alive, and like the monster which Dr Frankenstein in his scientific naïvety fashioned to solve the riddle of life, it has turned against him, confronting him as a powerful, alien, and hostile force.[7]

C. Wright Mills, the brilliant, maverick American sociologist, was also concerned with the specific character of modern society and its problems. He discovered that the liberal democracies of the West were on the way to becoming mass societies similar in character to those in communist or fascist states. The mass society thesis was not invented by Mills; it was a standard weapon in the arsenal of aristocratic critics of the bourgeois social order in nineteenth-century Europe. But whereas the reactionaries attacked the opening up of the élites to mass penetration and the subsequent devaluation of all values, Mills belongs to the camp of democratic critics of mass society.[8] According to this view, mass society is antithetical to liberal democracy and not, as the conservatives held, identical with it. Liberal democracy, in one classical presentation, is a political form which is characterized by the pluralist and public nature of power. The individual in 'face-to-face' discussion of public issues with his equals in a variety of corporations, associations, and clubs helps form public opinion, which is then translated into law, administrative principles, and executive acts. This assumes that discussion is freely carried on by rational human beings, that the various interests involved are in the last instance harmonious. The view which wins out (that is, public opinion) is 'the infallible voice of reason' (1957:300).

For Mills mass society is most readily distinguished from democratic, public society by the dominant mode of communication: 'In a community of publics, discussion is the ascendant means of communication, and the mass media, if they exist, simply enlarge and animate discussion, linking one *primary public* with the discussions of another. In a mass society, the dominant type of communication is the formal media, and the publics become mere *media markets*: all those exposed to the content of given mass media' (1957:304).[9]

The publics are no longer those bodies which mediate individual and political power. Rather, a process of atomization has occurred; the individual has become a homogenized unit of a mass which is now manipulated by the power élite which has a monopoly on the media – the mass media. The mass society is determined by technique – to be more precise, the technique of mass communications. It is facilitated by bigness, by urbanization, and by the consequent impersonality of social relations. Mills gives us no insight into either the logical or historical relations between technique and the power élite, and hence we are not sure if the former spawns the latter, the latter the former, whether they both arise simultaneously from some prior conditions, whether the élite can rule without mass communication, or whether mass communications can exist without an élite. In any event, the mass is oppressed benevolently, although perhaps more insidiously, by means of propaganda, thought control, and hidden persuasion.[10]

Unlike Marcuse and Ellul, Mills does argue that the members of the élite do not bear the same relation of servitude to the 'machine' as the mass. The former make decisions from a position of power whereby the latter are manipulated. The question of the content of these power decisions is not raised: does technique dictate to the power élite or does the power élite use technique as the instrument of its power? In any event, it is clear that the élite/mass relationship is determined by the mode of communication. The solution lies in the establishment of a true public with popular access to the means of communication.

It is no wonder that C. Wright Mills became the patron saint of the New Left students (Viorst 1979:185; cf Bone 1977:2–3). Although he died in 1962, at the dawn of the new activism on the campus, his message, addressed to the intellectuals, was taken to heart by the younger generation flooding into the universities. Mills' writings gave expression to one of the faces of sociology. If functionalism represented the theory of submissiveness of the intellectual and the 'mindless empiricism' represented the practice of the same, then Millsian radicalism represented the theory of intellectual defiance in face of the powers that be. In modern society the intellectual was liberated from the bonds of feudal patronage only to become substantially bound by the laws of the market. The mediate producers were divided in a secondary way among themselves; there were those who became the spokesmen of capital, forms of its personification; others became the radical critics of society. Yet their criticism was the vehicle through which they asserted their own one-sided claims to power.

C. Wright Mills was never able to resolve the ambivalence of his own position. The sentiment underlying his critical sociology was populism;

yet his message to the intellectuals was clear: *they* were to become the new agent of social change, the new historical subject of social transformation. In his letter to the New Left Mills wrote: 'It is with this problem of agency in mind that I have been studying ... the cultural apparatus, the intellectuals, as a possible, immediate, radical agency of change ... if we try to be realistic in our utopianism ... a writer in our countries on the left today *must* begin with the intellectuals ... Who is it that is thinking and acting in radical ways? All over the world ... the answer is the same: it is the young intelligentsia' (1960b:70).

But as early as the 1940s Mills had written about the political potential of the intellectual. And the ambivalence persisted through his last writings. For, as F. Perlman asks: 'If Mills' statement about the freedom of the intellectual is taken seriously, then the basis on which the intellectual is to engage in political action is not clear; is he to struggle because he's one of the powerless people, or because he's already the freest member of American society?' (1971:21). This is the problem of the New Left in particular, of the mediate producers in general.

9

The anti-ideology of the early New Left

In spite of the fact that the primary thrust of the student movement was practical and not theoretical, emotional and not intellectual, New Left student groups were notoriously prolific producers of radical literature. An office might be a luxury, but a mimeograph machine a necessity. The activist students produced not only leaflets, communiqués, and calls to action but pamphlets and books which were thoughtful statements based upon attempts at serious analysis and collective discussion.

'The Port Huron Statement'

At the 1962 convention of the American SDS in Port Huron, Michigan, a document was put together which was to serve as the manifesto of the New Left in the sixties. The *Port Huron Statement* (PHS) represented an attempt by SDS to criticize and rewrite American domestic and especially foreign policy. It began with the now famous words which faintly echo the beginning of the American Declaration of Independence: 'We are people of this generation, bred in at least modest comfort, housed now in universities, looking uncomfortably to the world we inherit' (SDS 1964:3). It would serve us well to note that the PHS begins in this way. By keeping this firmly in mind we can relate the general criticisms raised in the document to the specific conditions of that generation of students housed in the universities in the early sixties.

At first reading, the assertions and accusations made in the PHS appear to be entirely transparent and easily understood. A group of concerned students armed with the values underlying an as yet unfulfilled dream of humanity has drawn up a systematic critique of a society which has failed to act in conformity with those values.

Fundamentally, the PHS is supposed to be at once a manifesto against hypocrisy and the basis of a program which will establish relations of 'reason, freedom and love' among men. Although the analysis is not systematically developed in this regard, the forces responsible for maintaining the hypocritical status quo include: private financial interests, the administrative bureaucracy, the military, war profiteers, professors and administrators who have sold their 'skills and silence,' the idolatrous worship of things, a complex technological and social structure, and student apathy. The ameliorative forces, on the other hand, are made up in part of participatory democracy, real publics, individual involvement, personal commitment, in short, of everything based upon 'love, reflectiveness, reason and creativity' (7). In our naïvety we accept this at face value.

If, however, we situate the PHS in its historical and social context, if we view it as a product of a particular group of people concerned about their own changing position in society, we are forced to penetrate the abstract-humanistic and universalist cast of criticism by grasping the concrete social conditions of life of that same group of people and to show how and why that criticism has been expressed in this moralistic and humanistic form.

In directing their attention to the larger society beyond the campus, the framers of the PHS attempted to show that in many ways the university was but a microcosm of American society. However, if we recall that the students are looking at the larger society through the eyes of the campus, then it makes greater sense to suggest that they are portraying American society as a macrocosm of the university, which is a logical error, *pars pro toto*, and an unwarranted substantive comparison.

Like the students, Americans are generally viewed as manipulated, empty, powerless people who have withdrawn in resignation from public life, 'from any collective effort at directing their own affairs.' The bond between the people and its leadership has become corrupted: 'With the great mass of people structurally remote and psychologically hesitant with respect to democratic institutions, those institutions themselves attenuate and become ... *progressively less accessible to those few who aspire to serious participation in social affairs.* The vital democratic connection between community and leadership, between the mass and the several élites, has been so wrenched and perverted that disastrous policies go unchallenged time and again' (12; emphasis added).[1]

From the point of view of the student situation, the above complaint encompasses the student protest against the massification of the university-trained élite whatever the substantive truth value of the apparent criticism. The students used the failure of the élite to realize completely the promise of democracy and to make a real commitment to peace as a way of making their own grievances plain. (In fact, peace had been maintained throughout the fifties after Korea, new initiatives in civil rights had been made, colonies were gaining their independence, and the liberal-Catholic John Kennedy had beaten Eisenhower's conservative heir, Richard M. Nixon, in the presidential race of 1960. But in the eyes of the younger generation which was used to getting its way when it wanted, these occurrences, which represented encouraging starts to the older generation of liberals, were seen by the young as being far too little, coming far too late.)

In the context of the explosion in tertiary education in the sixties and the concomitant tightening of the reins on the mobility of the youth of the middle class, 'real individual initiative or popular control' could not exist. Although the student was told he was 'free,' he was experiencing a deterioration in the conditions of élite training and, by extrapolation, of the élite itself.

In the section entitled 'Towards American Democracy' the message, lifted from the pages of C. Wright Mills, presents a radical-democratic critique of the organization of political life; in this form, the students were able to register a protest against their own exclusion from the political process: 'Mechanisms of voluntary association must be created through which political information can be imparted and political participation encouraged.' At the same time, the students cannot 'trust the corporate bureaucracy to be socially responsible or to develop a "corporate conscience" that is democratic' (48). There is only one answer: 'The allocation of resources must be based on social needs. A truly "public sector" must be established, and its nature debated and planned.' A 'truly public sector' would presumably be one in which the students had the power to set policy. 'Social needs,' whatever else they may be, are needs of the students themselves. This is not only a matter of qualitative but also of quantitative change: 'All the tendencies suggest that not only solutions to our present social needs but for our future expansion rests upon our willingness to enlarge the "public sector" greatly.'[2]

The PHS also attacked the military and the scientific establishments for perpetuating the cold war and perverting the ends of science. The military was a perfect target for the students. The cold war and space race had not only helped bring about changes in the economy which had revamped the character of middle class mobility but had also linked the university with these patriotic matters and humbled the traditionalist academic élite by openly making the university an adjunct to industry, the government, and the military. Furthermore, it is clear that the New Left students, who overwhelmingly came from the faculties of social sciences and humanities, did not share equally in the university bonanza of the sixties with students in the so-called hard sciences.[3]

It is the 'irresponsible elites' which favour warfare instead of welfare and the perpetuation of domestic injustice. These same élites are part of the archaic conditions which were in the process of transformation – a transformation characterized by the growing link between knowledge and production. This engendered a protest on the part of the students against the separation of knowledge and power in the training institutions and in the bureaucratic institutions which would later employ these mediate producers. The students wanted to be the 'responsible élite.'

In the last section of the PHS the claim to power on behalf of the 'knowledgeable,' or rather on behalf of those certified as 'knowledgeable,' was forcefully made. The old university élite has allowed itself to be bought by the representatives of the power élite: 'The extent to which academic resources presently are used to buttress immoral social practice is revealed first, by the extent to which defense contracts make the universities engineers of the arms race' (61). But this means that the universities have the power to change the focus of social priorities: 'These social uses of the universities' resources also demonstrate the unchangeable reliance by men of power on the men and storehouses of knowledge: this makes the university functionally tied to society in new ways, revealing new potentialities, new levers for change.' Hence, within the university, students can be a new and powerful constituency for social change: 'In each community we must look within the university and act with confidence that we can be powerful.'

Student concern with power is inversely related to the extent of their own powerlessness; the concern with humanity to their actual social isolation; the concern with hypocrisy to their exclusion from positions of 'creativity,'[4] authority, and power; their concern with reason to the unreasonableness of outmoded relations; their concern with freedom to the limitations on the formal freedoms of the middle class.

'Hochschule in der Demokratie'

Around the time of its exclusion from the SPD, the German SDS published a major treatise *Hochschule in der Demokratie* (HD; SDS 1965) on the question of democratization of the institutions of higher learning. The classical German university sought to preserve an autonomous field of action within an absolutist state. The state granted this 'ideal' autonomy to the university early in the nineteenth century in return for 'useful research results and employable civil servants' (191). With the industrialization which occurred in the latter half of the nineteenth century, the university was in fact transformed into an institution which responded to the new social demands made upon it. It began to produce specialized scientists and tangible research results. Even so, the myth of the classical university was reactivated after World War II.

The students, however, were not taken in by the lip service paid to autonomy and freedom. They knew that in 'late capitalist society' the university served two basic purposes: the production of qualified labour-power for the market and useful research results; and the reproduction of the social relations of power which stand in the way of rational engagement in the service of man. The university as an integral social institution can no longer emancipate itself from the economic and political forces of which it is a part. Hence, the formal recognition of the neutrality and autonomy of the academy stands in contradiction to its substantive social interests and biases. Since the university can no longer realistically avoid social engagement, it must commit itself to the fight for a rational society 'in which the free development of each is the condition for the free development of all' (4).

It is interesting to note that the German document begins precisely where the PHS ends, with a discussion of the university and social change. The emphasis given university affairs by the German SDS is itself a reflection of the élitist character of the German academy and its prominence as an economic and political issue. Since the Wilhelmine period the German university had been a national institution with deep ties to industry and the state. Students and professors had jealously guarded their corporate privilege, and this élitist and parochial claim was maintained down to the Nazification of the universities in the late twenties and early thirties (Faust 1973; Schäfer 1977). Even after World War II, the corporate and élite consciousness of the student body was expressed in the strength of the corporations which flourished at the German universities during the fifties (Negt 1971; Schäfer 1977). But the character of the university-trained élite was changing in such a way as to make these manifestations of corporate privilege anachronistic. The process of massification of the intellectual élite in Germany was subjectively expressed as a consciousness of exploitation and oppression rather than of élitist and corporate privilege.

The élitist character of the student movement in Germany, as in the United States, was expressed through the medium of radical democratic demands, humanistic values, and enlightenment language. The German students in sds set themselves up as the bearers of the truly universal and human interest in a society dominated by 'partial interests.' It is, of course, these partial interests which are responsible for turning knowledge and students into commodities, for subjecting pure science to business imperatives. Research becomes the private purpose of a small élite; education becomes the transmission of material to an anonymous, faceless mass which mechanically consumes the material in hopes of selling its labour-power at a higher price after graduation. It is 'the saleability of the intellect as a commodity,' the 'reification of knowledge,' which are the enemies of 'the principle of critical rationality' of which the students are the bearers (14).

Part of the secret of student radicalism is revealed in the following observation: 'Corresponding to the factual privilege of entrance to the university, which today is still the prerogative of specific social strata, is the claim upon a supposedly "academic" free style of student life which is diametrically opposed to the restricted working environment of their contemporaries in the factories and technical schools who must labour according to the achievement principle' (14–15). But in truth the radical opposition lies not in the professed gap between the free universities and the unfree factories and technical colleges, but in the growing similarity between the two.

The German students, like their counterparts elsewhere, did not look back to the old glories of the ivory tower, but forward to power in society. Hence, they were opposed to the conservatives, who wished to isolate the university from society, to make the university into a self-contained institution imprinting an élite consciousness upon its charges. They opposed this overt élitism because it was unrealistic, because the student élite as the potential intellectual élite was in the process of being massified.

But even though the sds students lined up with progressive forces by attacking overt élitism and preaching that the university must become a socially relevant institution, they did not want the university to be relevant to this society, dominated as it was by partial interests. Rather, they wished the university to be in the forefront of the struggle for a new society based upon the values of critical rationality in the service of man.

Classical education was the simple prerogative of the few; it was not a 'commodity' which the broad masses could 'purchase.' While remaining a privilege in the sixties, higher education had been devalued even as it became a necessity for the broad middle class. The authors of HD protest about the uselessness (read powerlessness) of higher education in the following observations concerning the humanities: 'The "uselessness" of such moral-scientific studies lends them the polish which is most useful as a decoration of social prestige, which distances its "possessor" from the graduates of the lower levels of our educational hierarchy who do not come to enjoy higher education' (29).

The conservatives wanted freedom from society; the technocrats wanted the university to serve the existing society,[5] the society dominated by 'partial interests.' The students wanted both autonomy and relevance, knowledge and power. The only way for the students to resolve the ambivalence of their position, the contradictory character of their demands, was by means of an attempt to transform society according to the abstract ideals of the academy: 'The goal of education should be that research and research results, that study and studying be recognized in the profession itself as politically relevant. In this way, action in one's profession and political action become identical. The separation of "existence as a citizen of the state" and as "otherwise a man" is overcome' (31; cf Wetzel 1976).

It is this union of knowledge and political power which the students were seeking. Speculative philosophy had lost much of its privileged economic and political foundation, and the positive sciences had no direct input into the determination of social and political policy. The critical science championed by the German SDS would be the realization of the union of science and power. The scholar would make history instead of merely contemplating it:

Such a decisive engagement must turn itself against a 'humanistic' education which is alien to reality and introverted, just as much as it must turn itself against a positivistic scientific concern which is reduced to description and the systematization of material. For the contemplative orientation of the scholar in relation to his material of knowledge which underlies description and systematization is reproduced in his relation to social praxis, which in its turn consists in accepting the 'given' as given (44).

The development of the student movement over the course of the sixties can be understood as an attempt to realize this claim to social and political power by means of an attack upon existing forms of social and political power. The failure of the New Left to translate this claim into fact led to the fragmentation and eventual disintegration of the movement. The demand for autonomy (which was a central value of the old academy) under the changing conditions of post-war society could not be advanced only on behalf of the university, but had to be made on behalf of all humanity. Just as Luther could only free men from priestly domination in so far as he turned them into their own priests, SDS could only demand autonomy for all men by turning them into students and by casting society as a gigantic university.

One interesting and characteristic expression of the recognition of élite massification was the theory of student syndicalism, which only gained currency in North America in the second half of the sixties but is already found fully articulated in HD. According to SDS, the relations of labour in the universities do not differ from those in other 'factories': 'in the university too, "management" with the power of disposition over the means of labour stands opposed to the dependent labourers who are separated from the means of labour' (84). Furthermore, the labour of teachers and students at the university is socially productive labour which can be 'transformed into economic *values* in the broadest sense.' Because of the central importance of this scientific labour for the whole of social production, such labour must receive just recompense according to its indispensable contribution (107).

The theoretical understanding of the student as an intellectual worker and the demand for a 'just' recompense for labour performed had a directly practical application in the fight over state policy regarding financial assistance for students. In 1957 the Bundestag voted in favour of a state-financed program of financial assistance (*das Honnefer Modell*) which would offer aid to those students who could not support themselves or whose families could not support them during their studies. Since university education in the eyes of the German government was a privilege and a means to individual betterment, the student was required to repay a substantial part of the government assistance at the conclusion of his studies.

Of course the SDS reacted with anger to the program, attacked the philosophy behind it, and launched a critique of the 'élitist' view of education which was fostered by it: 'Minister of Domestic Affairs Schroeder explained in April 1957 that the Honnef model was an "attempt to stop the general massification precisely at the point where it would have a particularly bad effect upon the life of our nation"' (135).

According to the sds, the government, imbued with 'social-conservative élite thinking,' wished to indoctrinate the future leaders of the state and society with a special élite consciousness. By emphasizing the individual achievement in higher education the state wished to create an intellectual élite with a superior self-consciousness. Students become future leaders, according to this conservative view, by working hard with the talent they have. They must earn the privilege of studying and prove themselves worthy of such a reward. But the students could not take this self-help rhetoric seriously under the changing conditions of higher education. The university diploma was fast becoming a necessity for increasing numbers of middle class youth. They were expected to toil hard for a lesser payoff. But when precious stones become as common as pebbles on the beach, no one can be bothered to exert much energy in gathering them. The German government, as we have seen, tried to stall the process of massification by weeding out the slothful from the ranks of those heading to university. But it was too late.

The tide had turned; there was no going back to the ivory tower, or, *dem Elfenbeinturm*, as the Germans called it. The only way for the new student cohort to move was forward, to set itself at the head of the erupting forces and to attempt to push them far beyond the limits which technocrats and reformers had ever intended. If the old élite was being destroyed by democratization, then democratization would become the battle cry of the new massified élite.

German students, like their North American counterparts, were caught between the conservatives and the technocratic reformers. The former offered them empty visions of old fashioned élitism, the latter offered them real existing social relevance without power. The students raised a third alternative which combined features of élitism and relevance inscribed upon the banner of radical democracy. When sds asserted 'we strive for *emancipation* of the student as a free intellectual labourer and the complete constitution of academic freedom' (138), it pleaded a special and privileged case for the students. The emancipation of the working class would have to wait until sds had the freedom and the power to impose the principles of critical rationality upon society as a whole.

There was no way in which the students could assert a directly élitist claim which would have had any relevance in the context of modern German 'know-how,' computer technology, progressive industrial psychology, data retrieval, and media hype. The arms-bearing student corps were clearly out of step with the times. The middle class had been made an offer it could not refuse – security, stability, and a higher standard of living. The price was not difficult to meet for those who had experienced depression, war, and total military defeat – limitation on the forms of social mobility (especially for their children) and direct and formal integration into the public and private bureaucracies. It was a price which was far more difficult for members of the younger generation to pay. Raised to be creative, in relative privilege, they did not accept the 'yoke' of massification, sweetened though it was, without a fight. The university was not the road to the top:

If parents ... refuse 'to buy' their children an academic education, then the state is not justified in doing this in their stead.

'The economy' beckons to this kind of consciousness in so far as it continues ceremoniously to value university studies as the actual 'road to the top,' *supposedly* to the pinnacle of society, while on the other hand it helps to block entrance to the university. (There is only an apparent contradiction here.) Even though in fact university study in no way means 'climbing' to the highest salaries, to the top of the income pyramid, nevertheless it is to be glorified in this way in the consciousness of the students as the road leading to the social élite. (137–8; emphasis added)

This promise of entrance to the social élite through university education was only partly fulfilled. University education granted entrance to the new massified élite of mediate producers, not to the centres of economic, social, and political power. The result was the student revolt of the sixties.

CUCND/SUPA: New Left 'anti-ideology' in Canada

In 1969, during the dissolution of the New Left in Canada, the movement was criticized by one of its erstwhile marginal leaders (Laxer 1969) for blindly following the lead of the American movement and for showing little appreciation of the Canadian social and political context and of Canadian traditions. If this criticism was partly justified, and a case can be made for it, it was certainly not the whole truth.

The roots of the first national New Left organization in Canada, the

CUCND, were nourished not by the American movement but by the British CND. It should also not be forgotten that the development of student syndicalism in Canada originated in the ranks of UGEQ before it had found a receptive ear in the American SDS. Finally, it is difficult to generalize at all about the Canadian movement, for regionalism in Canada militated against the formation of a centralized movement. If SUPA branches in Ontario were inclined to follow the American lead (and it is by no means clear that this was done blindly and unselectively), SUPA in Montreal and in Saskatchewan were less prone to do so.

By and large, Canadian student radicals did not compose lengthy manifestos or elaborate statements of philosophy and program. There is no single Canadian document comparable to the PHS or to HD. The tendency which developed within the Canadian New Left can best be described as a concern with analyses of particular questions – nuclear weapons, community organizing, and student power, for example.[6] Yet several small and mostly abortive attempts to develop a more systematic statement of purpose were made during the early and middle sixties.

At its federal conference in Toronto, 20–3 February 1963, the CUCND identified itself with a declaration, only fragments of which had in fact been drafted.[7] The first section of the declaration consisted of a statement of purpose which included assertions of principle in opposition to the 'Cold War military and political policies of both nuclear blocs.' In particular, the CUCND was uncompromisingly opposed to the stationing of nuclear weapons on Canadian soil.[8] In this struggle 'CUCND believes that students have a special role to play ... to eliminate war as a method of settling international disputes, and that the university community should take the lead in the mobilization of social forces internationally for the achievement of world peace' (CUCND 1963b).

Opposition to war and militarism is unexceptional. Yet historically not all student movements were antiwar; in fact many were rabidly militaristic, nationalistic, and xenophobic. It is true that all-out nuclear war could lead to the annihilation of all life on the planet. But this in no way simplifies matters, for student movements, like all social movements, we continue to argue, arise out of and are expressions of historically specific, not generally human, conditions. Antinuclear protest in the early sixties was conducted by specific social groups, notably students, and the reason for this is to be sought in the historically specific situation of precisely those groups. Even if there was a real threat to all humankind, the sociologically interesting question remains why only certain groups and not others seized upon it as an issue.

The answer to this question is to be sought in the changes occurring in the post-war era which affected the mobility of the middle class youth of the baby boom. The CUCND chose as its targets in this declaration the cold war, the space race, nationalism, patriotism, and militarism. All these matters were involved in the acceleration of the process of massification of the intellectual élite during the fifties and sixties. This massification and the growing importance of mediate production became centres of attention for educated youth. In the last instance, these changes appeared to be determined by the wants of the military-industrial complex during that period. Against this trend, the students seized upon radical democracy as a weapon:

So it has been with Canada and the US, as the democratic institutions and habits have shrivelled in almost direct proportion to the growth of her armaments. Decisions about military strategy, including the monstrous decision to go to war, are more and more the property of the Military and Industrial arms race machine, with the politicians assuming a ratifying role, instead of a determining one. This is increasingly a fact, not just because of the installation of the present military, but because of constant revolution in military technology. The new technologies allegedly require military expertise, scientific comprehension and the mantle of secrecy. As parliament relys [sic] on the armed forces, the existing chasm between people as makers of decisions becomes irreconcilably wide, and more alienating in its effects.

In this way, the universalist issue and appeal of peace served as a means of giving expression to the particular protest of educated youth against the perpetrators of the massification process.

In preparing its case against the military, industry, and the state, the radical students displayed a perspicacity in recognizing the forces of progress at work in the university and society. The German SDS, as we have seen, had been urging official contact with the GDR long before such a position became the cornerstone of Willy Brandt's *Ostpolitik*. The American SDS preached *détente* and recognition of Red China long before Nixon and Kissinger adopted them.[9] The Canadian New Left raised two questions which were later to play major roles in national politics – Canadian nationalism and Quebec separatism. Since the present work does not include a discussion of the student movement in Quebec, it is only noted here that the separation of the French-speaking universities in Quebec from cus and the formation of ugeq in 1964 can be seen as a 'dress-rehearsal' for the rise of the Parti québécois in the seventies. In the United States, the national question played no role (except in terms of black nationalism, which did not originate with the white student movement) – the United States was considered to be the 'heartland of imperialism' – and it was present in Germany as a problem of reunification of the two German states. It was raised in Canada by the New Left in terms of the analysis of the nation-state, the rejection of nuclear weapons, and the concern with specifically Canadian problems.

In many ways the rise of nationalism in Canada (and it had both conservative and socialist expressions) was part of the same dynamic which gave rise to the student movement, or rather which gave the latter its particular cast and hue. Canada has always stood under the economic and political shadow of great powers, France, England, and the United States. In a country composed of a string of economic regions, the north-south pull is often more compelling than east-west confederation. After World War ii, American capital penetration increased substantially, and the rationalization of the Canadian economy, especially in manufacturing and resource extraction, was conducted under the aegis of branch plants of American multinational corporations. Opposition to growing American influence was supplied by both conservative and radical intellectuals. It is not entirely clear why nationalism held such an appeal for these two groups.

Among both there was much talk in the sixties about developing a truly Canadian identity, and this can only in part be attributed to the growing unease with the status quo in the province of Quebec. The United States, an economic and military giant, is also the home of a vast network of cultural industries – artistic, cinematographic, educational, musical, phonographic – which support a large number of actors, artists, authors, editors, educators, producers, publishers, and technicians of every stripe. The sheer volume of production and the tremendous capital investment in these areas entirely eclipse the relatively meagre development of the cultural sector in Canada. Canadians who are active in cultural pursuits are at once drawn towards and repelled by the American cultural colossus. Fear and enticement are the conflicting, ambivalent moments in the Canadian intellectual and cultural milieu *vis-à-vis* the United States.

The conservative intellectual in Canada wishes to protect his monopoly over a small, traditional, élitist Canadian cultural apparatus. He would be content with his aristocratic pretensions. As the Germans say,

'Klein aber mein.' The radicals, on the other hand, very much wanted to have the power and scope enjoyed by the Americans, but they wanted it on their own terms.[10] In fact, both the conservatives and the radicals were enticed by and fearful of the Americans, in different ways. The conservatives were less ambitious, seeking only to defend their own turf from an overbearing foreign competitor. The radicals were more aggressive (they were generally younger) and wished to carry the attack to the cultural Goliath.[11] Professor George Grant, a conservative-nationalist philosopher, was, not coincidentally, an ally of the Canadian New Left (albeit a critical one) in the sixties, and a friend – a critical friend – of the flotsam and jetsam of the student movement in the seventies.

This tension was exacerbated at the Canadian universities during the sixties when thousands of American teachers, scholars, and administrators, came across the border to fill various posts within Canada's rapidly expanding university system. Some of these Americans were not of the highest calibre (although many of them, to be sure, were distinguished in their fields), and they were able to make lucrative arrangements with Canadian universities which were experiencing severe manpower deficiencies during those years of unprecedentedly rapid growth. However, at the end of the sixties, when a large number of Canadian PHDs were moving into the labour market, these Americans became an easy target for conservative and radical nationalists alike. The growth of neo-Marxism on the Canadian campuses was fed in part by this same anti-Americanism.

On the occasion of 'Students Remember Week' (9–13 November 1964) the CUCND published a pamphlet entitled *The University and Social Action in the Nuclear Age*. The so-called nuclear election in Canada had been fought and lost by the antinuclear coalition, and the CUCND was beginning to integrate the program of community organizing into its structure. In the first section of the pamphlet, 'The Dilemma of Social Action in the Nuclear Age' (written by Matt Cohen and Art Pape), an attempt was made to develop a political strategy which went beyond the single issue of nuclear disarmament (although nuclear disarmament would still be a central part of this new political strategy). Their message was clear: the old institutions, relations, and ways of doing things are not capable of handling the new tasks facing mankind. When they referred disparagingly to the threat to democracy, they were inevitably calling attention to the students' loss of prerogative in the life of society, to the massification of the traditional, intellectual élite, to the subservience of mediate production to the wants of capital: 'Thus at the root of our national hypocrisy is our failure to create democratic institutions which will make people and democratic values stand at the centre of policy-making. This failure is observed in all manner of problems that cry out for a rebirth of social imagination' (CUCND 1964:4). Who is it in contemporary society who enjoys a professional monopoly on 'social imagination'? If we read 'students' for 'people' we have a clearer idea of what in fact is being advanced. In the concluding passages we find a remarkably lucid appeal to the student to reject those changes occurring around him by advancing an independent claim to social power:

The dilemma before the student is profound. The university has equipped us for a set of optional roles to be played within our society; but in fact this set of options does not offer us real choice. Because our major social institutions are integrated parts of our nation-state and thereby of the inter-nation system, any business-as-usual role within those institutions must have the effect of being supportive in our drift towards war. If the student wants to act for a world of freedom and dignity for all men, he must find a way to use his personal power to continually challenge the society in the most fundamental ways possible.

Our social institutions are not geared to provide support for those who want to challenge the fundamentals of those same institutions. The university may provide one situation for such people, if they are skilled enough to have their services required despite their critical role. In fact most mainstream institutions will tolerate and support a small number of highly qualified people who are working to reconstruct social institutions.

That may be a solution for the few. Even they must guard against misunderstanding what they can accomplish in this way. They must avoid the tendency to begin as a social critic and end by becoming technical engineers trying to make structures do what they cannot hope to do. (6–7)

In other words, these students will not be satisfied with positions lacking the power to determine social policy. Let those who will settle for less (the technical engineers) beware!

Section 2 of the pamphlet, appropriately entitled 'The University as a Base for Action,' contains 'a compendium of excerpts from articles which have appeared in "Our Generation Against Nuclear War" and elsewhere.' This section is interesting, for it brings together statements from various sources which reinforce the views presented in this book concerning the partial as opposed to the generally 'human' interest advanced by the New Left. Here are a few examples:

In the post-war years ... autonomy for the intellectual has meant isolation. It has meant the ivory tower, the retreat from full participation in society ... Involvement, on the other hand, has meant to the post-war intellectual service in the establishment. And there has been very little leeway for any third kind of role for the intellectual to develop.

There is a new understanding, gained through direct participation in social movements, that power is something that can be created, ie, can be generated at the base of the social structure; and the intellectual can obtain power by involving himself in the emerging centres of power in society; the civil rights movement, the peace movement, the discussion of economic issues. So there is an end to the romantic vision of power as something that could not be touched and there is a beginning of self-conscious use of power for the accomplishment of certain goals.

Traditionally, the myth of progress with its promise of *certain* triumph in the future, provided an ideal justification for immediate frustrations. Contemporary Canadian students, however, as we have noted, lack any such belief; whether their aim is sensory gratification or the achievement of a moral goal, students cannot tolerate delay or defeat. (10–11)

The last ideological statement of the early Canadian New Left to be considered here is the draft prepared by the CUCND for its conference in Regina, Saskatchewan, 28 December 1964 to 1 January 1965 (the founding conference of SUPA). Entitled 'The Student and Social Issues in the Nuclear Age,' it represents an attempt to develop a critical alternative to Canadian domestic and foreign policy. In essence it restates the CUCND position on the nation-state, militarism, and nuclear disarmament, but it seeks to expand the scope of its treatment of domestic issues to include the question of the quiet revolution in Quebec and the growing separatist movement in 'la belle province.'[12]

The last two sections of the draft statement – 'Students, Universities and Society' and 'Students and the Future' – show that the students were acutely aware of the changes which were going on around them. Their understanding of how these changes were going to affect them is stated in the following terms:

A complex society requires great numbers of trained personnel; these trained individuals are the product in which the developed nations are investing in maintaining educational institutions.

The educational establishment is thus basically a conservative one. It aims to produce those capable of maintaining the society essentially as they find it; they will have to improve and update the major institutions, but not re-examine or reconstruct them fundamentally ...

Students, like most of their fellow citizens in North America today, have been willing to leave basic decisions about their environment and future to others. (CUCND 1964–5:11)

Students are being trained to fill positions which serve the interests of others who, unlike the students, have the power to make basic decisions for society. The question which follows from this view is of a strategic nature: how can this state of affairs be changed so that the students will be able to effect those fundamental social decisions?

First, the old élitism is shown to be out of date and, because of this, dysfunctional for society as a whole: 'Yet this whole concept of education is dangerously out of date in this age which demands of the developed nations the development of basically new attitudes and institutions, on a world scale. An educational system which does not create the potential for this kind of change works against the real interest of society' (11). But in order to ensure that these necessary changes will be implemented, society must see to it that 'independent and creative' people will be advanced in an educational system which values independence and creativity; of course, this can only happen when the university is fully integrated into society and its members are able to assume their rightful responsibility for making social decisions:

The university must become a special part of that educational system, by completing the process of giving the student the potential for independent intellectual work. But just as the university cannot prepare the student to take responsibilities ... also it cannot prepare him to take a critical role in society except by making that a central part of his work at the university. In other words, the university itself can only contribute to society the kinds of individuals required for an age of rapid change by itself adopting a role suited to that age. (12)

Of course, the students are not simply to remain the passive beneficiaries of these reforms. They must make an effort on their own to become 'relevant':

But new goals, structures and patterns of action for the university cannot be developed except through experience; students who would make the university relevant to the needs of the age must themselves attempt to become relevant to the age, using the university as a base. That will provide the experience and knowledge necessary to proscribe [*sic*] alternatives, as well as the potential for actually realizing them. A university-based movement for social change must itself come to embody the patterns which we would prescribe for the university as a whole. (12)

Writing allegorically about themselves, the students see that 'this loss of control poses a threat to the very existence of civilization' (13). But in spite of this: 'It is possible that men will be able to recognize their situation and take advantage of it to create a more just, humane and democratic social order on a world scale. Technology now makes material abundance for all possible. Human and social sciences are developing to the point where we can make real advances towards developing that kind of social order' (13).

This technocratic viewpoint expresses the élitist claim of the students under cover and in terms of the values of 'justice, humanity and democracy.' The same basic thrust underlay the more systematic and self-conscious theory of the new working class during the final years of the New Left.

10

Ideology in the periods of glory and transition

The purpose of the foregoing presentation and analysis of the representative documents of the early New Left has been to show how the changes in the mobility conditions of middle class youth and the concomitant changes in the educational system were met by the spokesmen of the student movement. In this way it has been possible to grasp the meaning of the historically specific appeal to democracy, humanity, reason, and justice which was a common feature of the New Left everywhere.

The development of the New Left in the sixties can be understood in terms of the attempts to resolve the ambivalence inherent in the student position by translating the student claim to power into an effective political force. The impossibility of this task led to increasingly fantastic assertions being made by the various factions of the New Left which had formed around different poles of the ambivalent unity.

During the first half of the sixties, the New Left everywhere grew out of the student campaigns for nuclear disarmament. In the United States directly, in Canada and Germany vicariously, the New Left arose out of the civil rights movement. After a while, however, the same issues raised in connection with peace and civil rights – powerlessness, irrationality, democracy, equality, and civil liberties – were raised in connection with the university itself. Students and intellectuals were thus seen as part of a broad popular movement for social change, although within this popular movement they more or less openly acted as if they were *primi inter pares*.[1]

At the annual convention of SDS in Pine Hill, New York, in June 1963, Paul Potter, a former national affairs vice-president of the National Student Association (who was to become president of SDS in 1964), delivered a speech[2] on the intellectual as an agent of social change in which he clearly outlined the role of the intellectual in the new movement:

Intellectuals want direct power. They no longer want to deal with power as an abstract symbol of the classroom and of lectures. They want to utilize power for social ends and from this insurgency comes autonomy. From this insurgency comes autonomy and there is the paradox. Autonomy is not isolation. Autonomy is involvement and this is the critical factor which I think we have submerged in our own particular ways of talking about university reform as the penultimate goal of our new society. (Potter 1963:33)

The way to achieving this 'direct power' is through the activities of the New Left in the early sixties:

For the first time, there are alternatives to the intellectual other than service to the Establishment or isolation from society, and those alternatives are being enunciated and proclaimed and implemented by social movements in the society. For the first time there is a base of power outside the university to which the intellectual can turn. There is an autonomous base of power which he can utilize in freeing himself from the strictures of the university system, in defending himself from the exposed position which he held in society until 1955 or later. (32)

The university is no longer an important end in itself. Rather, it is an institution which is to be used by intellectuals to achieve social power:

Yet in the past when intellectuals were cynical, they dreamed of the day when the university might be reformed. Today, that is receding, and instead, intellectuals are thinking increasingly of how they can use the University to accomplish pragmatic ends. So they are manipulating structures. Instead of the old academic entrepreneur – we have the insurgent intellectual – who milks foundations and the university system itself, who builds pyramids of people around him in order to work effectively in a social movement, be it peace research, be it civil rights, be it any of the number of things which any of you might name. And this is terribly important because this concept of exploiting the university underlies a new movement among a growing minority of intellectuals who are active. (33–4)

If we keep in mind the changes in higher education, mediate production, and middle class mobility, Potter's statements take on new meaning. The university has been inextricably tied to production, and the character of the university-trained élite has been transformed from a tightly knit, estate-conscious, conservative group to a mass educated stratum removed from the centres of power by several degrees. The only way for educated youth to realize its claim to positions of power and authority was through the assertion of its leadership in a mass democratic movement. For them power was attainable only through the 'power of the people':

There is an end, I think, of the old romance about power. Power was something that *Time Magazine* had, power was something that congressmen had, power was something that only the people at the pinnacles of bureaucratic structures could hold and the only way to obtain access to power was to serve those structures and exert minor influence on their peripheries. But there is a new understanding, gained through direct participation in social movements, that power is something that can be created, that it can be generated at the base of the social structure; and the intellectual can obtain power by involving himself in the emerging centers of power in society: the civil rights movement, the peace movement, the discussion of economic issues. So there is an end to the romantic vision of power as something which could not be touched and there is the beginning of self-conscious use of power for the accomplishment of certain goals. (34)

Compare this with the following assertions by Mario Savio, leader of the Berkeley FSM:

Many students here at the University, many people in society, are wandering aimlessly about. Strangers in their own lives, there is no place for them. They are people who have not learned to compromise, who for example have come to the University to learn to question, to grow, to learn – all the standard things that sound like clichés because no one takes them seriously. And they find at one point or another that for them to become part of society, to become lawyers, ministers, business men, or people in government, very often they must compromise those principles which were most dear to them. They must suppress the most creative impulses that they have; this is a prior condition for being part of the system. (Savio 1967:252)

The massification of the intellectual élite stifled the creativity and diminished the power of the new class of mediate producers. This was the source of the sharp antisystem bias of the youth of the sixties.

Late in 1965, Paul Booth and Lee Webb (1966:78–99; cf Gitlin

1980:78, 82) wrote an important paper entitled 'From Protest to Radical Politics,' which represented an attempt to channel the antiwar issue into a broader framework for social change and to warn radicals about the pitfalls of single-issue organizing. The paper was largely based upon the kind of viewpoint found in the PHS, as the following passage illustrates: 'We must find a way to end that war, and the solution to this question must incorporate the lessons we have learned. Vietnam is not a separate moral or political issue. It is a political issue, as is Mississippi racism, Chicago unemployment, university paternalism, and the public aid system, that can be dealt with only by attacking the way that decisions are made in America, who makes them, and the purpose of a society' (Booth and Webb 1966:81).

This same paper tried to outline the basis of a broad social movement built upon an alliance of the blacks, the poor, the students, and those opposed to the war. It was a warning to those who would build such a movement upon antiwar sentiment alone and an attempt to bring unity to the troubled ranks of the New Left. The dream of an interracial movement of the poor with which the students would be affiliated had dissipated in the wake of the black power movement and the failure of ERAP.

At about this same time, the chairman of the federal council of SUPA, Jim Harding, wrote a paper entitled 'An Ethical Movement in Search of an Analysis' (1966), which addressed problems in the Canadian movement similar to those which Booth and Webb had sought to outline in their article. Harding's paper, however, represented a qualified self-criticism of the explicit moralism of the early movement and called for a detailed analysis of Canadian society. SUPA had to become a political movement, an extraparliamentary opposition to American domination of the Canadian economy, informed by 'the ideas of student syndicalism which suggest that student consciousness and social action can be linked with the problems of minorities, the unemployed youth':

SUPA is an ethical movement, *and knows it!* Certainly the kinds of ethics it is developing are part of a process of social and historical conditions; in fact it is by reference to real conditions such as military and totalitarian technology that it has developed its ethics of non-violence and participatory democracy. But, it is at a stage in development where it is consciously concerned with the ethics of human relations which hopefully is a concern which can be linked with an overall and valid analysis of conditions.

Other groups also have a level of values, morals or ethics, but perhaps because they have adopted a political theory developed at an earlier stage of history they are unaware of this. Because they are unaware of the implicit values in their analysis, their values can become *bias*, and they cannot look at social conditions squarely. (Harding 1966:26–7)

But by late 1965 and early 1966 the original tactical, strategic, and theoretical views of the New Left could no longer bear the weight of the changes and defeats (and indeed very real partial victories) which had occurred. Rejected by blacks and poor whites, cut off from the cold war socialists and liberals, and unnoticed by the working class, the students were forced back to the campus, where they discovered a new constituency to represent – themselves. The war in Vietnam only helped the students to cast themselves in the role of victims. Student syndicalism was one of the ideological expressions of this newly found interest.[3]

Student syndicalist ideology was explicitly introduced to the New Left in North America by UGEQ, which had borrowed the theory from the Union nationale des étudiants de France (UNEF).[4] In 1964, Serge Joyal,[5] provisionary president of UGEQ, wrote a paper entitled 'Le Syndicalisme étudiant au Québec,' which was published by SUPA in English translation. Joyal considered the student to be an intellectual worker: 'Intellectual investments, just as much as financial investments, condition the equipment of society, and therefore, its capacity for production. The student, like the teacher, participates in the working world by this activity of training. He is the producer of a service which is indispensable to the progress of the nation, the service of intellectual investment ... A tight solidarity unites all the productive elements; intellectuals and manual workers are united in the common effort' (Joyal 1965:6).

Student syndicalism represented a direct response to the shock of the 'broken promise,' to the declassification of the future mediate producers (already visible in the 'multiversity'). It was largely a defensive ideology expressed in an aggressive form. This syndicalism of the future massified élite 'must be the collective expression of the group, of the future managerial class, firmly situated in society with rights and duties. This way, the student is less and less identified with his social origin, and interestingly as a "student," that is, as a component part of the active and dynamic population of the nation' (6). The increasing importance of the university to the middle class, as a means of maintaining social position or of achieving upward social mobility, is reflected in the student syndicalist position. Student syndicalism makes the student

aware of his strength on the social, political and economic levels; it makes him aware of the solidarity of all the component parts of society, intellectual workers and rural and industrial workers; it is a direct socialising force in the student; it integrates him in society, giving him the status of a young intellectual worker, and of a full citizen, active (committed) and responsible; it transforms the intellectual conditions of the student's work, so that schools are no longer outside society, indifferent and absent, but have a direct influence on society, especially on its economic life. (7)

The change in the character of student life, the change from a satisfied, self-conscious privileged élitist grouping to a radical, democratically oriented, massified educated élite asserting a claim to power is given expression in the following:

Services are no longer conceived in an egoistic way or niggardly way, but are viewed in their social perspective. Services based on exclusivity of membership, centred round the conservation of a few privileges and a status of assisted person, are directly opposed to the fundamental aim of student recognized as a young intellectual worker, a citizen of full status, active and responsible. (9)

The age of passivity is over, and the sanctimonious cult of paternalism and authority is out of date. There is *no* authority which holds a monopoly on truth, knowledge, and infallibility. (10)

Carl Davidson, vice-president of sds in 1966–7, systematized the student syndicalist position for the American New Left. His paper 'Student Syndicalism' (1967a) clearly outlined the conditions against which the student movement had protested. The universities have become mass institutions. No longer traditional and exclusive preserves of scholars, they have become ordinary institutions – corporations, knowledge factories: 'Concretely, the commodities of our factories are the *Knowledgable*. AID officials, Peace Corpsmen, military officers, CIA officials, segregationist judges, corporation lawyers, politicians of all sorts, welfare workers, managers of industry, labor bureaucrats ... They are products of the factories we live and work in' (Davidson 1967a:103).

In the sixties the universities were neither the preserve of a small, privileged class, nor mass democratic institutions. Since World War II they had become training institutions of diminished privilege, and their accreditation diminished in value; but at the same time they were becoming increasingly necessary for the broad middle class. Their graduates increasingly came to work for the public and private bureaucracies. Hence the students were in the ambivalent position of being both privileged and 'exploited' simultaneously: 'It is on our assembly lines in the universities that they are molded into what they are. As integral parts of the knowledge factory system, we are both the exploiters and the exploited. As both managers and the managed, we produce and become the most vital product of corporate liberalism – bureaucratic man. In short, we are a new kind of scab' (103).

The disappointment experienced by the first wave of the baby boom generation at the university turned to anger directed at the entrenched intellectual élite:

We are told we must learn to make responsible decisions, yet we are not allowed to make actual decisions. We are told that education is an active process, yet we are passively trained. We are criticized for our apathy and our activity. In the name of freedom, we are trained to obey.

The system requires that we passively agree to be manipulated. But our vision is one of active participation. And this is the demand that our administrators cannot meet without putting themselves out of a job. That is exactly why we should be making it. (106–7)

Somewhat later, during his term as inter-organizational secretary of SDS (1967–8), Davidson wrote an extended analysis of the university in which he developed a foundation for the student syndicalism/new working class perspective. In this paper, 'The New Radicals and the Multiversity' (1967b), we find a remarkably clear statement of the student malaise and a rationalization for the demands of student power. Citing extensively from a letter to the *New York Times* written by a despondent student, Davidson sought to illustrate the subjective expression of student alienation:

I begin to wonder just what this is all about: am I educating myself? I have that one answered ... I'm educating myself the way *they* want. So I convince myself the real reason I'm doing all this is to prepare myself; meantime I'm wasting those years of preparation. I'm not learning what I want to learn ... So maybe I got an A ... but when I get it back I find that A means nothing. It's a letter *you* use to keep me going ... I feel like I'm in a coffin and can't move or breathe ... My life is worth nothing. It's enclosed in a few buildings on one campus; it goes no further. I've got to bust. (Davidson 1967b:62–3)

In the demand for relevance and freedom, there is combined a backward- and a forward-looking element: the freedom and creativity of the traditional scholar and the relevance of the technocrat. But in this the students are merely demanding that society live up to the promise which it made to them, a promise which unintentionally but inevitably carried a double message:

What should education be about in America? The official rhetoric seems to offer an answer: education should be the process of developing the free, autonomous, creative and responsible *individual* ...

But what is the reality of American education? Contrary to our commitment to individualism, we find that the day-to-day practice of our schools is authoritarian, conformist, and almost entirely status oriented. (63–4)

In fact, Davidson knows what the problem is, even though he does not know that it is the current problem of the middle class: 'Quantitatively education has been rapidly increasing in the last few decades; but, as it grows in size, it decreases qualitatively' (64). As we have seen, as the gates of the university were forced open by the broad strata of middle class youth and as mediate production became immediately subsumed under the organization of capital, the traditional role and function of the university shifted in emphasis and meaning. Quite unwittingly, Davidson has hit upon the secret of the predicament of the middle class students in the sixties.

The 'knowledge industry' is big business which, according to Davidson, 'accounts for 30% of the Gross National Product; and, it is expanding at *twice* the rate of any sector of the economy' (66). He has also grasped the changes within higher education which have occurred as a consequence of the rise of the 'knowledge industry': 'Education is not being done away with in favour of something called training. Rather, education is being transformed from a quasi-aristocratic classicism and petty-bourgeois romanticism into something quite new ... In one sense, we are separated from life. In another, we are being conditioned for life in a lifeless, stagnant, and sterile society' (66).[6]

The university had now become the crucible out of which would pour the new working class. In this way, the university serves the needs of the ruling class. The students, as Mario Savio saw in 1964, have a 'process served upon them': 'Our rough edges must be worn off, our spirit broken, our hopes mundane, and our manners subservient and docile. And if we won't pacify and repress ourselves with all the mechanisms *they* have constructed for our self-flagellation, the police will be called' (73).

By means of this analysis, Davidson is able to 'understand the student revolt': 'What we are witnessing and participating in is an important historical phenomenon: the revolt of the trainees of the new working class against the alienated and oppressive conditions of production and consumption within corporate capitalism' (74).

The shift in focus from community organizing to the university, from an interracial movement of the poor and peace actions to a concern with student syndicalism and the new working class, introduced a powerful new element into the theoretical and strategic thinking of the New Left – a preoccupation with the concept of class and a growing interest in Marxism. During the latter part of 1966 and the first half of 1967, SUPA carried on an internal debate about class in its newsletter (Harding 1966b:2–5; Lomer 1966:15–16; Roussopolous 1966:17–19; Freeman 1967:10; Repo 1967:9; Shepherd 1967:16–17). This was part of a larger attempt to clarify and formalize the organization's ideological position.[7] Late in 1966 SUPA decided to prepare a manifesto which would set forth the fundamental principles and outline the basic analyses of the union. Perhaps the most active supporter of this idea was Don McKelvey, an American active in SDS, who had come north to work with SUPA in the mid-sixties.[8] In connection with this attempt to write a manifesto, McKelvey wrote a position paper on organizing the middle class around non-economic, social-psychological issues. Convinced that the 'lumpen-proletariat,' claimed by the early New Left as its constituency, could be and would be easily brought into the middle class by the state, McKelvey argued that the only pay-off for those interested in bringing about radical social change lies in middle class organizing. Although this position reflected the disappointments and defeats which the New Left had experienced in its community organizing experiments (and in the civil rights movement in the United States), it was also the expression of a new attempt on the part of the students to break out of their isolation by discovering the historical agency of social change of which they were somehow to be a part. This would ensure that students would once again have an important role to play on the world-historical stage, a role which was first promised and later denied them.

The incompatibility of the new emphasis on class with the early populist orientation of the New Left is clearly brought out in the following excerpt from a letter written by Stan Gray (a SUPA leader studying in England at the time) to Don McKelvey:

I don't think you see the incompatibility of the new left's present emphasis with the Marxist emphasis on class and workers control. If there is one thing which the new left, at least in Canada, has consistently sought to avoid, it is the radicalizing experiences and organizational importance of the productive process, and thereby of the working class as a class. Its line is participatory democracy in slums, schools, foreign policy, perhaps professions – but nothing about the struggle for control at the point of production. (Gray 1967:9)

Even those who still held to the communitarianism of the early New Left began, in the late sixties, to rationalize the holding of that view in class terms. In a letter to McKelvey from a member of SUPA on the subject of the proposed manifesto for the organization, a critique of middle class organizing is mounted. Instead, the writer of the letter would have SUPA base its strategy for revolution upon the outcasts of society – hoboes, tramps, beggars, and the like – who, in the eyes of this same writer, have a historical mission as a class to fulfil.

The question of class, which was to command a growing attention in the New Left, was raised in an atmosphere of isolation and desperation, and this led to an increasingly fantastic view of political and social reality. The fantasy grew as the students began to turn their attention to the university once more. The retreat to the campus had been completed by 1967.

11

Fists and flowers: ideology and the end of the student movement

During the last years of the sixties, the New Left in all three countries was racked with internal ideological strife which led to functional organizational paralysis and chaos within the movement. Those who contracted the disease of 'vanguarditis' at the end of the decade appeared to have rejected the fundamental tenets of the New Left in favour of the principles, strategies, and tactics of the Old Communist Left. An attempt will be made, however, to show that the spread of 'vanguarditis' was not something which engulfed the New Left organizations from without, but rather represented the development of an element inherent within the New Left itself. More specifically, the rise of vanguardism, centralism, and Marxism-Leninism within a radical democratic decentralist populist movement must be understood as part of the unravelling of those contradictory strands which until that point had been successfully, if tenuously, held together under more favourable conditions in an ambivalent unity.

Although the rise of vanguardism was found everywhere, and although the struggle between the various factions was carried out with bitter acrimony in Canada and the United States, the most theoretically sophisticated debate occurred within the German SDS. A paper written by Hans-Gerhardt (called 'Jascha') Schmierer (1969) of the Heidelberg SDS in which the theories of the anti-authoritarian New Left were assailed and in which a call is made for the establishment of a socialist vanguard organization provides an excellent example of the arguments adduced for vanguardism.[1] Perusal of this article will allow us to consider the nature of the ideological split in terms of the previous analysis of the character of the student movement.

There is a temptation now, as there was then, to begin with

ideological statements and to move from there to the interests which they represent, or to the conditions of which they are an expression. In so doing, one might 'find' that one tendency represented a 'petty bourgeois' class interest, another, a reactionary élitism of the children of the well-to-do, and so on. However, we have consciously followed the trajectory of the movement beginning with the analysis of its 'earthly core' and only then pursued its ethereal, ideological expressions. In so doing, one finds that the polarization of the New Left was not of a substantial but rather of a formal and external character.[2]

The split within the New Left revealed the secret dynamism of the student movement – its intrinsic ambivalence, the very components of which appeared in their palpably pure form within the various factions and tendencies of the late New Left. Removed from the actual mediate and immediate productive life of society, the students acted out a fantasy, because of the specific character of their reality, because their reality was one which needed the fantasy (Marx 1970:131). In this way, the politics of the students was devotional, religious in character.[3] The promise which was denied them in reality (that is, in society) would be redeemed by the students themselves by means of campus politics, by means of drugs, by acts of polymorphous sexual perversity, by the iron laws of Marxism-Leninism (which were at the same time grasped in a remarkably voluntaristic way), by means of terrorist acts or suicide. As we have already seen, Marxism was a general vehicle of expression upon which groups representing both ambivalent poles of the movement seized in the fray. Elsewhere in this work the reasons for the student fascination with the concepts of Marxism have been stated in a general way. Here there is an interest in following the process of dissolution of the New Left into its antagonistic component parts.

The two souls of the student movement

J. Schmierer's 'Zur Analyse der Studentenbewegung' represents an attempt to develop an explanation of the student movement and to prepare the ground for a 'discussion of the decisive question concerning the relationship of the student and workers' movements.' Schmierer takes issue with various other attempts, then current, to explain the student movement, attempts which he cites under the following headings: the theory of science as a productive force; the theory of marginal groups; the theory of the capitalization of science; the theory of the authoritarian state; and the theory of the new working class.

Although he doesn't explain the inner relations among these variously designated theoretical positions, it is clear that they all share a basic orientation which Schmierer feels is severely wanting. In terms of our previous analysis, all of them can be ranged around the polar position which has been characterized as seeking to substitute the part for the whole, students for the proletariat (that is, humanity), the university for society. Schmierer's own position represents one variant of the opposite polar view which is distinguished by the endeavour to deny the part in order to assert leadership of (or alternatively to be rescued by) an illusory whole.

In fact, Schmierer's analysis of the student movement, which, for all his Marxism-Leninism is really an analysis of the ideology of the student movement, approaches at points, albeit uncritically, some of the theses advanced in this book concerning the genesis and trajectory of the New Left.

According to Schmierer, the theory of 'capitalized science,' which views the student movement as a response to the increasing proletarianization of academically trained professions, and the theory of the authoritarian state, which views the students as a political vanguard capable of seeing the total process of repression on account of their position outside the process of social production, are both unable to grasp the relationship between the student and workers' movements.[4]

Capitalized science theory, in part, saw an inherent antagonism between capitalist irrationality (*pace* interpreters of Max Weber!) and the commitment of science to reason and efficiency. For Schmierer, however, the real task facing the student movement was not the laying bare of the relationship between science and capital but situating science within the struggle between the bourgeoisie and the proletariat:

The problem is not: 'Why do scientists submit themselves to the pressure of valorization of capital against their better judgement [*Einsicht*]' but rather: 'How is it that the specific situation of students and scientists allows a minority of them to break through the appearance of scientific rationality of capitalism and to recognize the contradictions of capitalism behind it and to place themselves on the side of wage labour in the basic contradiction between wage labour and capital?' Science is not per se anti-capitalistic; rather, determinate conditions allow students and scientists today to take the point of view of the proletariat and, on the basis of that perspective only, to break through the ideological character of bourgeois science and to put their training at the disposal of the proletariat. (SDS 1970:2)[5]

The student movement cannot be explained by the theory of capitalized science ('scientization of production,' 'economic penetration of science'), for the student movement grew out of those faculties (that is, philosophy and the humanities) 'which have little or no relevance for immediate production' (2):

To this point the student movement has been less the uprising of the productive force 'science' than the revolt of a conceited 'free-floating intelligentsia'[6] which clearly and poignantly learned that the moulding of society did not stop before it, that its moral protest against the war in Vietnam and the emergency laws and its abhorrence of the bourgeois milieu would no longer be tolerated because the necessity of manipulating and moulding society above all has as its prerequisite the moulding of the ideologists. (2–3)

But even though this attempt to understand the student movement as a revolt of the scientific producers was ideological, according to Schmierer, it allowed the student movement to advance beyond itself 'to create for the stirred up students a political identity which they could not have brought forth out of their own midst. The socialist interpretation of the student movement ... is the real service of SDS' (3). Socialists will see that the students are doomed to act as the footmen of capital, having no say in the determination and execution of their social function. The students

are trained to carry out the imperatives of authority ... they later have to function as the agents of capital. Since they are simultaneously excluded from every [position of] authority at the university, it is possible for them to differentiate between their later function of having to mediate authority to those below and not being able to influence the content [*Sinn*] of this authority at all (the lifeblood of authority is the hiding of this differentiation). At the same time it becomes clear to them that they can utilize their knowledge professionally only when it directly serves to benefit authority ... The expansion of capitalistic planning to include aesthetes must necessarily lead to frictions in the consciousness of the aesthetes. (3)

In his own ideological fashion Schmierer has expressed the ambivalent character of the student movement under changing conditions (that is, 'the expansion of capitalistic planning to include the aesthetes'). But since he does not begin at the beginning, with those changing conditions, but in the middle, with their ideological expression, he cannot come to grips with the real motor force of the student movement or with its historical meaning. He cannot do this without renouncing his own fantastic revolutionary politics, his own claim as the maker of history. Yet on the basis of the analysis of the changing conditions of life of middle class youth, of the valorization of capital, and of the university, one can appreciate the kernel of truth which Schmierer reveals in his ideological criticism. After referring to Lukács' theory of reification he goes on to say:

The imposition of this objective structure [reification] of the so-called intellectual professions in the university apparently comes into contradiction with the individualistic petty bourgeois ideology of the students. It becomes exacerbated by the 'massification' of the university and the ever worsening conditions of competition which call forth in many students an early resignation *vis-à-vis* their careers. (3)

One can wholeheartedly agree with Schmierer's understanding of the other tendency in SDS: 'The attempt to comprehend the borrowed class consciousness as the autonomous result of the student movement led to the construction of the theory of "science as a productive force"' (4). But Schmierer entirely fails to see his own Marxism-Leninism-Maoism as yet another way of rationalizing his own (the socialist students') lack of importance on the world-historical stage. He recognizes the élitism in the movement (expressed in the ideology of the 'other' tendency), but he does not see the élitist claims which he himself is advancing. Intellectual labourers are indeed labourers, but they are privileged within the class of social labour and hence they will invariably come down on the side of capital:

Science is rather the privilege of a separate stratum into which the individual labourer is able to rise only in a few cases. The greater the importance of science for the functioning of society becomes, the more the number of scientific labourers increases, the more the illusion of an autarchy of science within a society (which only observes that society) disappears as well. Since the products of the scientist's labour, his inventions, analyses, theories, enter into the production process of society, they thereby necessarily come under the command of capital, viz. a state committed to capital. Thus the scientist's own labour is alienated from him; it stands opposed to him as an alien power.

The scientific labourer enjoys the privileges of the capitalist class, privileges 'which are based upon the misery of the working class proper,' and hence he does not fulfil his 'historically given task' of explaining the roots of the alienation which intellectual labour and 'the working class proper' both suffer.[7] And so, socialist revolutionaries should not, according to Schmierer, look to the scientific labourers for leadership in the class struggle: 'Since science is privileged in comparison to labour in its relation to capital, it must be reckoned that it will fight on the side of capital until the workers [that is, the workers proper] put the question of power in a practical way' (5).

Having shown to his satisfaction that the theory of science as a productive force and the theory of the new working class derived from it are insufficient as an explanation of the student movement and as a basis for a socialist strategy, Schmierer proceeds to consider marginal group theory and the theory of the authoritarian state. If the 'new working class' theory saw the revolutionary potential of the students as scientific labourers because they stand at the centre of modern social production, the marginal group theory attributes their revolutionary potential to their privileged position outside the sphere of social production. According to the latter view, the centre of society has been brought under the control of the authoritarian state by means of modern technology and technique. Only those who are structurally excluded from this authoritarian manipulation or, to use another term, this one-dimensionality represent a potential for revolt. The central contradiction of modern society ceases to be that between capital and wage-labour; it is now the contradiction between the inhuman apparatus and a suppressed humanity which comes to the fore.

Schmierer confesses that he does not understand how the two theories – science as a productive force and the marginal group – can both be valid explanations of the student movement: the former is based upon the exploitation of intellectual labour under capitalism, the latter upon the privilege of university youth: 'On the one hand, they had to explain why it was precisely the students who revolted; on the other hand, they had to interpret their rebellion as exemplary. Thus, they could only insist upon the exemplary situation of the students, in order, at the same time, to deny it' (7).

Once again Schmierer has hit upon the fundamental ambivalence of the student movement. However, he sees it as a result of the 'motivation of the student revolutionaries.' Instead of dealing with the objective and subjective sides together, he treats the matter in a thoroughly one-sided, subjective fashion, ideologically. Elitism and populism were equally ambivalent expressions of a movement arising out of an ambivalent reality, as has been demonstrated here. Schmierer further shows us that he is lost at sea when he argues, against Dutschke,[8] that the capitalization of the university (which led to contradictions between the old élitist structure and the new achievement hierarchy) 'allowed a minority of students to free themselves from the drag-rope of the technocrats and to develop out of the critique of the technocratic reform of the university an anti-capitalist consciousness which is in no way identical with the immediate interests of the students' (7). To be sure, we are never told how these atypical students were able to free themselves of false consciousness or what social roots are given expression in their 'anti-capitalist consciousness.' They are considered to be traitors to their class, that is, to the student estate.

Finally, Schmierer argues that both of the theories of the tendency he opposes are seriously called into question when, 'on the one hand, state repression of the students is intensified and when, on the other hand, a specification of the relation between student movement and workers' movement becomes not only necessary but also possible through the intensification of class struggles in Western Europe.' It is not clear that these are the compelling reasons which call these theories into question. In any event, Schmierer gives us no further reason to believe that this is so. Yet his allusion to the intensification of class struggles in Western Europe seriously calls his own views into question; those who saw the rebirth of the revolutionary proletariat in Western Europe in the late sixties were conjuring with the product of their own imagination. They were in fact saying: 'Here is the pure socialist movement; it will lead me out of this morass' (variant one); 'I will lead it to its future, which is guaranteed by history' (variant two).

During the last years of the New Left, everyone wanted to present a 'materialist analysis' of the movement, and Schmierer was no exception: 'The student movement must be explained socio-economically out of the situation at the university and out of the valorization of science in capitalism'. Even though he doesn't do this, he argues with plausibility that the students qua students can never develop a proletarian consciousness, that the student movement as a student movement can never be socialist: 'The class consciousness of the students is borrowed. Students are as students not in a position to construct a consistent theory of society. Such a theory ... is only possible from the standpoint of the proletariat' (7). SDS was a socialist movement, but it was not able to make the broad masses of students into socialists. The failure of SDS in this matter is directly related to the lack of leadership, to the failure to gauge the limits of the student movement, to the misleading theories of marginal groups and the new working class. The socialist student leadership, according to Schmierer, should have constituted itself as a revolutionary vanguard in order to attempt to 'reconstruct the workers' movement.' It failed to do this because it did not draw the crucial distinction between petty bourgeois students at the university and 'the working class proper':

SDS did not understand itself as a socialist organization which works in the student movement as the agent of the working class and class consciousness in the working class; rather, it wanted to relate the student movement directly to the working class or to see it as the whole of suppressed humanity. The uncritical applications of the new working class and marginal group theories are the expressions of this attempt to make socialist politics without class analysis. (8)

We can clearly see the reason for the rise of variants of Marxism-Leninism within the disintegrating student movement. The students had been beaten both in society and on the campus. The weakness and vulnerability of the student movement had been made clear. It was now time for those select few to abandon the moribund vehicle of the student movement for a much more powerful historical agency (in theory and in fantasy). This agent was the proletariat, 'the working class proper.' Of course, they did not mean the German, American, or Canadian proletariat, as it lives and breathes. They meant the proletariat as the historical subject-object, the philosophical category, the fantastic vehicle which would realize the 'promise' made to them. It was the fantastic means for realizing the promise, because the promise was not to be realized in fact.

12

Conclusion

The New Left student movement died at the end of the sixties because, paradoxically, it both won and lost its struggle. In fact there are noticeable differences between the university and society of the eighties and those of the sixties, changes which can be directly or indirectly attributed to the student rebellion of the sixties. In this sense the students were successful. Yet the changes which occurred were changes pro forma; they were not part of a substantial transformation of society sought by the New Left. Even in the university the changes which have been institutionalized have not substantially altered the relations within the academy: students are not paid intellectual workers, professors still submit grades, the diploma or degree is a credential which is still a necessary if not a sufficient basis for finding 'clean' employment, and the university is still the life-blood of the social reproduction of the middle class.

The thesis of this book is that the student movement of the sixties was a movement of privilege, against privilege, for privilege – at a time in which the character of privilege itself was changing; that owing to the very nature of the student generation and the relations and conditions of the society in which the students found themselves, their assertion of privilege, as we have seen, took the form of its opposite – the radical-democratic assault upon privilege. The deeply rooted ambivalence of the student movement (which was an expression of the highly ambivalent character of that student generation) was appropriately manifested both in the substantial and in the formal and ideological elements of its dissolution.

Substantially the movement collapsed for the following reasons: the closing-off of the lucrative job market for university graduates and the general reversal of economic prosperity by the end of the sixties; the combination of the easing of requirements, formal concessions, skilful management of crises by the authorities, selective use of force by the agencies of the state, and the growing violence of elements of the New Left; and the transition from the university to the economy made by the first wave of the baby boom generation in North America, of the 'massified intellectual élite' in both North America and Germany.

As the New Left student generation moved into the professions and occupations of expanded mediate production, its radicalism, which was concentrated at the campus, was diluted and diffused within the economy and society. Imperatives of professional life, family life, and financial obligations made the ideals of the New Left seem distant and abstract. And membership even in the massified élite was relatively privileged in society as a whole. Finally, many of the most active students selected occupations and professions which allowed them the illusion at least of acting in a way consonant with their former New Leftism. The radical journalist, for example, working for a mass-circulation daily can imagine that he or she is not objective, but rather a committed journalist taking a stand with the oppressed, with the 'people.' The same is true for the social worker, teacher, professor, trade-union organizer, research worker, and many others.

Of course there were other, less diffuse heirs of the student movement. The meteoric rise of feminism in the public mind at the end of the sixties was due in large part to the efforts of the young women in and around the New Left. Leading figures and participants in the environmental and antinuclear movements in the seventies had been active in or influenced by the student movement in the sixties. In Germany, where some universities have remained more or less politicized throughout the seventies, students have been fighting primarily a defensive battle to protect the pro forma gains won a decade earlier. Otherwise they have been involved in altercations with the authorities over the construction of nuclear power plants, squatters' rights, *Berufsverbot* (blacklisting), and nuclear weapons proliferation.

To this extent there has been a certain continuity with the sixties, even though the successive waves of the baby boom generation have decisively shown a general lack of interest in political protest. With the last cohort of the baby boom now in the universities, we can expect to see the end of the potential for an aggressive, independent student movement capable of maintaining its momentum over any period of time. However, there is another basis to the continuity of the more limited activism of the seventies with the student movement of the sixties, for both are expressions of bohemianism in bourgeois society. We have seen that the New Left was fed in part by the eruption of bohemia into the middle class during the sixties. And, although the developments in the seventies cannot be addressed or analysed in this work, one could suggest that they emanate in large part from the 'dark side' of society, from its negative image. Bohemia is the ambivalent shadow of middle class life, feeding upon it and protesting against it simultaneously.

But the fallout from the student movement in the advanced countries of capital has been carried into other geographic regions of the world. A street in a northern Iranian village bears the name Movement of the Second of June. Former president Amin of Afghanistan had been a student at Columbia University during the late sixties, a fact which perhaps explains in part the sentiment expressed in the following report:

In a manner that seems eager to minimize any dependency on the Soviet Union, Mr Amin and Mr Taraki avoid references to Marxism, Socialism or Communism in their statements. But they call their friends 'comrades,' have busts of Lenin in their offices and have raised the red banner.

But the blueprint for the future they affirm is always something called 'working class ideology.'

One paradox at the mass demonstration was the absence of the working class. When this was noted to Fatah Nirwad, the deputy secretary of the press section in the Ministry of Foreign Affairs, he said, 'It is not necessary that the workers should be leading. A working class party does not mean that the majority is constituted by workers, but rather that the members are equipped with the ideology of the working class.'[1]

With hindsight one could add that a working class party does not mean that the majority is constituted by workers if the members are backed by Russian tanks.[2]

But if the students in the Third World indeed tell us something about the truth of the student movement in the capitalist world, the truth has only been dimly comprehended. In Germany the high degree of politicization of the students at the universities throughout the seventies has made an internal objective assessment of the reality of their situation next to impossible. Recent analyses in Canada and the United States of the student movement of the sixties have demonstrated little critical acumen.

In her journalistic account of the New Left in Canada, Myrna Kostash (1980) has not been able to establish any critical distance between herself and the (myth) of the movement, her work being a congratulatory ode to those who 'lived' the revolution.

Wini Breines' (1980) approach is more scholarly, but she is nevertheless guilty of this mysticization of the New Left movement as well. In defending the 'antiorganizational impulse' of the early New Left and certain tendencies of the later movement, Breines draws a contrast between 'strategic' and 'prefigurative' politics. The former implies instrumental rationality, the rational matching of discrete ends and discrete means, the organizational imperative; the latter designates 'an essentially antiorganizational politics characteristic of the movement, as well as of parts of the new left leadership; it may be recognized in counter-institutions, demonstrations and the attempt to embody personal and antihierarchical values in politics. Participatory democracy was central to prefigurative politics' (Breines 1980:421). According to her analysis, 'the new left *chose not to be strategic.*' (422) Consciousness and politics are for her independent elements which may possibly be accounted for by material factors which structure the choice made in favour of prefigurative politics. (This contrasts starkly with the view advanced in this book, that consciousness is always the consciousness of historically specific social individuals and does not, therefore, allow consciousness and the so-called material factors to be treated in isolation from one another.)

But the real object of Breines' concern is the organization theory of Robert Michels, according to which the tendency to oligarchy is a feature of all organizations regardless of their particular ends, forms, or purposes.[3] Since the New Left consciously rejected 'organization' and affirmed 'the movement,' Breines can state that 'theirs was a challenge to Michels.' But far from offering a challenge to Michels, the New Left, if we follow Breines' thesis, is further grist for his mill, for the 'prefigurative' New Left proved itself (to the glee of the Michelsians) to be ineffective, and the 'strategists' became undemocratic. Yet Breines is absolutely faithful to the spirit of the early New Left, for 'winning' (which is an instrumentalist notion) has never been the goal of student moralism. In their religious orientation to questions of social and political change the devout students will always prefer martyrdom to mere 'worldly' success.[4]

But the most serious objection to Breines' analysis concerns its ahistorical, abstract, and wholly formal character. She tears the organization question out of its historical context and considers it a matter of wilful choice on the part of the members of the New Left. She does this without considering that the formal opposition between 'movement' and 'organization' is itself peculiar to specific historical conditions and by no means a timeless categorical truth. In addition, the distinction which she draws between strategic and prefigurative politics is one of degree and not one of kind, as she suggests. The former emphasizes the parsimonious linking of particular means to discrete ends. The latter defines all behaviour in terms of some absolute value orientation. But if prefigurative politics was a choice made by large elements of the New Left, then it is in fact a subset of strategic politics (and this is probably closer to the historical truth).

Furthermore, true to the ethos of the New Left, Breines rides roughshod over history in her discussion of what she calls 'depoliticization': 'One of the central purposes of new left politics may be defined as the attempt to unite private and public life, which goes back to the idea of the polis in ancient Greece and is at heart profoundly political' (426). But the basis of the polis (one should begin with the relations of the polis, not with the 'idea') was not 'the attempt to unite public and private life' (which was not a desideratum but the actual condition of life of those who belonged to the master class), but the formal and substantial bondage of the class of social labour.[5] Conjuring with the image of the polis not only shows a lack of historical consciousness but seeks to embellish the particular ideals of the student generation of the sixties by lending them the trappings of some supposedly universal ideal, such as the 'idea of the polis.'

In fact, the only question of substantial historical import concerning the significance of the student revolt in the sixties is this: did it in some way make a contribution to the struggle for the substantial liberation of the class of social labour? All the indications lead us to answer in the negative.

The New Left students of the sixties participated in a movement which changed the face of the universities, revamped the foundations of middle class life, altered the character of sexual norms and mores, sensitized the public to environmental and ecological issues, seriously eroded the Protestant work ethic (especially among those under forty-five), and improved the formal position of women and minorities in society. Although these matters affect the lives of hundreds of millions, the substance of human freedom has not been enhanced thereby. The radical transformation of the substantial processes and relations of labour and production is not among the accomplishments of the student movement.

The movement of the children of privilege was not part of an actual and substantial movement of liberation. Yet the wheel is still in spin, and further judgement of it will have to fall to generations as yet unborn.

Postscript

The popular media take great delight in putting before the public catch-word characterizations of different decades. The thirties has been presented as 'the dirty thirties,' the decade of the depression; the forties as the 'war-torn' decade; the fifties as 'the silent fifties,' the decade of conformity. At the beginning of the eighties the media passed judgement on the seventies by drawing a comparison between it and the sixties. In relation to 'the activist sixties,' the seventies was portrayed as 'a non-decade,' as a stretch of time in which we were really only marking time. It is, of course, impossible at present to know how the eighties will fare at the hands of the pundits. Some observers are already calling attention to the similarities between the thirties and the early eighties, especially in terms of the deepening economic crisis and the growing mood of 'appeasement,' above all in Western Europe. Recent peace demonstrations involving many hundreds of thousands of individuals have led to predictions that a powerful mass peace movement is in the process of being formed. The election of the Green Party to the German Bundestag has been taken as a clear sign of potential political discontent.

For the activist vanguard of the baby boom generation in Canada and the United States, the seventies was a period of transition – from student life to middle class, professional life. This group, consisting of those born roughly between 1945 and 1950, entered the labour force just before the economic boom was lowered on the rest of the 'big generation.' This relatively fortunate set of individuals maintained its activist proclivities, but not in their New Left form. In opposition to the universalism and maximalism of the student movement of the sixties, the newest members of the educated middle class in the seventies directed their energy to the realization of particularistic and locally relevant goals. At the same time they turned their gaze inwards, flaunted their egoism, and gave themselves over to a series of fad diets, physical fitness programs, and the strangest assortment of psychotherapies. The counter-culture of the sixties had been tamed by middle class life, just as middle class life had been formally overhauled by the counter-culture.

In Germany veterans of the New Left found homes as young professionals in a wide variety of radical political groupings – the DKP, ML groups, 'green' and 'coloured' environmental organizations, feminist groups, alternative children's centres, and, at the end of the seventies and early eighties, in the peace movement and in the Green Party. This continuing political activism, which is more explicitly ideological than in Canada or the United States, is due in part to the further rapid expansion of German higher education in the seventies (leading to a further acceleration of the massification of the intellectual élite) and the growing nationalistic hostility of the educated German middle class to the four-power occupation forces, especially the United States. (For historical reasons, this nationalism can only be given covert and indirect political expression.)

Canadian and American university students in the seventies learned a lesson from the experiences of their immediate predecessors. At the same time they were confronted with an increasingly difficult job market for university graduates. This has led to a growing conformity among the student bodies; but it would be wrong to consider this conformity an expression of passivity or resignation. On the contrary, it is the conformity of contract, wholly formal and instrumental. These students know their rights, and not a few of them in recent years have challenged their professors on grades by bringing parents and legal counsel to meet with representatives of the administration. The number of such confrontations leading to litigation has increased dramatically in the last ten years.

Many of these students are angry as well. Their anger, however, is not channelled into political outlets. There are few causes to support, few ideological positions to be defended. It manifests itself in vandalism, alcohol and drug abuse, and a lack of community spirit or college allegiance (beyond the level of football, that is). It is the kind of anger which lies behind punk-rock nihilism.

The universities have also changed, both in form and content. In Germany the absolute power of the full professor was broken, but the politicization of faculty decision making has led to a serious erosion of scholarly integrity. In Canada and the United States student input and representation in both curricular and extracurricular matters has been institutionalized, and *in loco parentis* rules no longer exist. (Perhaps it would be closer to the truth to say that parental rules themselves no longer exist.) Academic standards have fallen directly and indirectly as a consequence of the student movement. Veterans of the movement who made careers in public and high school teaching brought much of the 'do your own thing' ethos with them into the classroom. As a result the level of literacy and numeracy of a whole generation of potential university students has been compromised.

Former activists who became university teachers brought into their various disciplines, especially in the humanities and social sciences, whole new perspectives and methodologies, many of suspicious provenance and questionable scholarly significance. At the very least, the core of many areas of scholarship was ripped apart, as colleagues could no longer agree on what was central and what was peripheral.

As the students became less and less interested in the content of their education and more and more concerned about formal requirements, the morale of concerned faculty members sunk lower and lower. This was further exacerbated by the growing financial pressures placed upon the university and by the worsening career prospects for university graduates. The university degree having been devalued in society, it was now being devalued in the university.

What are the prospects for the rebirth of political activism in the universities in Canada and the United States? In this book it has been argued that the university was a gift to the middle class in the fifties and sixties, a time of relative prosperity and security for that class. The political sixties gave expression to these conditions and relations of the children of privilege in the ways outlined above. If a politicization of the campuses in North America were to occur in the mid-eighties, it would be an expression of a different set of conditions and relations; thus it would have a different character.

The French student revolt of 1983 is the ironic last gasp of the movement which began in the sixties. The New Left responded to the first stages of the massification of the intellectual élite in a formally anti-élitist but substantially élitist manner. The New Right today is responding to the final stages of the massification in an explicitly élitist manner. When the final assault is made upon the last hold-outs of the old fashioned intellectual élitism (those in the medical profession, for example) the democratic form of protest vanishes, revealing its essential élitism.

The sociologists and philosophers in May 1968 with the force of a whole generation behind them took to the streets of Paris for the same basic reasons as the medical students in May 1983. The fact that the former were self-conscious leftists who identified themselves with the cause of a downtrodden humanity whereas the latter were consciously out to defend their threatened privilege is to be explained by the different objective conditions and consequent tactical options facing students in the sixties and the eighties.

The peace movement of the eighties does not have its centre in the universities. Although scholarly research has yet to provide us with reliable data, this new movement appears to be borne by the young mediate producers and supported by a larger middle class constituency. The middle class, hard pressed by the economy of the eighties, divided against itself, with no class interest but only a life-style to defend, has raised the banner of peace. In part this is a protest against a hideously large war expenditure (globally and nationally) when state deficits are enormous. At the same time, it is indirectly a supplication for peace for the middle class itself, a supplication addressed to the military, the banks, and the state.

Abbreviations

CDU	Christlich-Demokratische Union
CGT	Confédération générale du travail
CND	Campaign for Nuclear Disarmament
COMECON	Council for Mutual Economic Assistance
CORE	Congress for Racial Equality
CPUSA	Communist Party of the United States of America
CUCND	Combined Universities Campaign for Nuclear Disarmament
CUP	Canadian University Press
CUS	Canadian Union of Students
CUSO	Canadian University Students Overseas
CYC	Company of Young Canadians
DGB	Deutscher Gewerkschaftsbund
DKP	Deutsche Kommunistische Partei
ERAP	Economic Research and Action Project
FDP	Freie Demokratische Partei
FRG	Federal Republic of Germany
FSM	Free Speech Movement
FU	Freie Universität (Berlin)
GDR	German Democratic Republic
HD	*Hochschule in der Demokratie*
KBW	Kommunistischer Bund Westdeutschland
KdA	Kampf dem Atomtod
LID	League for Industrial Democracy
ML	Marxist-Leninist
MSB Spartakus	Marxistischer Studentbund Spartakus
NDP	New Democratic Party

OECD	Organization for Economic Cooperation and Development
PCF	Parti communiste français
PHS	*Port Huron Statement*
PL(P)	Progressive Labor (Party)
RAF	Rote Armee Fraktion
REP	Radical Education Project
ROTC	Reserve Officers Training Corp
RSM	Radical Student Movement
RYM (II)	Revolutionary Youth Movement (II)
SANE	Committee for a SANE Nuclear Policy
SB	Sozialistisches Büro
SCLC	Southern Christian Leadership Conference
SDS	Sozialistischer Deutscher Studentenbund
SDS	Students for a Democratic Society
SEW	Sozialistische Einheitspartei West-Berlin
SHB	Sozialdemokratischer Hochschulbund
SNCC	Student Nonviolent Coordinating Committee
SPD	Sozialdemokratische Partei Deutschlands
SPU	Student Peace Union
SUPA	Student Union for Peace Action
SWP	Socialist Workers Party
UGEQ	Union générale des étudiants du Québec
UNEF	Union nationale des étudiants de France
VDS	Verband Deutscher Studentenschaften
VISTA	Volunteers in Service to America

Notes

Introduction

1 The role of the media in the development and disintegration of the American SDS is examined in detail in Gitlin (1980). Cf Cutler (1973:47).
2 Günter Grass, the famous German novelist and political activist, anticipated the scene portrayed by the mass media in the late seventies in 1969 when he wrote: 'How many of the young revolutionaries are going to vote loyally and meekly for the Christian Democrats when their exaggerated expectations remain unfulfilled and they have, after leaving the university, sacrificed more and more [of their youthful idealism] in the interest of their career, which of course will not prevent them later on, in their circle of friends, as well-to-do men in their thirties, from remembering pleasantly their revolutionary past with a glass of Moselle wine ... ' (cited in Mehnert 1977:94).

None of the former student activists interviewed (see note 14 below) denied that many of their erstwhile comrades were leading fairly conventional middle class lives by the end of the seventies. There was, however, little agreement among the respondents concerning the significance of this recent state of affairs. One Canadian, for example, emphasized the lack of impact which the movement had upon the personal lives of its members: 'Well, when the movement dissipated around 1970, the people we're talking about graduated around 1970, and interestingly enough they went on to what they were going on to anyway. In other words, this radicalism seems to have made very little change in their own personal lives. Maybe a few became union organizers instead of middle management in the factory, but the difference between those two is pretty minor. I'm a lawyer anyway, and I was going to be a lawyer; and most everybody I know who went through the movement is little changed from probably where they were going to be headed. The professors have become professors, the doctors have become doctors. Maybe they spent a little while being a doctor in a community clinic, or being a lawyer in a community clinic, but really the change is small. I don't know what other change there could be.'

Another former Canadian student activist argues in a very different tone that the middle class life-style does not basically affect the political consciousness and activities of the former radical youth: 'I think a number of things survived: a newspaper here, or a radio station there, or an organization here, and what not. The fact that people have gone on and some of them made families, and some of them made middle class careers, and some of them not, and so on, that's a phenomenon that occurs in and around also, and it isn't the most significant thing ... And people got caught up in looking at that, as if that were remarkable. But no, it isn't. There's no reason why people taking bourgeois forms can't continue to have political shape to their lives.'

3 Although some authors of works on the radical movements of the sixties have drawn a fine distinction between the New Left and the student movement, I do not choose to do so. There were, to be sure, New Leftists who were not students and student activists who did not belong to some New Left organization or other. The distinctions are important and must be maintained in historical studies of particular organizations, regions, and campuses. However, in considering the radical movement as a whole, nationally and internationally, analytically and not historically, these distinctions serve no purpose. This decision is supported by the fact that only one former activist out of 100 or more contacted took issue with the identification of the two movements (cf O'Brien 1971a). For a review of the literature on the German movement concerning this issue see Otto (1977:15–25); cf Westby (1976:26).

4 Klaus Allerbeck (1971:181) argues that the survey data show that German university students from working class backgrounds, unlike their American counterparts, are even more politically radical than middle and upper strata students. But there were so few German university students from the working class during the sixties (1961: 5.4% of students, 1970: 12.6% of students) that they were a rarity, even within the New Left (cf Langguth 1976:27). Allerbeck himself acknowledges this when he writes: 'The German data do not support any "revolt of the privileged" or "children of affluence" explanation (though it has to be stressed that due to the low percentage of children of workers among German university students the vast majority of the students can claim by no means to be underprivileged with reference to worldly goods)' (1970:10).

Further, it should be kept in mind that Allerbeck is not trying to explain the rise of the student movement as such. He is far more interested in predicting individual participation in, or support for, student movements (1970:11). Finally, he seems to associate privilege only with the very wealthy, ie, those 'mit besonderer Wohlhabenheit' (1973:181), and his criticism that the students were going to get élite jobs doesn't take into consideration the fact that the élite jobs themselves had declined in value (1973:183).

Flacks and Mankoff (1971:55–67) have attempted to show that the class base of the student movement broadened considerably after 1969. They are supported in this by the research of Gold, Christie, and Friedman (1976). See also Wood (1974). There is no doubt that this did occur in the United States, and that it was almost entirely associated with a general turning against the war effort among large elements of the American populace. In retrospect we can see that it signalled the end of the student movement rather than a deepening of its roots among the lower class youth.

In a very recent critical study of the New Left, Conlin (1982) has put special emphasis upon the privileged position of radical students in the sixties. Not only does he suggest that the movement achieved nothing (371), he argues that it killed what remained of a 'real left' in America. One can sympathize with the sentiment which motivates this author, but his severe criticisms quickly degenerate into little more than namecalling. Instead of an analysis of why the New Left arose and took the course it did Conlin presents us with a moralistic 'children of indulgence' thesis which is simply dismissive of the experiences of an entire generation. Ironically, the New Left itself was characterized by this same kind of moralism.

5 A Canadian who was active in the New Left during the late sixties explicitly made the link between the bright future prospects of the sixties youth and their moralistic activism: 'It was easy to get a job; it was easy to move around. Money in a sense, in a certain sense, was not that hard to come by; it was almost as if one didn't have to think about these things. And it had been that way since the late fifties. And that climate itself allowed one to say: "No, I don't want to do this. I'm going to ask you, society, to be held accountable for the ideals and whatnot that you've taught me."'

6 Cf Ericson (1975). Ericson shows the growing influence of the radicals and the Marxists in the Modern Languages Association in the United States. Many former student activists see the rise of neo-Marxism and other 'radical' theories within the disciplines as one of the accomplishments of the New Left.

7 The hostility to political ideology was most marked in North America. The German students were more closely linked to the socialist movement and the Marxist tradition than their American and Canadian counterparts.

Compare the articles published by the Radical Education Project (REP) of the American SDS or printed in the influential CUCND journal *Our General Against Nuclear War* with those in *Neue Kritik*, the theoretical organ of the German SDS.

8 In fact the attempt will be made below to show how the explicit moralism of the early New Left was transmogrified in later years and appeared implicitly in 'Marxist' garb. There was an inner connection between the sectarianism and moralism of the New Left which was rooted in the specific social character of the movement. Of course, not all the New Leftists of the early and middle sixties became Marxists, Stalinists, or terrorists after 1967. Some had dropped out of the movement by then, and others continued on with their anti-authoritarian politics and commitment to participatory democracy. One former activist with SDS in New York during the early sixties explained that the students involved in the late sixties were different people with different aims than those of the earlier cohort: 'I think the question is based on a false premise, which is that the people who remained in SDS at the time of the split were the same people who were in SDS in the early sixties, and that just isn't true. It was a different generation of people with different needs; most of our friends had got out by then because it just wasn't doing the kind of work that we wanted to do.' The perplexing thing about the later movement was its ability to bind together, at least for a time, the most contradictory elements within it. As we shall see, this unity of extremes within the movement broke apart and the different strains sought their embodiment in separate groups and factions.

Kelman makes the following observation: 'SDS inevitably gave up on organizing a movement of saints and settled, as it had to, for organizing a movement of psychopaths' (1970:281).

9 In each country I established contact with former leaders of prominent New Left groups, and in all cases they willingly provided the names and addresses of former participants. The interviews were structured but open-ended, and the questions were designed to elicit the present views of the sixties activists concerning the growth and trajectory of the New Left. All but two of the interviews (one in Canada, one in Germany) were recorded on cassette tapes and later transcribed verbatim. Twenty-one Germans were interviewed during December 1977 and January 1978 (all these interviews were conducted in German and later translated by me into English); twenty-three Canadians were interviewed during February, March, and April 1978; twenty Americans were interviewed in May and June 1978. For the most part, those interviewed had been primary and secondary leadership people in their respective national New Left organizations at

the federal, regional, and local levels. Although by no means a representative sample of the leadership of the movement, let alone of the rank-
and-file, they constitute a good cross-section of the movement's former élite
in each country. The former activists who were interviewed were associated with the following groups: CUCND, SUPA, CUS, SDS in the United States
and the FRG, and the Sozialdemokratischer Hochschulbund (SHB). Thus the
concern of this book is the 'mainstream' movements of the students in these
three countries. Excluded from detailed consideration are the movements
of the black and Hispanic students in the United States, the Québécois
students in Canada, the students descended from aboriginal peoples of
North America, and the 'Old Left' student groups in all three countries.

10 I was a member of the CUCND (high school branch) from 1960 to 1963,
loosely associated with SUPA 1966–7, involved with CUS 1968–9, and a
founder of the Radical Student Movement (RSM) at the University of Waterloo in 1968.

11 This is not to suggest that earlier studies have not been able to advance our
understanding of the dynamics of student activism. In the first place, without the numerous empirical studies of various aspects of the movement
which have been conducted and analysed in the last two decades it would
be difficult to say anything intelligent at all about the student radicalism
of the sixties. Second, many of the earlier attempts to fathom the roots of
the movement were accurate in locating them in the changes which have
occurred and were occurring in society, the economy, and the university,
and I am grateful to them for their pioneering efforts, even though they did
not pursue the inner thread which ties the whole together. Finally, those
scholars who have brought out the continuity and discontinuity of the
student radicalism of the sixties with earlier student movements have
helped discover the historical significance of the New Left student movement.

Chapter 1

1 Compare the discussion of intergenerational differences and relations in
Keniston (1968, 1971). See also Cutler (1973), Gerzon (1969), and Laufer
and Bengston (1974).

2 Even for children who were 'red- and pink-diaper babies,' a sizeable minority in the early New Left, studies show the same consistent result: the
parents tend to be less radical than their children in practice. In fact, it was
precisely because of this 'cautious' attitude of their parents, their unwilling-
ness to act on the basis of their political and social values, that the younger

generation was so angry. See Allerbeck (1973); Flacks (1967); Keniston (1968); Lipset (1976); Westby (1976). Wood (1974:55) sees this for radical parents and their radical children, but not for liberal parents and their radical children.

3 Satin (1960:18). The same developments occurred in Canadian urban centres. In Germany the growing affluence was manifested in different forms, but if anything the contrast with the late forties was even starker than in North America.

4 Fromm (1955:160; see also Jones 1980:47–55). In Germany, Alexander Mitscherlisch (1970) was writing of the society without the father. There the situation was complicated by a lost war, which meant a physical absence (killed, missing in action, captured) and a moral absence (discredited Nazi values and beliefs) of the fathers.

5 The fifties had a somewhat different impact upon the youth of Germany. The older generation had both lost a war and rebuilt the country. The contrasts between the generations in Germany were even more pronounced than in North America. If the forms of relative privilege differed in the two areas, then the content was the same. In both cases the university became the focus of heightened interest and anxiety for the new generation of middle class youth.

6 After the war political re-education programs were organized by the American occupation forces in Germany to root out Nazi values and to instil a respect for democratic political beliefs and practices. The political ideals of German youth in the fifties became those of the American victors. Thus the New Left student revolt in Germany was as much directed against the disjunction of American ideals and American social reality as it was against the German establishment. A former German student activist explains: 'The ideals of the American Revolution had become after 1945 the ideals of bourgeois youth. And then the dispute with the American war in Vietnam was also basically a dispute with ideas of the American Revolution and the reality of parliamentary democratic life in the United States. This dispute was perhaps more intense than in any other country, perhaps more intense than in America itself ... And out of that, too, it is of course of interest here that in the ambiguous American war in Vietnam the components 'idea of democracy in America' and 'reality of democracy' again played a very strong role.' The importance of America for the development of the political consciousness of German youth is emphasized by another former leader of the German SDS: 'After the war America had unbelievable influence in Germany. America was really *the* golden country in every way. Hence, when something was wrong in America, that was something entirely different

than in France of the Fifth Republic, which was also a very peculiar democratic community with this presidential constitution under DeGaulle.'

Chapter 2

1 Levinson (n d); Marshall Goldman has characterized the changes in the following way: 'Who would have dreamed back in 1959 that one day the Chase Manhattan Bank would open an office at 1 Karl Marx Square, or that the chairman of the New York Stock Exchange and the national commander of the American Legion would go to Moscow as honored guests? Who would have imagined that Pepsi-Cola, that erstwhile symbol of capitalist imperialism, would be produced and sold in the Soviet Union? Is nothing sacred?' (1975:3–4).

2 The terms 'mediate production' and 'mediate producers' are taken from the system developed by Krader in his recent writings (1977, 1979, n d). Derived from Hegel and Marx, this aspect of Krader's system portrays the class of social labour as divided internally according to the following relations: 1 / immediate producers, or those who are engaged in the process of the human transformation of nature to the satisfaction of some human want, and 2 / mediate producers, or those who are engaged in the processes which technically develop and plan, organize, or supervize the process of social production as a whole. In opposition to the class of social labour stands the class of non-producers, composed of those who are engaged neither in mediate nor in immediate production. Krader (n d) has characterized the relations between the mediate and immediate producers in the following way: 'The mediate producers, engineers, skilled technicians, applied scientists, specialists with advanced training are a class ... separated by marks of privilege, preferential treatment, better working conditions and pay within the social class of labor from the class of immediate producers ... By the play of subjective interest upon the mediate producers in civil society they are separated from the process of social labor, the unity of which is disrupted thereby.'

3 On the human capital school see Bowman (1966:111–37). Conservative critics, especially humanists, were horrified at the liberal-technocratic attempt to turn knowledge into a commodity, to link it to the crass relations of the market. Knowledge was the preserve of the intellectual élite, and the ivory tower existed not in society but in the timeless empyrean (cf Nisbet 1969:54–6).

Student radicals also objected to the technocratic assertions of 'human capital.' Like the conservatives they felt that knowledge was debased when it was pressed into the service of partial interests. But, unlike the conservatives, the radicals wanted knowledge to be democratic (free admissions, no grades, student stipends, and the like) and relevant to human as opposed to sectional and private interests ('a free university in a free society'). In pursuing this goal the students were quite unconsciously raising their own claims to social domination, as we shall see. The massification of the college-trained élite was reflected in the radical-democratic form of the new élitism.

4 This is not to suggest that the development of human capital theory was part of a vast conspiracy to dupe a guileless population. Theory does not play an immediately active role in history. Rather, it gives expression to material interests and relations in a variety of historically specific ways.

5 Marx (1972a:329, 351). Marx neglected to point out that the process of the self-valorization of capital is an appearance only, a process *as-though*. Krader has recently written: 'Capital being a form separated from the human substance, which is labour, is made into an animistic creature, treated as though it had a life of its own, which was capable of self-valorization (*Selbstverwertung*), and made into a fetish object' (n d).

6 Marx (1972c:838) referred to the 'topsy-turvy world' (*die verkehrte Welt*).

7 It has been argued by some that the lower and working classes have also looked to the university as a means to achieve upward social mobility. But those who have accomplished this are exceptions to the rule. In class terms the university is a formal, not a substantial, means of advancement for these class-individuals. The middle class has always been vastly overrepresented, the lower and working classes underrepresented as a proportion of the student body (cf Porter 1965; Squires 1979:20–1; Healey 1971). Michael Miles put it well when he wrote: 'Equal educational opportunity for the poor is, moreover, a myth within a myth. There has been no change in the last several decades in the correlation between education and social mobility, education and income, education and occupational states' (1971:177; Jencks and Riesman 1977).

The OECD reports that 'the proportions of students from less favoured social categories have increased (except in Norway and the United Kingdom). The increase is very clear in Germany (from 5.4 to 12.6 per cent) ... *but in all countries the group of young people originating from this class (that is 45 to 65 per cent of the total) remains very clearly under-represented*' (1974:29; emphasis added).

8 The theory of human capital attempted to flatter the new mediate producers by making them into little capitalists who 'owned' their skills as capital. That this undertaking had any possibility of success is due to the fact that the separation of 'intellectual' and 'manual' labour, of the 'labour of the head' and 'the labour of the hand,' has attained the fixity of a popular

prejudice in civil society. To call the ditch-digger a capitalist because he 'owns' the skill of pitching dirt is patently absurd. To call the physicist a capitalist because he owns the skill of splitting atoms is accepted as economic wisdom by some. Adam Smith (1863:8) (and following him Karl Marx 1966) understood that 'by nature, a philosopher is not in genius and disposition half so different from a street-porter, as a mastiff is from a greyhound, or a greyhound from a spaniel, or this last from a shepherd's dog.'

9 The German working class, which was weakened but not decimated by the war, was one of the most skilled in the entire world. The German capitalist class too, while weakened, emerged from the ashes of the Reich (with allied support) with the means to build new empires. Those who profited shamefully from the slave labour of 'non-Aryans' in the camps and factories, and from the sale of Zyklon B, were now profiting respectably from the labours of 'Aryan' as well as 'non-Aryan' workers.

10 Adapted from tables 2-4 and 2-5 in Bell (1976a:134–6)

11 Szymanski (1972:103). As a percentage of the total labour force in the United States, wage and salary workers increased from 75.1 per cent in 1940 to 89.5 per cent in 1969. Cf Jencks and Riesman (1977:9n, 70).

12 For an empirical look at the changes in job qualification in the fifties and sixties (respectively) in the United States see Folger and Nam (1964:19–33) and Rodriguez (1978:55–67). For a wider discussion see Berg (1970).

13 Thorstein Veblen (1957) criticized the domination of the university by the business ethic and by businessmen during the early part of this century in the United States. Mass disaffection with the university's traditional form by middle class youth did not occur at that time for two reasons: first, the middle class had certain alternatives with regard to career, mobility, and security which did not involve the university. By 1960 the university had become much more central to the life plan of a broader range of middle class youths since other alternatives had been largely eliminated by the direct subsumption of the middle class under capital. Second, the university had become much more directly part of the 'military-industrial complex,' feeding mediate producers into social production which had become increasingly dependent upon them. On the growth of the American universities from the Civil War to World War I see Bledstein (1976). On the increasing importance of higher education in middle class life plans see Collins (1979).

14 Children of professionals could not inherit the credentials of their parents. Children of grocers, five and dime store proprietors, and so on could become partners with, and eventually replace, their parents in these businesses.

However, under conditions of strenuous competition from the growing chain stores, the situation of the small proprietors had become difficult. But even if there had not been a decline in such opportunities for the children of small businessmen, the profits which would have accrued to them may not have been as great as the salaries they would have received as professionals in either the public or private sphere. As Keller and Vahrenkamp (1974:39) point out: 'Already in the year 1961 more than 50% of specialty retail businesses projected a smaller income than the industrial worker' (except where otherwise indicated, translations from German texts are my own). Of course, the professions most highly prized by middle class parents were medicine, dentistry, and law, for, in addition to gaining financial security, these professionals could still be their own 'bosses.'

As a bottom line, university education was viewed by the middle class as a hedge against unemployment. It had a correct perception that university graduates fared relatively well during the depression of the thirties. See Jencks and Riesman (1977:108).

15 Martin Trow (1973) has argued that universal secondary education had been achieved in the United States by World War II. Elsewhere he has argued that the character of secondary education in the United States had changed after the war: 'Secondary education in the United States began as an elite preparatory system; during its great years of growth it became a mass terminal system; and it is now having to make a second painful transition on its way to becoming a mass preparatory system' (1977:111). Randall Collins (1979) has seen the development of education in the United States as an Anglo-Protestant attempt to control the Catholic working class immigrants who came to the United States in successive waves during the nineteenth and early twentieth centuries.

16 Ringer (1978). This is not to say that the intellectuals, especially those without independent means, did not suffer material want at times. The constitution of an intellectual proletariat in Germany during the first quarter of this century is only too well known. The *völkisch* and reactionary response to the declassification of the intelligentsia in Germany is part of the tragic history of that period. The relationship between the intelligentsia and the socialist movement has been an ambivalent one (see Michels 1932; Lafargue 1970).

17 I am reliably informed that in the 1950s at one of Canada's leading universities the president, in officially welcoming new faculty at a public ceremony, still posed the question: 'And are you, sir, a Christian gentleman?'

18 For an interesting discussion of related changes in the US economy see Edwards (1979).

19 As Collins suggests, 'By their very numbers, college graduates could no longer count on élite status, since they came to exceed the number of élite positions available (even including those positions they could create). But the colleges had carried out a *fait accompli*, and there was no turning back. Now college graduation had become the requirement for many positions for which no such education had been required before. College education, once an incidental accompaniment of high status, now became the prerequisite of mere respectability' (1979:129). Although Collins understands the impact of this change upon the young generation, he doesn't fully grasp that the intellectual élite itself was being massified. He seems to make a similar error to the one we encountered in the writings of Allerbeck, according to whom only those with great wealth are to be counted among the élite.

Birnbaum expresses the idea of the massification of the new intellectual élite in a roundabout way as follows:
We may state the contradiction experienced by the present student generation in another, more aphoristic, manner. They are inculcated with bourgeois humanist conceptions of individual intellectual and cultural attainment – precisely as a preliminary to bureaucratic employment in a society which may properly be deemed post-bourgeois. Insofar as the universities have attempted to adapt to the newer social forms of a changed process of production, they have organised intellectual work in a bureaucratic manner all the more repellent because of its formal dissonance with the intellectual content of an historically elaborated system of high culture. (1969:237)

20 The Horatio Alger myth which served as the basis of a social mobility fantasy in the twenties did not survive the depression and war untarnished. On the question of the relationship of the generations to the changing conditions of middle class reproduction, see Bruce-Briggs (1979:197–8).

21 The growing income and prestige of the professoriate created a widening gap between teacher and student (cf Lipset 1976:19).

22 Enrolments had increased to 900,000 by the end of the seventies.

23 One former American student leader, now a professional sociologist, said it in the following way: 'At the time I was particularly impressed with what I thought of as anticipatory alienation. In 1962/63 you projected your career forward, and where were you? You were in some large organization that provided a service and you had got there through professional or other training because you were motivated to do good or to be a good person, to make a living in reasonable comfort while doing good, doing well by doing good. That's what everybody wants to do, right? But so often that organization doing that service was perceived as and felt to be, more or less accurately, one that was producing the opposite of its service. So if you wanted to

be a teacher you found yourself on the front line of a racist institution. If you wanted to be a doctor or a lawyer you were all wrapped up in arrogant control. If you wanted to be a journalist you knew ahead of time that you were going to have to cut and trim and otherwise suppress the truth. And so, for a lot of the student movement, I think that their alienation from the society was an anticipatory one, and had to do with probable destinations. And that frequently got formulated about the university.'

24 Philanthropy, after all, is the simple prerogative of the wealthy. The promise was not that of power to manipulate others or to acquire a personal fortune, but power to do good, to be creative, to help one's fellow man.

25 The question concerning the way in which the students were made aware of this process is an important one. Clearly the changes which were occurring both in the university (impersonalization, bureaucratization, large classes) and in the economy, especially in the public sector, made an impression upon the student generation. The 'New Frontier' was their 'New Deal' and Kennedy was their man. But their New Deal was also a raw deal because it created low-key bureaucratic jobs for the newly educated 'masses,' not high-power positions of authority and responsibility.

26 According to Adam Smith the Athenians in classical antiquity carefully protected the privilege of citizenship and thus prevented its debasement: 'The city of Athens never contained above 23 or 25000 free citizens of the military age. This number was very small compared to the extensive territory they possessed, having the property of most of the islands in the Aegean sea, besides many cities and colonies in Thrace and Asia. The revenue arising from this territory must have been very considerable, and was wholly the property of this small number, who were intituled to many benefits out of it. The(y) had frequent distributions of money or corn; they had their children maintain'd at the publick expense when necessary in the Pironeum, which was then reckoned no disgrace; the(y) had also an allowance for their attendance on the courts and the assemblys of the people, and at last had even one to enable them to attend on the theatres. Had they been very free in communicating the citizenship, the share of the publick stock which fell in this way to each of the old citizens would have been proportionally diminished; and they therefore always opposed admitting of any new members into the city' (1978:305).

27 In this sense, the university was not the ultimate target of the student radicals. As Mehnert observes: 'In the last analysis, campus problems as such did not stand in the foreground of the conflict, either at Berkeley or in other universities ... The true enemy was "society"' (1977:29–30).

28 It must be emphasized that this societal élite was itself in the process of

being transformed from a relatively small and homogeneous 'intellectual class' to a massified stratum of (still relatively privileged) educated labourers.

29 Gramsci (1971) subsumes the conservatives partly under the heading of 'traditional intellectuals.' Yet he fails to make the distinction between form and substance explicitly. Benda (1969) in his classic work brings out the subjective side – the transformation of the consciousness of the intellectuals from scholarly disinterest to political engagement. Both his puzzlement about and scorn for this development would have been considerably blunted had he taken up the objective and social side of this process.

Chapter 3

1 In 'A Brief to Members of Parliament' presented on 13 November 1963 by the CUCND, we read: 'For us, members of the CUCND, the dilemma begins with the basic values which we hold – a society based on the worth and dignity of the individual, which recognizes equality and self-government as the rights and needs of all men. We recognize that we have learned these values, and come to hold them ourselves, by meeting them in the culture that surrounds us.

But we find that our society has not in fact developed ways to live and act according to those values. As a society, we continue to pay lip-service to these phrases but have rejected them in our public actions.

Our public policies are filled with contradictions: in the name of protecting freedom, we threaten to destroy all freedom through nuclear destruction; in the name of democracy, we form sacrosanct alliances with despotic governments; in the name of a decent standard of living we destroy food surpluses while millions starve.' But part of the promise made to the younger generation which was never explicitly raised as an issue by the New Left had a much less altruistic content: it was the promise to the young that the university would be the means to enter the power structure. The protest over the unfulfilment of the universal promise of society was driven in part by the outrage at the unfulfilment of the particular promise made to the students. The two promises were construed as one by the youthful activists.

2 This is not to suggest that the Canadians were not deeply influenced by the civil rights struggle in the United States. As a former SUPA leader pointed out: 'Don't underestimate the number of people who were down – dozens and dozens of people were down from Canada, were in Mississippi for the voter registration drives and the other places. And a whole bunch of those people were later in SUPA.'

3 The organizational histories of the American and German SDS have their parallels. At an early stage both of them engaged in bitter struggles with their respective 'parent' organizations, and on similar grounds. Both of them declined during the same period (1968–9), ostensibly on account of similar factional feuds. See Fichter and Lönnendoncker (1977); Sale (1974).

4 Unlike students in North America, who had been somewhat sympathetic to the left in the earlier decades of this century, the German students of the sixties were the first generation to be attracted in a significant way to left-wing politics. (Left-wing student groups in the pre-Nazi era were relatively small and made no major impact upon German student politics.) One German respondent put the matter in these words: 'After 1918 it was the students who were the active core which beat down the revolt of the proletariat. Armed battalions of students in Saxony and Thuringia, but also in many industrial cities of the Ruhr area and in Silesia, once again restored the old relations of ownership and domination. Students were the first section of the population in Germany in 1930 to turn to the politics of National Socialism in a major way.'

5 In fact, when Americans talked about the student movement in the early sixties, they were invariably referring to the white, middle class, civil rights movement.

6 The international appeal of civil rights was so strong that even the German university students participating in a sit-in at the FU in the mid-sixties would sing 'We Shall Overcome' as an expression of their commitment and solidarity.

7 This is, of course, an over-simplification. The works of the Frankfurt School were available to the students, even if they were not readily at hand, and there were a handful of professors such as Wolfgang Abendroth who acted as resource persons. Yet it is fair to say that the mass publication of Marxist and otherwise left-wing literature in the FRG was a result of the student movement, not a cause. Bernd Rabehl told me that Berlin SDS often had to resort to distributing mimeographed copies of classical works of Western Marxism because they were only available in the libraries.

The dearth of Marxist literature at the beginning of the sixties in Germany is underscored by the following story told by one of the former student activists: 'If one ordered some kind of Marxist books from the GDR in 1959 or 1960, anything from Marx or the like, it was confiscated. One was only allowed to order one copy for "personal use." It happened to me a few times – when, as chairman of the group, I ordered, for example, thirty copies of the *German Ideology* (because we wanted to organize a study group) I had to go to the customs office, where I was handed one copy and the other twenty-nine were confiscated. And there was no Marxist or socialist literature at all here in the Federal Republic. The first, I remember, which appeared in a real, regular West German publishing house was *The History of the Russian Revolution* by Trotsky. The thick unabridged edition was published by Fischer. And then things proceeded apace: from then until the mid-sixties there was an increasing tendency for Marxist literature to appear in bourgeois publishing houses. And now the restrictions concerning the importation of literature have ceased.'

8 The students met official resistance when they attempted to criticize the role of the French in Algeria in the early sixties and the American effort in Vietnam somewhat later. Yet these same students were encouraged in their actions against the regime in the GDR (cf Lönnendoncker et al 1975).

9 One of the former Canadian activists interviewed during the course of this study remarked: 'I suppose at the time we felt that the reasons that we had to act were because no one else was acting, because certain problems seemed to contradict everything that we had been taught. That is to say, the gap – I always like to put it like this – between the rhetoric and the reality got to be too large; we therefore attempted to bridge the gap.'

10 One of the watchwords of the student left was 'relevance' or 'social relevance.' But the university was not to be made relevant to society as it was, but to the society which the student left had as an ideal. Hence, the students put themselves in the impossible position of making an argument for relevance to a situation which did not exist, ie, which was irrelevant. Clark Kerr also argued for relevance, but for a relevance to the existing institutions. The FSM students and Clark Kerr are thus opposite extremes; the former represent the relevant in the ideal, the other the relevant *sans phrase*. As Birnbaum has written: 'It is significant in this connection that both the technocratic innovators who would thoroughly rationalise the universities and the younger socialists who would make of the academies new bases for revolutionary action wish for a changed relationship of high culture to *praxis*' (1969:237). The best single study of the Berkeley FSM is Heirich (1971). On relevance see Scott and Lyman (1970:57–67).

11 The new vision of the university as a multiversity was being developed in works such as Kerr's *The Uses of the University* (1963). Individuals like Kerr were hard-nosed liberals who were as much opposed to the utopianism of the students as they were to the ivory tower concept of the university cherished by many conservatives. Thomas Mann presented a caricature of this type in the person of Lodovico Settembrini in *The Magic Mountain*. Ralf Dahrendorf played a similar role in Germany. See Leibfried (1968).

On the differences between the pre-war and post-war university see Shils (1969); Ben-David (1974).

12 See the reference to 'unwashed youths with beards, long-haired girls in

leotards, all sitting intransigently in public buildings or on sidewalks or in Times Square' in Olson (1963).

13 Alceste, the main character in Molière's *Le Misanthrope*, was a kind of proto-bohemian. He demanded that people be scrupulously honest with each other at all times. The consequence of this would be the separation of mankind into the truly superior and the jackasses. Modern bohemia demands honesty *and* egalitarianism (cf Rousseau 1969). For a discussion of the differences between the 'beats' and 'hippies' see Conlin (1982).

14 Cutler writes about the failure of the projects as follows: 'This effort failed largely because most of the organizers could find no workable common ground, either psychological, economic, or political, with their chosen clientele' (1973:41).

15 Not surprisingly, the populist thrust so prominent in the early and mid sixties in the American and Canadian movements was severely muted in Germany. There were no community action projects in Germany at the time, for populism – the German cognate of 'populist' is 'völkisch' – was thoroughly identified with the Nazi regime (the Nazi newspaper had been called *Völkischer Beobachter*). Some observers of the German peace movement in the eighties have seen it as the expression of a new populism (see Pohrt 1981).

16 In January 1966 the Selective Service System indicated that draft deferments for college students would no longer be automatically granted (see Viorst 1979:400; Sale 1974:253). Furthermore, the draft threatened those with 2s deferments for eight years, not merely for one. The new draft law of 2 July 1967 abolished deferments for graduate students and led to heightened tensions on the campuses (see Jones 1980:93–6).

17 Just as the protest against the war in Vietnam began with the middle class, so too did the environmental movement of the last decade. As long as environmental hazards were confined to working class areas of industrial towns, there was little 'public' outcry. As soon as the suburbs, the 'houses on the hill,' were threatened in a direct and major way, a large-scale campaign was mounted against pollution and for environmental protection (cf Wildavsky 1979).

18 The common thread which runs through all the schools of recent Marxism is the exaggerated historical role accorded intellectuals, or that which intellectuals create – theory. In fact, not only has Marxism become compatible with the most extremely divergent doctrines, it has been seen as their highest expression or completion. As Hook has written: 'The oddest syntheses result. I have known professors and graduate students, suddenly stirred into a passion of social protest by some current evil, who have convinced themselves shortly after reading Marx that he was *au fond* a

phenomenologist, an existentialist, a positivist, a Spinozist, a Kantian, a Freudian, a Bergsonian, an anticipator of Samuel Alexander (all they had in common were their ethnic origin and their beard!) – and, of course, an Hegelian. There are some Catholic writers who rather cautiously suggest that, despite Marx's atheism, Aristotle and Aquinas would not have disowned him. Some Protestants, and not merely pro-Soviet figures like Karl Barth and Niemöller, declare that Marx is essentially a more religious man than many of his religious critics' (1975:7–8).

19 The student syndicalists argued that the student is a young intellectual worker who should be paid a wage by the state for intellectual training. In the end the community benefits from his services, and hence the public power should provide the necessary financial support during the training period. This was not charity, it was wages for work.

20 One former activist interviewed claimed that these radical media personalities in the United States during the late sixties had really taken Stokely Carmichael as a role model: 'Stokely makes his reputation by becoming more of a media figure than an actual grass-roots leader. The black/white split occurs, but I think the thing that is important is the black/white split occurring. In fact, Stokely becomes a role model for ambitious white kids who see the movement as a route to prominence. So Abby and Jerry take over, and to a certain extent, Tom Hayden and Rennie Davis too begin to imitate Stokely, and begin to look for these garish newspaper headlines through outrageous actions. And you simply can't reconcile outrageous actions and a desire for public relations with the kind of work that was really pleasing that we were doing' (cf Young 1977:349).

21 Of twenty-five key leaders from the early years still active in Canada in 1968 and 1969, only one had become involved in a vanguard party. Apparently this was not true for Germany or the United States, where considerably more of the early New Leftists (although a distinct minority) went over to the authoritarian camp.

22 In West Berlin the party is called the Sozialistische Einheitspartei West-Berlin (SEW). The student group of the party in West Germany was called the Marxistischer Studentenbund Spartakus (MSB Spartakus), and it increased in strength in the seventies as a consequence of the organizational and ideological collapse of SDS.

Chapter 4

1 Demographers have told us that the student movement was a direct result of the enormous size of the post-war generation. (See Jones (1980) for a

discussion of the importance of size in the life of a generation.) But even if we grant that the tremendous increase in the number of potential and actual university students in the sixties exerted great pressure upon the institutions of higher learning, we may not conclude that social and political activism on the part of the students was the 'natural' response to this condition. There is no reason why an extremely large student cohort should automatically develop radical political ambitions instead of 'drop-out' or conformist attitudes. There is no purely 'natural' necessity in human history. It is thus erroneous to suggest, as Westby (1976) has done, that there is a natural history of the student movement.

2 He refers to the following features of this process: the earmarking of external funds for manpower training, the predominance of research over teaching, the application of industrial principles to university operations, the deterioration of undergraduate education, the disintegration of community, the 'urbanization' of higher education, the creation of student ghettos, and the concomitant rise of the youth culture.

3 To argue that protest is associated with periods of relative prosperity is to assert a law-like relation without explaining its specific socio-historical character.

4 The criteria which determined entrance to middle class positions were in the process of changing (cf Lasch 1978).

5 It is not the democratization *per se* which led to the erosion of standards but the social context of the democratization.

6 Konrád and Szelényi (1979) have recently treated this topic. They argue that the development of what Bahro (1977) has called 'real existing socialism' in eastern Europe represents the conquest of society by the intellectuals, who are becoming a class. They don't believe that the intellectuals in the West have constituted themselves as a class since they have been weak and badly divided. On the history of the 'new class' theory see Bell (1976: 86–99) and Gouldner (1979:94–101). See also Bruce-Briggs (1979:1–18).

7 Kristol identifies the material interest of this new class not as money, but as power: 'They are not much interested in money, but are keenly interested in power. Power for what? Well, the power to shape our civilization – a power which, in the capitalist system, is supposed to reside in the free market. The "new class" wants to see much of this power redistributed to government, where *they* will then have a major say in how it is exercized' (1978:28).

8 Schelsky writes in this connection: 'The restructuring of the schools and universities into parishes of the social faith of salvation, into social churches, must, of course, "critically" dissolve the identification with, or the feeling of

belonging to, other institutions, particularly to the state, its judiciary, or even its police or military, which have not yet been captured by the faith of salvation. "Critical sociology," "critical peace research," "critical philosophy," "critical pedagogy," and whatever other kinds of critically founded standpoints there are have functionally become the same as exorcism and witch-hunts for the traditional Christian clergy' (1977:398).

9 Marx and Engels attacked this position: 'The division of labour first becomes an actual division from that moment when there arises a division of material and mental labour. From this moment on, consciousness *can* actually imagine itself to be something other than the consciousness of the existing practice, *actually* representing something without representing something *actual* – from this moment on, consciousness is in a position to emancipate itself from the world, to pass over to the construction of "pure" theory, theology, philosophy, morals, etc' (1969:31).

10 Cf Marx and Engels: 'We have shown that making thoughts and ideas independent is a consequence of making personal relations and relationships independent. We have shown that the exclusive, systematic occupation with these thoughts from the side of the ideologists and philosophers and therewith the systematization of these thoughts is a consequence of the division of labour, and the German philosophy especially a consequence of the German petty bourgeois relations. The philosophers have only to resolve their language into the common language out of which it is abstracted in order to recognize it as the twisted language of the actual world and to understand that neither thoughts nor language constitute their own realm for themselves, that they are only *expressions* of actual life' (1969:433).

11 It's not that Schelsky is opposed to philosophers and ideologists but that he is opposed to the 'new' philosophers and ideologists. Schelsky indicates that he is more comfortable with the old élitism of the intellectuals than with the new.

12 Gouldner sees the New Class explicitly as a new bourgeoisie which monopolizes 'cultural capital' and shares a culture of critical discourse. The former concept of cultural capital is derived from the human capital theory in economics, the latter concept of the CCD is borrowed from the work of Basil Bernstein (1971, 1973, 1975). Unlike Schelsky, Gouldner sees a potential good in this new class. It is the potentially universal class.

13 But cf Marx (1972e:405–6), where 'the entire economic structure of society' is seen to revolve around the form of labour, not the ownership of the means of production.

14 Cf Ehrenreich and Ehrenreich (1978:322, 327) where a similar point is made. Arguments such as these not only serve to make Marx into some

kind of guru, they also demonstrate a profound lack of appreciation of his texts. There was no volume 3 of *Capital* in Marx's lifetime. He left behind a massive collection of notes which Engels, and later Kautsky, tried to edit and systematize. Cf Lukács (1971:46) who ought to have known better.

15 Today, the middle class gains its privilege from the education and jobs which it has as a consequence rather than from the little capital it owns. But it is precisely this separation and opposition of mediate and immediate production which creates the basis of contemporary middle class life. This means that the middle class today is no longer composed primarily of classical petty bourgeois elements and that substantially and potentially its interest is that of the class of social labour as a whole. Yet the possibility of a unified movement of social labour developing in the near future is extremely small. This, and only this, is the crisis of Marxism in the twentieth century. In the absence of such a movement the Marxist has got religion and repeats the daily prayer, questioning: 'I lift up my eyes unto the mountains, wherefrom shall my help come?'

Kelman (1970:136) describes two kinds of revolt in any class society, both of which are justified: the revolt of the lower classes for material betterment and the revolt of a section of the élite for meaning in life. He is giving expression to the actual strivings, during the sixties, of the immediate producers and the potential mediate producers respectively.

16 Daniel Bell (1979:186–7) sees the new class as a 'mentality,' as the 'endpoint of a culture in disarray,' and not a 'new class' in the 'socio-cultural sense.'

17 Feuer (1969). For a critical discussion see Flacks (1970–1:152); Halleck (1970:105–22); Levin and Spiegel (1979:26–7); Westby (1976:185–93).

18 Marx and Engels made this point forcefully in this criticism of Max Stirner: 'The standpoint at which people are satisfied with such tales about spirits is itself a religious one, because people who adopt it are soothed by religion, they regard religion as *causa sui* (for both "self-consciousness" and "Man" are still religious – instead of explaining it from the empirical conditions and showing how definite relations of industry and commerce are necessarily connected with a definite form of society, hence, with a definite form of State and hence, with a definite form of religious consciousness. If Stirner had looked at the real history of the Middle Ages, he could have found why the Christian's notion of the world took precisely this form in the Middle Ages, and how it happened that it subsequently passed into a different one; he could have found that "*Christianity*" *has no history* and that all the different forms in which it was conceived at various times were not "self-determinations" and "further developments" "of the religious

spirit," but were brought about by wholly empirical causes in no way dependent on any influence of the religious spirit' (Marx and Engels 1968a:164). This is a specification of the argument advanced in the first chapter of the same work directed against Feuerbach: 'The phantoms formed in the human brain are also, necessarily, sublimates of their material life-process, which is empirically verifiable and bound to material premises. Morality, religion, metaphysics, all the rest of ideology and their corresponding forms of consciousness, thus no longer retain the semblance of independence. They have no history, no development' (38; see also Marx and Engels 1969:25, 215, 245–6).

Historical specificity was the most fundamental basis of Marx's critique (1966:96, 111) of P.J. Proudhon. On these grounds Marx also criticized the True Socialists in Germany, the Utopian Socialists, Classical Political Economists (especially the Physiocrats), the theory of natural law and the social contract, and the German Historical School of the 1870s (cf Marx and Engels 1968b:especially part II); Marx 1978; see also Korsch 1964).

19 As Konrád and Szelényi write: 'The intellectuals of every age have described themselves ideologically, in accordance with their particular interests, and if those interests have differed from age to age it has still been the common aspiration of the intellectuals of every age to represent their particular interests in each context as the general interests of mankind. The definition of universal, eternal, supreme (and hence immutable) knowledge displays a remarkable variability over the ages, but in every age the intellectuals define as such whatever knowledge best serves the particular interests connected with their social role – and that is whatever portion of the knowledge of the age serves to maintain their monopoly of their role' (1979:14).

Of course, all human beings think, yet not all humans are 'intellectuals.' According to Sorel, 'The intellectuals are not, as is so often said, men who think: they are people who have adopted the profession of thinking, and who take an aristocratic salary on account of the nobility of this profession' (1950:184n). Being an intellectual is not related to the activity of exercising the intellect, but to specific social relations. As Gramsci wrote: 'All men are intellectuals, one could therefore say: but not all men have in society the function of intellectuals ... This means that, although one can speak of intellectuals, one cannot speak of non-intellectuals, because non-intellectuals do not exist' (1971:9; cf Krader 1976:257).

20 This is not to suggest that ideas are somehow unreal, illusions, or that they are merely reflections of material conditions. Ideas and consciousness are real, but they cannot be divorced from or treated apart from the individuals

whose ideas and consciousness they are, or from the historically specific context in which they exist, without mysticizing them. Ideas cannot be reduced to material or social relations, for they are expressions of these relations, and a relation and its expression are not the same. Ideas do not have a life of their own; they exist as part of the socio-historical world of real individuals. But because ideas are, by definition, non-material, they cannot simply be deduced from the material conditions and social relations to which they give expression. The material and the ideal are each different orders of natural being; the one is not reducible to the other. Krader has expressed it tersely as follows: 'The human order is a veritable order, for it has a condition which is not directly present in the natural order, namely, that of mediate relation, concretely and abstractly by labor, abstractly by consciousness which is an order *of itself*; it is not an order *in itself*, for it is a reordering of that which is already existent in the natural order; it is not an order *for itself*, save by an act of human arrogation' (n d).

21 Marxism has been burdened with a reflection theory of consciousness which is defective in a variety of ways. It stands in contradiction to its revolutionary thrust both in theory and in practice, for the self-activation of the human subject-object is thereby excluded. It is also a simplification and falsification of the process of consciousness, which is not an absolute and unchanging feature of mind but a variable and historically specific process in society. As Krader instructs us: 'The mirror reflection in respect of the mind or the consciousness as either bears upon reality, or reality bears upon either, has nothing to say about passive reflectedness, active reflecting, subjective and objective, mediate and immediate reflecting, reflectedness, reflection, distortion, hallucination, interestedness. The hypothesizing, searching, probing, integrating, catalytic, analytic activity of the conscious mind, or the mind becoming conscious is the materialist theory of the consciousness.'

22 The fact that the élitism of the student movement appeared in the guise of its opposite is one of the most fascinating and at the same time most perplexing of its characteristics. One could seek to explain it by means of the theory of resentment developed by Nietzsche (1956[1887]) to account for the origin of Judeo-Christian morality and refined by Scheler (1961) to provide a more general tool of sociological analysis. (For a comparison of the use of 'resentment' in Nietzsche and Scheler see DeGré 1979.) Accordingly, the New Left could be seen as an attempt at subverting the liberal democratic society at first by championing its ideals and later by a kind of transvaluation of its values. The resentment of the 'children of privilege' against those who failed to keep the promise is the motor of the New Left.

One could also call upon Max Weber's simplification of the theory of resentment (1958:190, 276) to explain the course of the student movement. According to this view, the New Left could be understood as an attempt to provide a generation of disappointed youth with a compensatory ideology which promises a better world 'after the revolution.'

I think that the democratic yearnings of the New Left are to be explained in terms of the conditions of life of the children of privilege. The psychological element is secondary and derivative.

23 In their recent work, Rothman and Lichter (1982) have made 'ambivalence' (especially in relation to authority) into a key explanatory variable determining the psychological predisposition to student radicalism in the sixties. According to their research, early New Leftists in the United States were 'protean' rebels from primarily Jewish homes with cold and distant fathers and intrusive, narcissistic mothers. Towards the end of the sixties, the composition of the movement changed with an influx of 'rigid' rebels from primarily non-Jewish homes with intrusive, punishing, and inconsistent fathers and submissive mothers. Both the Jewish and non-Jewish radicals, the authors tell us, were negative authoritarians, each attempting to resolve the different kinds of ambivalence arising out of their respective family dynamics.

Rothman and Lichter are not trying to explain why the movement arose when it did. To their credit they recognize that only a sociological explanation can do this. (Their own attempts at presenting such a sociological explanation are rather feeble, to say the least.) They do, however, seek to explain the historical course taken by the New Left during the sixties by means of the differences in the character of the ambivalence of the protean rebels (who were dominant in the early years of the decade) and the rigid rebels (who constituted the majority of radicals at the end of the sixties).

Although their data are interesting, their explanation of the trajectory of the New Left is rather shaky. In the first place, they admit that many radical students were not authoritarian. Second, they grant that authoritarianism (which is a characterological development out of the struggle with ambivalent feelings in relation to one's parents) has no necessary connection with extremism of the right or left. If authoritarianism is indifferent to political ideology, then it cannot explain the vicissitudes of politics. Finally, even if we grant the authors all their arguments concerning the psychology of the student rebels, we have a perfectly good sociological account of the course of the New Left in the sixties which doesn't require an analysis of endopsychic processes. (At the same time, their work should be accepted as an important contribution to the psychoanalytic literature and should prove to be of use to analysts and therapists in the treatment of certain of their patients.)

Although nothing which I have written here is incompatible with the data collected and analysed by Rothman and Lichter, my use of the term 'ambivalence' refers solely to the sociological situation of middle class university students in the sixties.

24 A former American SDS leader sees the success of PL within SDS as a result, in part, of the anti-intellectualism of the early New Left: 'It is true that all through the early years there was such an anti-intellectualism and an anti-ideology tendency in the organization that anybody who had his bent towards that would have been attracted to PL, or would have quit and joined any of the more Marxist organizations.'

25 The following presentation has been greatly influenced by Hegel (1970: 312–17, 1973:140, 265–86, 1974:442–94); Lukács (1971); Marx and Engels (1969:102–438).

26 The moralism of both the egoist and altruist arises out of the social conditions which create one-sided individuals, ie, egoists and altruists (or a 'mixture' of both within the same individual). Far from being antagonists, the egoist and the altruist are complementary beings, expressions of an antagonistic actuality. See Marx and Engels (1969:228–9). It is incumbent upon us to grasp the basis of the apparent opposition, ie, the material conditions and relations which give rise to the appearance. See Marx and Engels (1969:229); Marx (1973:178); Marx and Engels (1968b:52).

27 The student radicals of yesteryear were on the defensive in the late sixties, and they have been kept there ever since. Today they are fighting to maintain jobs which have been slowly disappearing and to cope with a falling standard of living, although it is, in relative terms, a high standard of living.

The university, meanwhile, seems to have fallen into line as the trainer and certifier of middle class youth. To be sure, the traditional pomp and circumstance is still paraded about, and public relations officers still package phrases about the 'community of scholars,' but just below the surface it is the dollar which rules, and woe to the administrator who fails to recognize this fact.

In the early eighties there are some indications that various attempts may be made to restore the lost élitism and scholarship of old. If these attempts are made on a broad scale, the authorities responsible will have to face the wrath of the middle class, *ceteris paribus*.

28 From his vantage point as a practising psychoanalyst, Irvine Schiffer has called attention to this ambivalent relationship between the students' uni-

versalist political ideology and their egoism, between their appeal to radical democracy and their own élitist self-assertion: 'The clash of ideologies is never more demonstrable than it is in the exhibitionistic displays of the adolescent as he confuses a political ideology with a niche in a society that values fame or notoriety. In such a paradox, the adolescent demonstrates against violence by acts of violence; he repudiates the double standard of the system by exerting the most strenuous efforts to qualify for some special niche in that very system; he demands a classless society in which his particular exhibitionism lifts him out of the classless; his communal slogan is "to let it all hang out," yet he is determined to let "his" hang out just a little bit further than his fellows.

'In their quest for their particular niche in politics, young adults are far from being willing to settle as some unimportant appendage in the political body that involves them' (1973:133).

29 As Kruger and Silvert argue, 'Some may even have become dimly aware that as members of a still relatively privileged stratum, they may serve their own interests best if they advocate radical change in the interest of the disadvantaged' (1975:164). Cf Bruce-Briggs (1979:206): 'While capitalism does permit hostile intellectuals by providing the *necessary* conditions of affluence and liberty, that is not a *sufficient* explanation. The argument that these people dislike capitalism because it does not buy and sell enough of what they want to sell and buy strikes me as much more reasonable.'

30 Edward Shils (1974:293) is right in his view that the New Left was a response to the failure of the authorities to solve problems (eg, war and poverty). But it is only because of the deeper relations of that generation in and to society that the movement took the critical course it did. Shils' argument in this respect is similar to that of Feuer (1969).

31 The FU in West Berlin is situated in the suburb of Dahlem, literally a stone's throw from major American military and diplomatic installations.

32 A similar kind of ambivalence existed in relation to the Jews. There is an uneasy mixture of a rather forced philo-semitism and a suspicious admiration of the PLO on the part of many young German radicals (cf Broder 1981).

33 In Germany the struggle was very much directed by an alliance of students and junior faculty (the so-called *Mittelbau*) against the full professors (*Ordinarien*), who had been jealously guarding their traditional privileges in the face of changing post-war conditions.

34 Regis Debray (1979) has recently made a similar argument with respect to the French situation. It is interesting to note that Raymond Aron saw the student revolt as a 'rejection of modernity,' while Debray sees it as an unwitting instrument of modernization.

Chapter 5

1 A former field-worker for the American sps referred to the practice of the organization during the late sixties as 'participatory democracy, which, in retrospect, has to be the most undemocratic form I've ever functioned in.'

2 Recession did not hit Germany until the mid-seventies, and the education boom continued until then. This explains, in part, the continued strength of the fragmented student left in Germany during the early and mid-seventies (cf Langguth 1976:102–3).

3 Cf Lockhart (1971). This relatively discouraging situation found expression not only in commission reports and learned theses. By 1969–70 the mass media were full of stories about the deteriorating employment opportunities for graduates. See, for example, Hechinger (1970); Malcolm (1970); Rice (1970); 'The New Face of Unemployment' (1970); 'Story of a Science Depression' (1971).

4 'To a great extent university education was a routing toward élite occupational status. As we argue in this book, this routing has become much less clear. For one thing, there is now an over-supply of university graduates. In addition, economic expansion in Canadian society has not been at such a rate that manpower has been opened. Third, community colleges have emerged and their graduates have come to compete directly in the labour market with university graduates. Fourth, although we do not contend that university education in Canada was ever strictly vocational in character, it is nonetheless clear that trends in university curricula have tended to reduce whatever vocational content might have existed' (Harvey 1974: 62–3).

5 Taken by itself, the beginning of the end of the lucrative job market for university graduates should not be over-emphasized as a factor leading to the disintegration of the student movement. However, it should not be ignored entirely. It most certainly did drive a wedge between the radical leaders and the mass of university students, especially after 1969.

6 Referring to the sixties they conclude: 'While, in the last decade, in all provinces considered, academics had no problems finding employment, at the end of the sixties employment bottlenecks arose for this group of persons for the first time.'

It is interesting to note that none of the Germans interviewed cited a change in employment prospects for university graduates as a reason for the collapse of sps.

7 The musical *Hair* is a particularly good example of its genre. In it we find an antiwar message couched in astrological and humanistic language set

to music. Cf Ernst Schikaneder's *Die Zauberflöte*, in which 'natural man,' Papageno, refusing to fight for wisdom, replies to the servants of Sarastro: 'Fighting is not for me. I am a man of nature who is satisfied with sleep, food and drink; and if I could perhaps catch a beautiful woman ...'

It is interesting to note that some neo-conservatives in particular have never forgiven private enterprise for promoting the images, ideals, and values of the hedonistic and thus economically subversive counter-culture (see Bell 1976b; Kristol 1978). On the perversion of the hippie movement in San Francisco see Conlin (1982:235–7).

8 The important thing to understand about these 'defeats' is that they were seen by many outside, and some inside, the core of the movement to have been real victories. The most visible rise and rapid spread of the counter-culture is a case in point. The abolition of *in loco parentis* regulations at the university is another. For many students sympathetic to the New Left, these were the changes they wanted; if they were open to the rhetoric of revolution, and some indeed were, they were content with their concrete achievements. But cf Calvert and Neiman (1971:10). Clecak (1973:243) points out that the New Left had to find some way of accounting for its minor achievements within the framework of its general defeat.

9 We are not looking at the baby boom generation as a whole here (the last members of this big generation are only now in the universities), but at its first student cohort (1964–8). The fate of this group was highly instructive for those coming immediately thereafter. The defeat (ie, the 'victory') of the movement during these years and the increasing cost both of participation in the movement and of failure in one's studies could not but have deeply affected the following cohort.

10 Clecak (1973:253) perceptively remarks that the New Left abandoned 'real people' for illusions when 'real people' failed to measure up to the standards which the New Left set for them. The best source on the Weathermen to the fall of 1970 is Jacobs (1970). One of the best studies on the making of a terrorist is Powers (1971). For a journalistic account of the Baader-Meinhof gang (Red Army Fraction) see Jillian Becker (1978). For an autobiographical account of a non-middle class terrorist see Baumann (1975).

11 This calls to mind a cartoon in which two obviously henpecked husbands are discussing the power relations in their respective families. 'In my family,' the one husband boasted, 'I make all the big decisions. My wife decides the small matters such as where we go on our vacation, what kind of car we should buy, in what neighbourhood we live and so on. I get to decide whether Reagan should send in the marines, whether the dollar should float and whether we ought to increase our expenditure on the space program.'

12 It is ironic that this proclivity, which has been associated with the 'traditional' female roles of teacher, nurse, social worker, and nun, should appear in the midst of a movement which was dedicated to the eradication of precisely these stereotypes. But, as Lessing has written: 'Not all are free who mock their chains.' Shakespeare believed that there was a 'natural' relationship between man and woman governing their social roles which was to be maintained. But at the same time he called attention to the economic foundation of this apparently 'natural' relationship. In the *Comedy of Errors*, for example, Adriana asks Luciana about men: 'Why should their liberty than ours be more?' To which Luciana replies: 'Because their business still lies out o'door' (act 2, scene 1). In *The Taming of the Shrew*, Katharina, in giving advice to the 'headstrong women,' explains why some women owe their husbands obedience: 'And, for thy maintenance, commits his body / To painful labour, both by sea and land, / To watch the night in storms, the day in cold, / While thou li'st warm at home, secure and safe' (act 5, scene 2).

13 This can be seen most clearly in the collapse of SUPA in the spring/summer of 1967. If one compares the last issues of the *SUPA Newsletter* with the first few issues of the *New Left Committee Bulletin*, one can see the shift from articles on community organizing, class theory, and the war in Vietnam to those dealing with feminist issues. (In addition, a number of older male leaders published letters of·resignation from the executive in the *Bulletin*.) See this material in the CUCND/SUPA archives in the McMaster University Library, Hamilton, Canada.

Chapter 6

1 In a delightful editorial piece entitled 'Karl Marx comes to Canada' (*Saturday Night* 1979:4), typical readers of Canadian 'Marxist' magazines and journals are humorously (although credibly) caricatured: '*This Magazine* ... Typical reader: a left-leaning school teacher who lives in the Annex district of Toronto, reads Antonio Gramsci as well as Sylvia Plath, and doesn't wear Roots shoes – this year.

   '*Canadian Dimension* ... Typical reader: a CUPE organizer in Saskatoon who wears wire-rimmed glasses and has read both Santiago Carillo on Eurocommunism and the biography of Joe Davidson.

   '*Studies in Political Economy* ... Typical reader: a graduate student who has *Das Kapital* on his bedside table, reads the *New Left Review* from cover to cover, understands Italo Calvino, and gets sentimental about Doris Lessing.'

2 Sidney Hook, one of the relatively few American intellectuals who actually knows the texts of Marx, has sketched the new constituency of Marxism in the sixties and seventies: 'The intellectual historian of the future will be challenged by a striking phenomenon of the latter half of the twentieth century – the second coming of Karl Marx. In this second coming he appears not in the dusty frock coat of the economist, as the learned author of *Capital*, nor as a benevolent reformer whose beard has been trimmed by the Fabian Webbs and other tribunes of the welfare state, nor as the revolutionary *sans-culotte*, the inspired pamphleteer of the *Communist Manifesto*. He comes robed as a philosopher and moral prophet with glad tidings about human freedom valid beyond the narrow wishes of class, party, or faction. In his train flock not the industrial workers of the world but the literary intellectuals of the capital cities of the world, not the proletariat, extended to embrance all wage earners, but many elements of the professoriat, not the socially disinherited but the psychologically alienated, not the hungry and poverty stricken youth of the slums but a varied assortment of artists and writers, idealistic young men and women in search of a cause, some square, some beat, and some Zen' (1975:1–2).

Unfortunately, Hook's explanations of the 'recurrent allegiance to Marx' (1975:51–6) are less satisfying, primarily of a psychological rather than a sociological character.

3 For the German experience of those who joined vanguard parties see: *Wir warn die stärkste der Partein* (1977).

4 Lewis Feuer (1969) has emphasized the suicidal tendencies in the history of the student movement. His psychological characterization, while not inaccurate, is inadequate, for it does not grasp the primary social-historical character of student ambivalence, marginality, and interest.

5 Rowntree and Rowntree (1968c:13). The Rowntrees included an appendix on the condition of Canadian youth, and in it they concluded that in Canada youth '*as youth* do not play a unique class role.' Nevertheless, they advanced the argument that the Canadian student is a worker.

Chapter 7

1 Marx and Engels (1969) criticized the separation of theory and practice.

2 Michels was accused by Sombart of being motivated for this reason. Michels' general response was penned in self-defence.

3 The works of Herbert Marcuse found resonance among activist students because they saw in them a flattering theoretical confirmation of their historical importance. The real social-historical 'truth' of this position lies

in those changes which hve been discussed above. The development of social service occupations in the public and quasi-public sphere and a concomitant 'professionalization' of familial, psychological, sexual, and health relations and the problems thereof were the means whereby the new generation 'created' new social policies.

4 In the same way, the Russian revolution occurred on the basis of the weakness of both capitalism and the proletariat, not on the basis of their strength (cf Krader 1978).

5 A similar kind of fantasy can be observed with respect to the position of women in classical Greece. In his excerpts from Morgan's *Ancient Society*, Marx wrote the following concerning women and their position portrayed in mythology: 'But the relation of the goddesses on Olympus shows a past memory of an earlier, freer and more influential position of women. Juno domineering, the goddess of wisdom springs out of the head of Zeus etc' (Krader 1972:121). Krader explains the reference: 'The recollection of a prior state of greater freedom and influence in the position of women accounts for half of the mythology of Juno and Minerva. The other half of the account is that the projection into heaven of the ancient freedom of equality of the women is the inversion of their actual position in Greek society; it is also the justification in the mythology of their constraint in that low position, and the expression of the hopeful fantasy of its betterment in another world' (1972:14).

6 George Orwell, himself an unrepentant socialist, was untiring in his criticism of the élitism of the middle class socialists of the thirties: 'As with the Christian religion, the worst advertisement for Socialism is its adherents.

'The first thing that must strike any outside observer is that Socialism in its developed form is a theory confined entirely to the middle class. The typical Socialist is not, as tremulous old ladies imagine, a ferocious-looking working man with greasy overalls and a raucous voice. He is either a youthful snob-Bolshevik who in five years' time will quite probably have made a wealthy marriage and been converted to Roman Catholicism; or, still more typically, a prim little man with a white collar job, usually a secret teetotaller and often with vegetarian leanings, with a history of Nonconformity behind him, and, above all, with a social position which he has no intention of forfeiting. This last type is surprisingly common in Socialist parties of every shade ... In addition to this there is the horrible – the really disquieting – prevalence of cranks wherever Socialists are gathered together. One sometimes gets the impression that the mere words "Socialism" and "Communism" draw towards them with magnetic force every fruit-juice drinker, nudist, sandal-wearer, sex maniac, Quaker, "Nature Cure" quack, pacifist and feminist in England ...

'Sometimes I look at a Socialist – the intellectual, tract-writing type of Socialist, with his pullover, his fuzzy hair, and his Marxian quotation – and wonder what the devil his motive really *is*. It is often difficult to believe that it is a love of anybody, especially of the working class, from whom he of all people is the furthest removed ...' (1958:173–9).

Tom Wolfe caught the 'double-track' thinking in the middle class radicals of the sixties: 'From the beginning it was pointless to argue about the sincerity of Radical Chic. Unquestionably the basic impulse, 'red diaper' or otherwise, was sincere. But, as in most human endeavours focused upon an ideal, there seemed to be some double-track thinking going on. On the first track – well, one *does* have a sincere concern for the poor and underprivileged and an honest outrage against discrimination. One's heart does cry out – quite spontaneously! – upon hearing how the police have dealt with the Panthers ... On the other hand – on the second track in one's mind, that is – one also has a sincere concern for maintaining a proper East Side life-style in New York society. And this concern is just as sincere as the first, and just as deep' (1970:48–9). Wolfe has grasped the ambivalence of the New Left precisely – ie, real sincerity inextricably bound to real élitism.

7 Of course, this is not true for those early activists who maintained a commitment to the goals of civil rights, nuclear disarmament, and community organizing and who rejected the Marxism of the later years of the movement.

8 Mehnert noticed this during the course of his research: 'One American SDS girl explained that she would cease to exist the moment she stopped fighting and frankly confessed that she and her friends would not know what to do if the university administration were to grant all their demands, leaving them nothing to protest against and forcing them again to face themselves' (1977:348).

9 An English translation of *Marxism and Philosophy* appeared in 1970, and *Monthly Review* published a short collection of his essays. There was somewhat more interest in Korsch in West Germany.

10 The GDR launched a renewed critique of Korsch at the time of his 'popularity' among the West German students (cf Albrecht 1975).

11 The mushrooming of Marxist schools and theories is on the one hand a reflection of the real tensions within the middle class and on the other hand a product of the commoditization of knowledge, where fashions are created not in the academy (where they are given their official stamp), but in the market-place, where success is measured by effective consumer demand.

12 Marx and Engels shared a low opinion of student radicalism in the nine-teenth century. Engels' condemnation of the Berlin student radicals of the 1840s and 1890s is well known. Marx was just as hard on the student followers of Bakunin. See Marx and Engels 1971:269, 272–7; 1973:382–3; Engels 1967:449, 450, 454; Lipset and Altbach 1969:vi–vii. For a criticism of the 'Uni-Marxisten' in terms of the separation of theory and practice see Wetzel (1976).

Chapter 8

1 It is impossible to compose a definitive list of the sources of New Left theory. Yet the following names were mentioned by the former partici-pants during the course of the interviews: T. Adorno, A. Camus, E. Fromm, P. Goodman, M. Horkheimer, K. Mannheim, H. Marcuse, S. Melman, C. Wright Mills, A.S. Neill, and J.-P. Sartre. Nevertheless, it should be kept in mind that Canadian and American activists of the sixties who were inter-viewed generally believed that books and the theories contained therein did not play a great role in the development of the movement. Some sugges-ted that many of these authors were known to the students only through secondary sources or the mass media. For example, few students actually read Sartre; some, however, did become familiar with his philosophy through W. Desan's popular work *The Philosophy of Jean-Paul Sartre* (1965).

2 Mills wrote: 'If the writer is the hired man of an "information industry," his general aims are, of course, set by the decisions of others and not by his own integrity. But the freedom of the so-called free lance is also minimized when he goes to the market; if he does not go, his freedom is without public value ... *The means of effective communication are being expropriated from the intellectual worker. The material basis of his initiative and intellectual freedom is no longer in his hands*' (1963:296–7; cf Constable 1980).

3 DeGaulle was once reported to have said in response to a question concern-ing the free reign accorded J.-P. Sartre by the French state, 'On n'arrête pas Voltaire' (cf Levitt 1979:652).

4 Not many observers have appreciated just how strikingly Simmel's cri-tique of modern culture anticipated much of what the New Left advanced during the sixties (cf Simmel 1968).

5 There can be no radical disagreement with these portrayals of the appear-ance of the modern condition. However, they are distortions, for they begin in the middle, with the fetish character of modern relations. As such they confound the apparent power of the fetish and the fetish as an expression of social alienation. Machines, technology, industry, bureaucracy, mass soc-

iety, capitalism, and so on are declared to be the source of the modern predicament. But these are abstractions which appear not only to be concrete, but to be the active subjects of history, entering into relations with one another and the human race. Indeed, it appears as if the machine enslaves man, as if technology determines the content of human life, as if bureaucracy reduces men to numbers, to things, as if the mass media program our thoughts, as if capitalism chains us to the imperative of the profit motive. But it is incumbent upon science to grasp the apparent as apparent, to begin, not in the middle with ethereal representations, but with the earthly core, ie, with the historically specific relations of human beings in society and to nature (cf Marx 1972b:441–2; Krader 1976).

6 There the word *Bedürfnis* is rendered 'needs' instead of wants. On 'wants' and 'needs' see Krader (1979:67–76).

7 Marcuse and Jean-Paul Sartre were the two philosophers of freedom and human liberation 'adopted' by the New Left. But far from advancing a rational theory of human liberation which encompasses the objective and subjective equally, they mysticized the theory of the substance of freedom. By separating the existential from the substantial, the subjective from the objective, consciousness from labour, emphasizing the former and suppressing the latter (even as the positivists elevated the objective and eradicated the subjective), they were in a practical sense intellectual pied pipers who led a generation of middle class youth out of the bourgeois enclaves into a fantasy world which brought mental confusion to a considerable number, and worse to a handful of others. On Marcuse, cf Young (1977:343–5).

8 Cf Kornhauser (1959). Kornhauser describes the differences between the aristocratic and democratic views of mass society, and he sees them as essentially complementary, each necessary for the theory of mass society. Here they are taken as manifestations of the ambivalent poles of intellectual life in civil society.

9 The popularity of the writings of Jürgen Habermas (1968) among the New Left students in Germany before 1969 was related to the theme of 'herrschaftsfreie Kommunikation' (communication without domination) which he developed in his works. Habermas (1970) criticized the late SDS for violating its earlier principles. The students replied in *Die Linke antwortet Jürgen Habermas* (1968).

10 Kornhauser still believed that the pluralism of American corporate and associational life was capable of counteracting the modern tendency towards mass society. This was the liberal face of cold war politics, and it did not speak to the younger generation for the reasons outlined above. Pluralism implied mobility, differentiation, and decentralization of power. The stu-

dent generation was experiencing massification; Mills and Marcuse spoke to these students in a meaningful way.

Chapter 9

1 It is, of course, the students themselves 'who aspire to serious participation in social affairs.' According to Viorst the PHS 'seemed to be saying, critical as it was of other élites, that a student élite had now to be forged on the campuses to realize the New Left's vision of the future. This élitism remained with the New Left throughout its history' (1979:193).
2 The quotation marks are absolutely crucial here. The students don't want to expand the existing public sector, the public sector of petty bureaucrats and corrupt officials. They want to expand the 'true' public sector as it exists in their imagination, a 'public sector' rationally organized in the interests of humanity, ie, a 'public sector' organized by the students. 'How shall the "public sector" be made public [without quotation marks], and not the arena of a ruling bureaucracy of "public servants" [with quotation marks]?' ask the PHS authors, rhetorically. It is done, they inform us, by opposing 'bureaucratic coagulation,' by instituting planning at all levels, and by 'experiments in decentralization ... based on the vision of man as master of his machines and his society' (for 'man' we read students and their abstract view of man). Statements like these in the light of the career trajectory of students have given ammunition to critics like Irving Kristol who write about the New Left as an expression of a new class, a new class closely aligned with the public sector.
3 Methodologically, particularly in North America, the social sciences were modelled after the positivistic natural sciences. Yet they remained 'poor cousins' of physics and chemistry since they could demonstrate neither the same degree of theoretical sophistication nor the same level of practical success. In addition, the students in social science routinely deal with questions of national, international, and world-historical import while they remain politically impotent and socially isolated. The 'radicalism' of the humanities students was fed by a latent conservatism which dismissed the technocrats as philistines and bourgeois upstarts, not from a proletarian, but from an 'aristocratic' position.

Again, it must be said that these students, for the most part, were honest, dedicated, sincere, moral souls who were deeply disturbed by the world around them. They were genuinely committed to humanistic, enlightenment values. But sociologically this commitment was fuelled by and gave expression to the character and experiences of that generation.
4 Creativity as a social phenomenon is a function of privilege. The bohemian

revolt against this connection between art and exchange-value in civil society is both a confirmation of and a protest against this state of affairs. Bourgeois society gives rise to bohemia; without the former, the latter could not exist (see Kreuzer 1968; Michels 1932).

5 In addition to the conservative professors and the radical students, there was yet a third group opposed to the technocratic reformers, namely, the radical professors such as the members of the Frankfurt School. Although the conservative professors and the radical professors opposed the technocrats on different grounds, both were equally abstract in their opposition (cf Marx's criticism of both the Left and Right Hegelians in *The German Ideology* (1968a). Scholars such as Allan Bloom, Robert Nisbet, and Helmut Schelsky continued to see in the university a timeless institution. Whereas these conservatives, oblivious to the actual situation, were looking backwards to preserve 'a shape of life grown old,' the radicals were developing utopian schemes, composing *Zukunftsmusik*. To be sure, the conservatives overwhelmingly outnumbered the radicals among the full professors and *Ordinarien*, in part because the severity of the impact upon senior academicians was far less than upon the students and junior faculty.

6 This is not to say that these matters were not part of the concern of other national New Left groups. However, the Canadian New Left on the whole managed to spend less time worrying about the grand synthesis than its American or German counterparts.

7 The table of contents lists eleven headings, less than half of which correspond to sections in the declaration fragment,

8 The New Left in Canada emerged out of a concern with the threat of nuclear war and the question of nuclear disarmament. It maintained this exclusive focus until the dissolution of the CUCND, and as one primary concern until the dissolution of SUPA in 1967. (The scope was broadened with the founding of SUPA in January 1965.)

9 The same can be said about the student attitude to the war in Vietnam. To paraphrase a pejorative appellation from the forties: the students were 'prematurely antiwar.'

10 In a similar way, Adam Smith described the differences between Whigs and Tories: 'The bustling, spirited, active folks, who can't brook oppression and constantly endeavouring to advance themselves, naturally join in with the democratical part of the constitution and favour the principle of utility only, that is, the Whig interest. The calm, contented folks of no great spirit and abundant fortunes which they want to enjoy at their own ease, and don't want to be disturbed nor to disturb others, as naturally join with the Tories' (1978:320).

11 The following excerpts from a letter in the *Toronto Daily Star* (Horowitz,

Gonick, and Sheps 1967) were reprinted in a *supa Newsletter* (1967:11–12):
'The majority of Canadians are nationalist; most of us want to preserve our
country's independence ...

'But the problem is not merely one of foreign investment and trade dependence. For with the dominant presence of the American branch plant
and with the American monopolization of non-agricultural trade, come
American values, American tastes, American ways of life and thought,
American laws, and American foreign policy. There is no reason to fear
political annexation, but total economic cultural integration is not only
threatening; it is happening.

'We are Canadian nationalists because we are not satisfied with being a
comfortable satellite of the United States. A miniature replica of the Great
Society is not our vision of the future of Canada. We are anxious to dimin-
ish the economic and cultural influence of the United States in order to
preserve the *possibility* of building in this country, a society better than the
Great Society.'

12 It should be pointed out that no clear position was taken by the cucnd in
this regard. Rather, the Quebec question was grasped as an opportunity for
re-examining the 'goals of Canadian society' and renewing 'social imagination and action in relation to those problems.'

Chapter 10

1 The German sds officially and publicly declared itself to be part of the
international New Left after its members were expelled from the spd in
1961. Until that time it had paid lip service, at least, to the social democratic view that the student organization was the representative of the spd
and trade unions (ie, the German workers' movement) at the university.
hd, which was written in an eighteen-month period during 1960–1, already
went beyond this view in many ways.

2 A version of this speech was reprinted in Potter (1963:30–6).

3 The roots of the interest and ideology of student syndicalism are as old as
the university itself. A great dispute arose at the end of the twelfth century
in Bologna concerning the status of the student corporation. The students
claimed the right of corporate self-organization on the basis of Roman law
according to which guilds of merchants and craftsmen were formed. But it
was held by many law masters that the students were not of the class of
those 'qui professionem exercere noscuntur'; they were more like appren-
tices of those who practised a trade or profession. Azo, in his gloss upon that
section of the codex which guarantees the right of professions to elect a
leader with judicial powers, excluded the students in the following words:

'ergo scolares, quia non exercent professionem sed sub exercentibus sunt discipuli, non possunt eligere consules, sicut nec discipuli pellipariorum. Magistri ergo possunt eligere consules, quia ipsi exercent professiones' (Denifle 1956:170n).

The student syndicalism of the sixties stands in a mediate continuity with the corporate movement of the twelfth-century students (cf Kibre 1948, 1962).

4 UNEF was also the source of the theory of German student syndicalism. Greg Calvert, national secretary of the American SDS in 1966–7, had studied in France in the early sixties, and he brought back to America many of the theories of the French student left.

5 Serge Joyal is currently minister of state of the government of Canada.

6 The New Left in fact was reacting not to the increasing differentiation among the universities but to the growing homogenization of the university system. Having let the cat out of the bag, Davidson tries to seal it up again: 'Just as different factories can produce different *kinds* of commodities, different universities produce different *kinds* of students. A type of educational "pluralism" has been developing over the last few decades. The traditional Ivy League schools shape the sons and daughters of the ruling and managerial élites. The state colleges and universities develop the sons and daughters of the working class and petty bourgeoisie into the highly skilled sectors of the new working class, the middle sector white collar workers, and the traditional middle class professionals. Finally, the new community and junior colleges serve the increasing educational needs of, for the most part, the sons and daughters of the working class' (69). But the New Left had its roots precisely in the Ivy League schools and the more prestigious state universities. Until 1968, at least, one could be fairly certain that the greater the proportion of working class students, the weaker the New Left groups on the campus would be.

7 The very fact that SUPA felt a need to formulate an ideology is significant and indicates a turning against the ethos of the early movement.

8 McKelvey had written to Al Haber asking about the circumstances surrounding the writing of the PHS. It's clear that McKelvey viewed the PHS as a kind of model for the drafting of the SUPA manifesto. See the correspondence in the CUCND/SUPA collection at the McMaster University Library, Hamilton, Canada.

Chapter 11

1 This article was part of a collection of four which circulated within SDS in 1970. This small compendium included another article by Schmierer (SDS

1970). The other two represented an attack upon Schmierer's position and a defence of the anti-authoritarian, new working class, science-as-a-productive-force theories (Krahl 1971; Roth 1970).

Schmierer's writings became part of the theoretical foundation of a number of Marxist-Leninist groups at the time (cf Kukuck 1974:40). In the seventies, Schmierer became a leading figure in the Kommunistischer Bund Westdeutschland (KBW) (cf Kukuck 1974:136–57; Langguth 1976:165–84).

2 Karl Marx, in his famous monograph on the French upheavals of 1848–51 (1968a), asserted that the large landowners who ruled France during the Restoration were Legitimist (supporters of the House of Bourbon) whereas the financiers and big industrialists who ruled during the July Monarchy were Orleanist. Legitimism and Orleanism were the political colours of different fractions of the class of capital. The leading circles of the army, the university, the church, the legal profession, the press, and so on could be found on either side, though, as Marx assures us, 'in various proportions.' Clearly the interests of this group of dignitaries was not substantially related to the interests of one or the other fractions of the bourgeoisie; support for the one or other fraction was more a matter of circumstance, inclination, tradition, training, and ephemeral interests.

3 In the late sixties the discovery was made by the New Left that every issue arising in every area of life was political in character; everything from relations between the sexes to child rearing and the care of the mentally ill was defined as a political problem. Hence, the phrase 'political economy' was prefixed to a plethora of topics in the social sciences in hopes that changing the name would transform functionalist sociology into its opposite. (Students of Marx's texts will recognize the ludicrousness of those who hoist the banner of 'political economy' and think they are performing a radical service in the name of Marxism. Marx himself was untiring in his critique of political economy, the opposite of which he considered to be communism).

In the middle of the 1840s, in doing battle with the Young Hegelian school of critical criticism, Marx and Engels noted that the proponents of this school reduced all questions to questions of religion, much in the same way that the New Leftists (and their academic progeny in the seventies) had reduced all questions to questions of the political economy. Since Marx set religion and politics on the same plane in social life, one can only assume that what he had to say about the Young Hegelians with respect to religion would apply equally well to the New Left concerning politics: 'The advance consists in the fact that the supposedly dominant metaphysical, political, juridical, moral, and other ideas as well are to be subsumed under religious or theological ideas, in the same way that political, juridical, and moral consciousness is to be taken as religious or theological consciousness, and political, juridical, and moral man, 'Man' in the last instance, is to be explained as religious. The dominance of religion is assumed. Slowly but surely each dominant relation is explained as a relation of religion and transformed into a cult, a cult of law, a cult of state, etc' (Marx and Engels 1969:19). Today we have the political economy of law, political economy of the state, and so on.

4 The theory of the authoritarian state attaches less importance to the class struggle between bourgeoisie and proletariat. Instead, it views the decisive contradiction in modern society residing in the essential antagonism between the authoritarian state and those who struggle on behalf of the true interests of humanity. Schmierer himself assumes that revolutionary change depends upon the 'proletariat proper' and that the student movement is doomed unless it is able to understand itself in terms of its relationship with the movement of the working class.

5 For all of his concern with real, historically specific conditions which lay behind the student revolt, Schmierer never moved beyond the dogmatic assertions of a system of philosophy in which 'the proletariat proper' appears as a logical category.

6 The free-floating intelligentsia (*die freischwebende Intelligenz*) was a concept originated by Alfred Weber and developed by Karl Mannheim. Mannheim (1936) believed that the intellectual who is not bound to the perspective of any one of the social classes is able to float above all class perspectives and hence to synthesize a dynamic view of the whole of social reality which is a close approximation to the social 'truth.'

The reference to 'the productive force "science"' concerns the New Working Class theory according to which scientists are productive labourers who are exploited by capital. Unlike the old factory proletariat, so the theory goes, the young intellectual labourers will not be bought off with higher wages and better working conditions, but will raise the revolutionary demand for control of the production process. Schmierer dismisses this line of thinking in much the same terms as some neo-conservatives.

7 Schmierer does not develop the notion of mediate production. Since those who do not labour in the immediate process of production are, by definition, not immediate producers, they do not belong to 'the working class proper,' according to Schmierer.

8 Rudi Dutschke was one of the sDs leaders at the FU Berlin. He was a student of philosophy, a charismatic figure, and a powerful speaker, who became the leading spokesman for the anti-authoritarian tendency in sDs. He was

shot by a mentally confused individual in April 1968, and this attempt on his life set off a storm of violent protest against the Springer chain of newspapers, which the students held responsible for whipping up anti-student sentiment among the German population. Dutschke died in 1979, according to reports, from an accident which was not unassociated with the brain damage incurred at the time of the shooting.

Chapter 12

1 Kaufman (1979). Herbert Marcuse (1972) might have discovered not some-thing new about the students in the Third World, but in the Third World the truth about the student movement in the capitalist world: 'If, in the Third World, the students are indeed a revolutionary avant-garde, if they are by the thousands the victims of the terror, then their role in the fight for liberation indicates a feature of the global revolution in the making, namely, the decisive force of a radical consciousness. In the Third World, the militant students directly articulate the rebellion of the people; in the advanced capitalist countries, where they do not (yet) have this avant-gardistic function, their privileged position allows (and commits) them to develop such consciousness in theory and practice on their own base – the base of departure of the larger fight' (1972:54–5). Cf the following state-ment by Mehnert: 'The Third World gave to the New Left not only an ersatz proletariat but also an ersatz nationalism' (1977:114; cf Viorst 1979:477).

2 In the same way, Angola's Marxist government is supported by Cuban troops, who are at the same time protecting the investments of Gulf Oil and Texaco: 'Angola's economy is kept afloat by revenue from the American Gulf Oil Co, which produced an average of 135,000 barrels of oil a day last year. It provides the government with an estimated $500 million a year in taxes and royalties.

'Gulf's operations are protected by Cuban forces in the Cabinda enclave, where a third guerilla movement, the Front for the Liberation of the Enclave of Angola, is fighting the government.

'Another US oil company, Texaco, recently was reported to have invested in Angola although it has not begun production' (Heinzerling 1978). Cf Hegel: 'The liberation of the colonies shows itself as the greatest advantage for the mother state, just as the freeing of the slaves is the greatest advan-tage for the masters' (1973:393).

3 For Michels it was precisely those organizations with an explicitly demo-cratic ideology existing in a hostile environment which were most likely to become oligarchic.

4 Mehnert writes: 'I have asked young people at demonstrations in various countries why they carried around the portrait of Che Guevara, a man who failed, as if it were an icon. In Berkeley, a girl answered: "Out of defiance. We know that we will be crushed as he was. That's why we feel one with him"' (1977:150)

5 Hegel wrote: 'The difference here ... is that between a slave and the contemporary labourer or day labourer. The Athenian slave perhaps had easier work and more intellectual labour than our servants do as a rule; however, he was nevertheless a slave, because the whole scope of his activity was made over to the master' (1973:145).

Bibliography

Adorno, T. 1967 *Prisms*. London: Neville Spearman

Albrecht, R. 1975 *Marxismus – bürgerliche Ideologie – Linksradikalismus*. Frankurt-am-Main: Verlag-Marxistische-Blätter

Allerbeck, K. 1970 'Alternative Explanations of Participation in Student Movements: Generational Conflict.' Paper presented to the International Political Science Association, 8th World Congress, Munich, 31 August–5 September

– 1971 'Eine sozialstrukturelle Erklärung von Studentenbewegungen in hochentwickelten Industriegesellschaften' in K. Allerbeck and L. Rosenmayr, eds *Aufstand der Jugend*. Munich: Juventa, 179–201

– 1973 *Soziologie radikaler Studentenbewegungen: eine vergleichende Untersuchung in der BRD und den vereinigten Staaten*. Munich and Vienna: R. Oldenburg Verlag

Altbach, P.G. 1967 [1966] 'The Student and Religious Commitment' in M. Cohen and D. Hale, eds *The New Student Left*. Boston: Beacon, 22–6

Bacciocco, E.J. 1974 *The New Left in America: Reform to Revolution*. Stanford, Ca: Hoover Institution Press

Bahro, R. 1977 *Die Alternative: zur Kritik des real existierenden Sozialismus*. Cologne and Frankfurt-am-Main: Europäische Verlagsanstalt

Bartley, R.L. 1979 'Business and the New Class' in B. Bruce-Briggs, ed *The New Class?* New Brunswick, NJ: Transaction, 57–66

Baumann, B. 1976 [1975] *Wie alles anfing*. Frankfurt-am-Main: Karl Marx Buchhandlung

Bauss, G. 1974 'Studentenbewegung in der BRD' *facit* 33:11–20

Becker, J. 1978 [1977] *Hitler's Children: The Story of the Baader-Meinhof Gang*. London: Panther Books

Bell, D. 1976a [1973] *The Coming of Post-Industrial Society*. New York: Penguin

– 1976b *The Cultural Contradictions of Capitalism*. New York: Basic Books

– 1979 'The New Class: A Muddled Concept' in B. Bruce-Briggs, ed *The New Class?* New Brunswick, NJ: Transaction, 169–90

Benda, J. 1969 [1927] *The Treason of the Intellectuals.* New York: W.W. Norton

Ben-David, J. 1972 *Trends in American Higher Education.* Chicago: University of Chicago Press

Berg, I. 1970 *Education and Jobs: The Great Training Robbery.* New York: Praeger

Berger, P.L. 1979 'The Worldview of the New Class: Secularity and Its Discontents' in B. Bruce-Briggs, ed *The New Class?* New Brunswick, NJ: Transaction, 49–55

Bergmann, U., et al 1968 *Rebellion der Studenten.* Reinbek: Rohwolt-Taschenbuch

Bernstein, B. 1971 *Class, Codes and Control* vol 1 *Theoretical Studies towards a Sociology of Language.* London: Routledge & Kegan Paul

– 1973 *Class, Codes and Control* vol 2 *Applied Studies towards a Sociology of Language.* London: Routledge & Kegan Paul

– 1975 *Class, Codes and Control* vol 3 *Towards a Theory of Educational Transmissions.* London: Routledge & Kegan Paul

Birnbaum, N. 1969 'On the Idea of a Political Avant-Garde in Contemporary Politics: The Intellectuals and Technical Intelligentsia' *Praxis* 5(1–2):234–49

Black, D., ed 1969 *Getting on with It.* Ottawa: Canadian Union of Students mimeograph

Bledstein, B.J. 1976 *The Culture of Professionalism.* New York: W.W. Norton

Bloom, A. 1971 [1969] 'The Democratization of the University' in R.A. Goldwin, ed *How Democratic Is America?* Chicago: Rand McNally, 109–36

Böckelmann, F., and H. Nagel, eds 1976 *Subversive Aktion.* Frankfurt-am-Main: Verlag-Neue-Kritik

Booth, P., and L. Webb 1966 'From Protest to Radical Politics' *Our Generation* 3(4) and 4(1):78–90

Bone, C. 1977 *The Disinherited Children: A Study of the New Left and the Generation Gap.* Cambridge, Mass: Schenkman

Bourdieu, P., and J.C. Passeron 1977 [1970] *Reproduction in Education: Society and Culture.* London and Beverly Hills: Sage

Bowles, S., and H. Gintis 1976 *Schooling in Capitalist America.* New York: Basic Books

Bowman, M.J. 1966 'The Human Investment Revolution in Economic Thought' *Sociology of Education* 39(2):111–37

Braungart, R.G. 1979 *Family Status, Socialization and Student Politics.* Ann Arbor: University Microfilms International

Breines, W. 1980 'Community and Organization: The New Left and Michels' "Iron Law"' *Social Problems* 27(4):419–29

Briem, J. 1976 *Der SDS*. Berlin: Verlag-Neue-Kritik

Broder, H. 1981 'Ihr bleibt die Kinder Eurer Eltern' *Die Zeit* (Canada Edition) No 10, 6 March

Bruce-Briggs, B. 1979 *The New Class?* New Brunswick, NJ: Transaction

Brzezinski, Z. 1968 'Revolution oder Konterrevolution – zum historischen Standort des Revolutionismus der "Neuen Linken"' in E. Scheuch, ed *Die Wiedertäufer der Wohlstandsgesellschaft*. Cologne: Markus-Verlags-Gesellschaft

Buscher, J., and K. Heinemann 1974 'Studentenbewegung im Klassenkampf' *facit* 33:3–10

Calvert, G., and C. Neiman 1971 *A Disrupted History: The New Left and the New Capitalism*. New York: Random House

Carnegie Commission on Higher Education 1973 *College Graduates and Jobs: Adjusting to a New Labor Market*. New York: McGraw Hill

Clecak, P. 1973 *Radical Paradoxes: Dilemmas of the American Left 1945–1970*. New York, Evanston, San Francisco, London: Harper & Row

Cohen, J., and D. Howard 1978 'Why Class?' in P. Walker, ed *Between Capital and Labour*. Montreal: Black Rose Books, 67–95

Collins, R. 1979 *The Credential Society: An Historical Sociology of Education and Stratification*. New York: Academic Press

Comte, A. 1973 [1853] *System of Positive Polity*. New York: Burt Franklin

Conlin, J. 1982 *The Troubles: A Jaundiced Glance Back at the Movement of the Sixties*. New York, London, Toronto, Sydney: Franklin Watts

Constable, M. 1980 'Left-Weberian Sociology as Ideology' MA thesis, Department of Sociology, McMaster University

Council of Europe 1967 *Reform and Expansion of Higher Education in Europe*. Paris: Council for Cultural Cooperation

CUCND 1963a 'A Brief to Members of Parliament' 13 November

– 1963b 'Declaration of CUCND' draft document, CUCND Collection, McMaster University Library, Hamilton, Ontario

– 1964 *The University and Social Action in the Nuclear Age*. Toronto: CUCND pamphlet

– 1964–5 'The Student and Social Issues in the Nuclear Age' Regina: draft statement, 28 December–1 January

Cutler, L. 1973 *The Liberal Middle Class: Maker of Radicals*. New Rochelle, NY: Arlington House

Dahrendorf, R. 1959 [1957] *Class and Class Conflict in Industrial Society*. Stanford, Ca: Stanford University Press

Davidson, C. 1967a 'Student Syndicalism' *Our Generation* 5(1):102–11
– 1967b 'The New Radicals and the Multiversity' *Our Generation* 5(3):60–89
Davidson, S. 1977 *Loose Change*. Garden City, NY: Doubleday
Debray, R. 1978 *Modeste contribution aux discours et cérémonies officielles du dixième anniversaire*. Paris: Maspero
– 1979 'A Modest Contribution to the Rites and Ceremonies of the Tenth Anniversary' *New Left Review* 115: 45–65
DeGré, G. 1979 [1943] *Society and Ideology*. New York: Arno Press
Denifle, H. 1956 [1885] *Die Entstehung der Universitäten des Mittelalters bis 1400*. Graz: Akademische-Druck-und-Verlagsanstalt
Desan, W. 1965 *The Philosophy of Jean-Paul Sartre*. Garden City, NY: Doubleday
Dickstein, M. 1977. *Gates of Eden: American Culture in the Sixties*. New York: Basic Books
Drucker, P.F. 1950 *The New Society*. New York: Harper
Durkheim, E. 1960 [1893] *The Division of Labor in Society*. Glencoe, Ill: The Free Press
Dutschke, R. 1968 'Die geschichtlichen Bedingungen für den internationalen Emanzipationskampf' in U. Bergmann et al *Rebellion der Studenten*. Berlin: Rohwolt, 33–93
Economic Council of Canada 1968 *The Challenge of Growth and Change*. Ottawa: Fifth Annual Review
– 1970 *Patterns of Growth*. Ottawa: Seventh Annual Review
Edwards, R. 1979 *Contested Terrain: The Transformation of the Workplace in the Twentieth Century*. New York: Basic Books
Ehrenreich, B., and J. Ehrenreich 1978 'The Professional-Managerial Class' in P. Walker, ed *Between Labor and Capital*. Montreal: Black Rose Books, 5–45
Elliot, M. 1979 'Sociology or a Marxist Social Science?: An Analysis of the Work of Karl Korsch' MA thesis, Department of Sociology, McMaster University
Ellul, J. 1967 [1954] *The Technological Society*. New York: Vintage Books
Engels, F. 1967 'Engels an Sorge' (27 Aug 1890) in *Marx-Engels Werke* vol 37. Berlin: Dietz, 449
– 1967 'Engels an Lafargue' (27 Aug 1890) in *Marx-Engels Werke* vol 37. Berlin: Dietz, 450
– 1967 'Engels au Kautsky' (18 Sept 1890) in *Marx-Engels Werke* vol 37. Berlin: Dietz, 454
– 1972 [1884] 'Vorwort zur ersten deutschen Ausgabe von Karl Marx' Schrift "Das Elend der Philosophie"' in *Marx-Engels Werke* vol 21. Berlin: Dietz, 175–87

– 1973 'Engels an Marx' (19 Nov 1844) in *Marx-Engels Werke* vol 27. Berlin: Dietz, 11

Ericson, E.E. 1975 *Radicals in the University*. Stanford, Ca: Hoover Institution Press

Erikson, E. 1962 [1958] *Young Man Luther*. New York: W.W. Norton

Evans, S. 1980 [1979] *Personal Politics*. New York: Vintage

Farber, J. 1970 *The Student as Nigger: Essays and Stories*. New York: Pocket Books

Faust, A. 1973 *Der nationalsozialistische Studentenbund*. Düsseldorf: Pädagogischer-Verlag-Schwann

Fendrich, J. 1974 'Activists Ten Years Later: A Test of Generational Unit Continuity' *Journal of Social Issues* 30:95–118

– 1976 'Black and White Activists Ten Years Later: Political Socialization and Adult Left-wing Politics' *Youth and Society* 8:81–104

– 1977 'Keeping the Faith or Pursuing the Good Life: A Study of the Consequences of Participation in the Civil Rights Movement' *American Sociological Review* 42:144–54

Fendrich, J., and A. Tarleau 1973 'Marching to a Different Drummer: The Occupational and Political Orientations of Former Student Activists' *Social Forces* 52:245–53

Feuer, L. 1969 *The Conflict of Generations*. New York: Basic Books

Feuerbach, L. 1976 [1841] *Das Wesen des Christentums*. Frankfurt-am-Main: Suhrkamp

Fichter, T., and S. Lönnendoncker 1977 *Kleine Geschichte des SDS*. Berlin: Rotbuch Verlag

Flacks, R. 1967 'The Liberated Generation: An Exploration of the Roots of Student Protest' *Journal of Social Issues* 23: 52–75

– 1970 'Who Protests: The Social Bases of the Student Movement' in J. Foster and D. Long, eds *Protest!: Student Activism in America*. New York: Morrow, 134–57

– 1970–1 'Review of Feuer's "The Conflict of Generations"' *Journal of Social History* 2:141–53

– 1971 *Youth and Social Change*. Chicago: Markham

Flacks, R., and M. Mankoff 1971 'The Changing Social Base of the American Student Movement' *Annals of the American Academy of Political Science*, 55–67

Folger, J.K., and C.B. Nam 1964 'Trends in Education in Relation to the Occupational Structure' *Sociology of Education* 38(1):19–33

Foster, J., and D. Long, eds 1970 [1969] *Protest!: Student Activism in America*. New York: Morrow

Freeman, J.M. 1967 'Who Are the Middle Class?' *SUPA Newsletter* 3(4):10, February

Fromm, E. 1955 *The Sane Society*. New York: Holt, Rinehart & Winston

– 1961 *Marx's Concept of Man*. New York: Ungar

– 1962 *Beyond the Chains of Illusion*. New York: Simon & Schuster

Galbraith, J.K. 1970 [1958] *The Affluent Society*. New York and Scarborough, Ont: Mentor

– 1971 [1967] *The New Industrial State*. New York: Mentor Books

Gerzon, M. 1969 *The Whole World Is Watching*. New York: Viking

Gillis, J.R. 1976 *Youth in History: Tradition and Change in European Age Relations*. New York: Academic Press

Gitlin, T. 1980 *The Whole World Is Watching: Mass Media in the Making and Unmaking of the New Left*. Berkeley: University of California Press

Gold, A.R., et al 1976 *Fists and Flowers: A Social-Psychological Interpretation of Student Dissent*. New York: Academic Press

Goldhammer, H. 1978 *The Adviser*. New York: Elsevier

Goldman, M.I. 1975 *Detente and Dollars*. New York: Basic Books

Goodman, P. 1964 [1962] *Compulsory Miseducation and the Community of Scholars*. New York: Vintage

Gordon, M. 1976 'The Communists of the 1930s and the New Left' *Socialist Revolution* 6(1):11–66

Gorz, A. 1968 [1964] *A Strategy for Labor*. Boston: Beacon

Gouldner, A. 1979 *The Future of the Intellectuals and the Rise of the New Class*. New York: Seabury

Gramsci, A. 1971 *Selections from the Prison Notebooks of Antonio Gramsci*. New York: International Publishers

Gray, S. 1967 *SUPA Newsletter* 3(7): 9 May

Haber, A. 1967 'From Protest to Radicalism: An Appraisal of the Student Movement' in M. Cohen and D. Hale, eds *The New Student Left*, Boston: Beacon, 34–42

Habermas, J. 1968 *Technik und Wissenschaft als Ideologie*. Frankfurt-am-Main: Suhrkamp

– 1970 [1969] 'Die Scheinrevolution und ihre Kinder' *Protestbewegung und Hochschulreform*. Frankfurt-am-Main: Suhrkamp, 188–201

Hacker, A. 1979 'Two "New Classes" or None?' In B. Bruce-Briggs, ed *The New Class?* New Brunswick, NJ: Transaction, 155–68

Halleck, S.L. 1970 'Hypothesis of Student Unrest' in J. Foster and D. Long, eds *Protest!: Student Activism in America*. New York: Morrow

Harding, J. 1966a 'An Ethical Movement in Search of an Analysis' *Our Generation* 3(4) and 4(1):20–9

- 1966b 'Bases of Conflict Within SUPA' *SUPA Newsletter* 3(1):14, November
Harris, S.E. 1972 *A Statistical Report of Higher Education*. New York: McGraw Hill
Harvey, E.B. 1974 *Educational Systems and the Labour Market*. Don Mills: Longman Canada
Harvey, E.B., and J.L. Lennards 1973 *Key Issues in Higher Education*. Toronto: OISE
Healey, F.G. 1971 *The Educational and Social Background of Students*. Strasbourg: Council for Cultural Co-operation of the Council of Europe
Hechinger, F.M. 1970 'PH D: It Has Become a Problem Degree' *New York Times* 19 July
Hegel, G.W.F. 1967 [1821] *The Philosophy of Right*. New York: Oxford University Press
- 1970 [1830] *Enzyklopädie der philosophischen Wissenschaften*. Frankfurt-am-Main: Suhrkamp
- 1973 [1821] *Grundlinien der Philosophie des Rechts*. Frankfurt-am-Main: Suhrkamp
- 1974 [1807] *Die Phänomenologie des Geistes*. Frankfurt-am-Main: Suhrkamp
Hegelheimer, A. 1975 *Texte zur Bildungsökonomie*. Frankfurt-am-Main: Ullstein
Heinzerling, L. 1978 'Angola's Marxist Regime Is in Trouble' *Hamilton Spectator* 15 April
Heirich, M. 1971 [1968] *The Spiral of Conflict*. New York: Columbia University Press
Hettich, W. 1969 *Growth and Characteristics of University Teaching Staff in the Social Sciences and the Humanities* Ottawa: Report to Canada Council
- 1971 *Expenditures, Output and Productivity in Canadian University Education*. Ottawa: Economic Council of Canada, Special Study No 14
Hettich, W.B., et al 1972 *Basic Goals and the Financing of Education*. Ottawa: CTF Project on Education Finance, Document 3
Holt, J.C. 1982 *Robin Hood*. London: Thames and Hudson
Hook, S. 1975 *Revolution, Reform and Social Justice: Studies in the Theory and Practice of Marxism*. New York: New York University Press
Horowitz, G., C. Gonick, and G. Sheps 1967 'An Open Letter to Canadian Nationalists' *Toronto Daily Star* 21 April; reprinted in *SUPA Newsletter* 3(7): 11–12, May
Hyde, A., with M. Rowan 1967 'The Student Union for Peace Action: An Analysis.' Toronto: SUPA mimeograph
Illich, I. 1976 [1971] *De-Schooling Society*. Harmondsworth: Pelican
Illich, I., et al 1977 *Disabling Professions*. London: Marion Boyars

Illting, W.M., and Z.E. Szgimond 1967 *Enrollment in Schools and Universities 1951–52 to 1975–76*. Ottawa: Economic Council of Canada Staff Study No 20

Jacobs, H., ed 1970 *Weatherman*. San Francisco: Ramparts Press

Jacobs, P., and S. Landau 1966 *The New Radicals*. Toronto: Random House

Jaffe, A.J., and F. Froomkin 1968 *Technology and Jobs*. New York: Praeger

Jencks, C., and D. Riesman 1977 *The Academic Revolution*. Chicago: University of Chicago Press

Johnson, T. 1977 'The Professions in the Class Structure' in R. Scase, ed *Industrial Society: Class, Cleavage and Control*. London: Allen & Unwin, 93–110

Jones, L.Y. 1980 *Great Expectations: America and the Baby Boom Generation*. New York: Coward, McCann & Geoghegan

Joyal, S. 1965 *Student Syndicalism in Quebec*. Toronto: SUPA mimeograph

Kahn, R.M., and W.J. Bowers 1970 'The Social Context of Rank-and-File Student Activists: A Test of Four Hypotheses' *Sociology of Education* 4(3):38–55

Kanzow, E., and K.H. Roth 1971 *Unwissen als Ohnmacht: Zum Wechselverhältnis von Kapital und Wissenschaft*. Berlin: Voltaire Verlag

Kaufman, M.T. 1979 'Afghanistan Regime Keeps Control with Core of Loyalists' *New York Times*, 9 September

Keats, J. 1965 [1963] *The Sheepskin Psychosis*. New York: Dell

Keller, S., and R. Vahrenkamp 1974 'Die Illusionen des Spätkapitalismus: Bildungsboom und Produktion' *Neues Forum* 241:38–43, 242:47–52

Keniston, K. 1968 *Young Radicals*. New York: Harcourt Brace & World

– 1971 *Youth and Dissent*. New York: Harcourt Brace Jovanovich

Kerr, C. 1966 [1963] *The Uses of the University*. New York: Harper Torchbooks

Kibre, P. 1948 *The Nations in the Medieval Universities*. Cambridge, Mass: Medieval Academy of America

– 1962 *Scholarly Privileges in the Middle Ages*. Cambridge, Mass: Medieval Academy of America

Kirkpatrick, J.J. 1979 'Politics and the New Class' in B. Bruce-Briggs, ed *The New Class?* New Brunswick, NJ: Transaction, 33–48

Knight, G. 1982 'Property Stratification and the Wage Form' *Canadian Journal of Sociology* 7(1):1–17

Kommission für wirtschaftlichen und sozialen Wandel 1977 *Wirtschaftlicher und sozialer Wandel in der Bundesrepublik Deutschland*. Göttingen: Verlag-Otto-Schwartz

Konrád, G., and I. Szelényi 1979 [1978] *The Intellectuals on the Road to Class Power*. New York: Harcourt Brace Jovanovich

Kornhauser, W. 1959 *The Politics of Mass Society*. New York: The Free Press

Korsch, K. 1963 [1938] *Karl Marx*. New York: Russell & Russell
- 1971a [1923] *Marxism and Philosophy*. London: New Left Books
- 1971b [1929] *Die materialistische Geschichtsauffassung*. Frankfurt-am-Main: Europäische Verlagsanstalt
- 1975 [1919] 'What is Socialization?' *New German Critique* 6:60–81
- 1978 [1932] 'The Passing of Marxian Orthodoxy' in D. Kellner, ed *Revolutionary Theory*. Austin: University of Texas Press, 176–80
Kostash, M. 1980 *Long Way From Home*. Toronto: Lorimer
Krader, L. 1971 'The Student Revolt in the United States' *Revue internationale de sociologie* 7(2):58–75
- 1972 *The Ethnological Notebooks of Karl Marx*. Assen: Van Gorcum
- 1973 *Ethnologie und Anthropologie bei Marx*. Munich: Hanser-Verlag
- 1976 *The Dialectic of Civil Society*. Assen: Van Gorcum
- 1978 'Die Asiatische Produktionsweise' in U.I.F. Wolter, ed *Antworten auf Bahros Herausforderung des 'realen Sozialismus.'* Berlin: Verlag-Olle-und-Wolter, 100–27
- 1979 *Treatise of Social Labor*. Assen: Van Gorcum
- n d Work in progress, typed manuscripts
Krahl, H.J. 1971 'Zum allgemeinen Verhältnis von wissenschaftlicher Intelligenz und proletarischem Klassenbewusstsein' in D. Claussen et al, eds *Konstitution und Klassenkampf*. Frankfurt-am-Main: Verlag-Neue-Kritik
Krauss, E. 1974 [1972] *Japanese Radicals Revisited*. Berkeley: University of Caifornia Press
Kreuzer, H. 1968 *Die Boheme*. Stuttgart: Metzler-Verlag
Kristol, I. 1977 'Memoirs of a Trotskyist' *New York Times Magazine* 23 January, 42–57
- 1978 *Two Cheers for Capitalism*. New York: Basic Books
Kukuck, M. 1974 *Studenten und Klassenkampf*. Hamburg: Verlag-Association
Kruger, M., and F. Silvert 1975 *Dissent Denied: The Technocratic Response to Protest*. New York: Elsevier
Lafargue, P. 1970 [1900] 'Der Sozialismus und die Intellektuellen' in *Vom Ursprung der Ideen: Ausgewählte Schriften*. Dresden: Verlag der Kunst, 221–47
Langguth, G. 1976 *Die Protestbewegung in der Bundesrepublik Deutschland: 1968–1976*. Cologne: Verlag-Wissenschaft-und-Politik
Lasch, C. 1978 *The Culture of Narcissism*. New York: W.W. Norton
Laufer, R.S., and V.L. Bengston 1974 'Generations, Aging and Social Stratification: On the Development of Generational Unity' *Journal of Social Issues* 30(3):181–205

Laxer, J. 1969 'The Student Movement and Canadian Independence' *Canadian Dimension* 6(3–4):27–70
– 1970 'The Americanization of the Canadian Student Movement' in I. Lumsden, ed *Close the 49th Parallel*. Toronto: University of Toronto Press, 275–86
Lee, J.M. 1978 'Of Vietnam and Gold and the Cauldron of '68' *New York Times*. 12 March
Lehndorff, S. 1974 'Studentenbewegung im Klassenkampf' *facit* 34:6–46
Leibfried, S. 1968 *Die angepasste Universität*. Frankfurt-am-Main: Suhrkamp
Levin, M., and J. Spiegel 1979 'Point and Counterpoint in the Literature on Student Unrest' in D. Light and J. Spiegel, eds *The Dynamics of University Protest*. Chicago: Nelson-Hall, 23–50
Levinson, C. n d *Vodka-Cola*. London: Gordon & Cremonesi
Levitt, C. 1979 'The New Left, the New Class and Socialism' *Higher Education* 8:641–55
– 1981 'The "Old" New Left: A Reassessment by Former Participants in Canada, the United States and West Germany' in P.G. Altbach, ed *Student Politics: Perspectives for the Eighties*. Metuchen, NJ: The Scarecrow Press, 53–75
Light, D., and J. Spiegel 1979 *The Dynamics of University Protest*. Chicago: Nelson-Hall
Light, P. 1964 'A First Person Report from Albany Georgia ... Feb. 20, 1964' *Dialogue for Peace*. Regina: Saskatchewan CUCND
Die Linke antwortet Jürgen Habermas. 1968 O. Negt, ed. Frankfurt-am-Main: Europäische-Verlagsanstalt
Lipset, S.M. 1976 [1971] *Rebellion in the University*. Chicago: University of Chicago Press
– 1979 'The New Class and the Professoriate' in B. Bruce-Briggs, ed *The New Class?* New Brunswick, NJ: Transaction, 67–87
Lipset, S.M., and P.G. Altbach 1969 *Students in Revolt*. Boston: Houghton Mifflin
Lipset, S.M., and S. Wolin 1965 *The Berkeley Student Revolt: Facts and Interpretations*. Garden City, NY: Anchor
Lockhart, A. 1970 'The Effect of Recent Techno-Economic Changes on the Mobility Patterns and Opportunities of the American Middle-Class, with Particular Emphasis on the Emergent Contradiction between Occupational and Educational Factors' MA thesis, Department of Political Science, Sociology and Anthropology, Simon Fraser University, Burnaby, BC
– 1971 'Graduate Employment and the Myth of Human Capital' in D.I. Davies and K. Herman, eds *Social Space: Canadian Perspectives*. Toronto: New Press

Lomer, N. 1966 'SUPA and Ideology' *SUPA Newsletter* 3(1):15–16, November
Lönnendoncker, S., et al 1975 *Freie Universität Berlin 1948–1973: Hochschule im Umbruch.* Berlin: Freie Universität Berlin, part IV
Lukács, G. 1971 [1923] *History and Class Consciousness.* London: Merlin
– 1972 [1954] *Die Zerstörung der Vernunft.* Frankfurt-am-Main: Suhrkamp
Luxemburg, R. 1974 *Gesammelte Schriften.* Berlin: Dietz
Lyons, R.D. 1970 'Science Jobs That Were' *New York Times.* 8 November
Malcolm, A.H. 1970 'Many New School Teachers Unable to Find Jobs as Nationwide Demand Shrinks' *New York Times* 19 July
Mallet, S. 1975 [1963] *The New Working Class.* Nottingham: Spokesman Books
Man, H. de 1928 [1926] *The Psychology of Socialism.* London: Allen & Unwin
Mannheim, K. 1928 'Das Problem der Generationen' *Kölner Vierteljahrshefte für Soziologie* 7(2):157–85; (3):309–30
– 1936 [1929] *Ideology and Utopia.* New York: Harcourt Brace & World
Marcuse, H. 1966 [1964] *One-Dimensional Man.* Boston: Beacon
– 1968 [1941] *Reason and Revolution: Hegel and the Rise of Social Theory.* Boston: Beacon
– 1972 *Counter-Revolution and Revolt.* Boston: Beacon
Marx, K. 1965 [1867] *Capital* vol 1. Moscow: Progress Publishers
– 1966 [1847] *The Poverty of Philosophy.* Moscow: Progress Publishers
– 1968a [1852] *The Eighteenth Brumaire of Louis Bonaparte.* New York: International Publishers
– 1968b [1849] 'Wage-Labour and Capital' in *Marx-Engels Selected Works.* Moscow: Progress Publishers, 72–94
– 1970 [1843] *Critique of Hegel's Philosophy of Right.* Cambridge: Cambridge University Press
– 1972a *The Ethnological Notebooks of Karl Marx.* Assen: Van Gorcum
– 1972b [1867] *Kapital* vol 1. Berlin: Dietz Verlag, Marx-Engels Werke (MEW) 23
– 1972c [1894] *Kapital* vol 3. Berlin: Dietz Verlag, MEW 25
– 1972d [1843] *Kritik des Hegelschen Staatsrechts.* Berlin: Dietz, MEW 1, 203–333
– 1972e [1905] *Theorien über den Mehrwert* vol 3. Berlin: Dietz Verlag, MEW 26.3
– 1973 [1939/41] *Grundrisse.* London: Penguin
– 1975 [1844] 'Critique of Hegel's Philosophy of Law: Introduction' in *Marx-Engels Collected Works* vol 3. London: Lawrence & Wishart, 175–87
– 1977 [1933] 'The Results of the Immediate Process of Production' in *Capital.* London: Penguin
– 1978 [written 1879/80] 'Critical Marginal Notes on Wagner's "Textbook of

Political Economy"' in T. Carver, ed *Karl Marx: Texts on Method*. Oxford: Blackwell, 179–219

Marx, K., and F. Engels 1968a [1932] *The German Ideology*. Moscow: Progress Publishers

– 1968b [1848] 'The Manifesto of the Communist Party' in *Marx-Engels Selected Works*. Moscow: Progress Publishers, 35–63

– 1969 [1932] *Die deutsche Ideologie*. Berlin: Dietz Verlag, MEW 3

– 1971 [1850] 'A. Chenu's "Les Conspirateurs" und Lucian de la Hoddes' "La naissance de la République en février 1840"' in MEW 7. Berlin: Dietz Verlag, 266–80

– 1973 [1873] 'Ein Complot gegen die Internationale Arbeiter-Association' in MEW 18. Berlin: Dietz Verlag, 327–471

– 1975 [1845] 'The Holy Family' in *Marx-Engels Collected Works* vol 4. London: Lawrence & Wishart

Mattick, P. 1978 'Review of Krader's "Asiatic Mode of Production"' *Internationale Wissenschaftliche Korrespondenz zur Geschichte der deutschen Arbeiterbewegung*. Berlin: Historische Kommission zu Berlin

Mauss, A.L. 1971 'The Lost Promise of Reconciliation: New Left vs Old Left' *Journal of Social Issues* 27(1):1–20

Mayo, E. 1975 [1945] *The Social Problems of an Industrial Civilization*. London: Routledge & Kegan Paul

Mehnert, K. 1977 [1976] *Twilight of the Young: The Radical Movements of the 1960s and Their Legacy*. New York: Rinehart & Winston

Meier, A. 1970 *Black Experience: The Transformation of Activism*. New Brunswick, NJ: Transaction

Metzenberg, H. 1978 'Student Peace Union: Five Years Before the New Left' Honour thesis, Department of History, Oberlin College

Meyer, J.W., et al 1977 'The World Educational Revolution, 1950–1970' *Sociology of Education* 50(4):242–58

Michels, R. 1932 'Zur Soziologie der Boheme und ihrer Zusammenhänge mit dem geistigen Proletariat' *Jahrbücher für Nationalökonomie und Statistik* 136:801–16, tr C. Levitt in *Catalyst* 15:1–25 (1983)

Miles, M. 1971 *The Radical Probe: The Logic of Student Rebellion*. New York: Atheneum

– 1977 'The Student Movement and the Industrialization of Higher Education' in J. Karabel and A.H. Halsey, eds *Power and Ideology in Education*. New York: Oxford University Press, 432–49

Mills, C. Wright 1957 [1956] *The Power Elite*. New York: Oxford University Press

– 1958 *The Causes of World War Three*. New York: Simon & Schuster

- 1959 *The Sociological Imagination*. New York: Oxford University Press
- 1960a *Listen Yankee*. New York: McGraw-Hill
- 1960b 'On the New Left' *Studies on the Left* 2(1):63–72
- 1963 *Power, Politics and People*. ed I.L. Horowitz. New York: Oxford University Press
Mitscherlisch, A. 1970 [1963] *Society without the Father*. New York: Schocken
Monthly Review 1969 'The Old Left and the New' *Monthly Review* 21:3–11
Moore, W.E. 1951 [1945] *Industrial Relations and the Social Order*. New York: Macmillan
Negt, O. 1971 'Die Zerstörung der Deutschen Universität' in *Politik als Protest*. Frankfurt-am-Main: Agit-Buch-Vertrieb, 9–24
'The New Face of Unemployment' 1970 *Time* 2 November
Newfield, J. 1967 [1966] *A Prophetic Minority*. New York: Signet
Nietzsche, F. 1956 [1887] 'The Geneology of Morals' in F. Golffing, tr. *The Birth of Tragedy and The Geneology of Morals*. Garden City, NY: Doubleday
Nisbet, R. 1969 'The New Philistinism' *Transaction* 6:54–6
O'Brien, J.P. 1971a 'The Development of a New Left in the United States, 1960–1964' PH D dissertation, Department of History, University of Wisconsin (Madison)
- 1971b 'The Development of the New Left' *The Annals of the American Academy of Political and Social Sciences* 395:15–25
OECD 1974 *Towards Mass Higher Education: Issues and Dilemmas*. Paris: Conference on Future Structures of Post-Secondary Education, 26–9 June 1973
Oglesby, C. 1977 [1976] *The Yankee and Cowboy War*. Berkeley: Medallion
Oglesby, C., and R. Shaull 1967 *Containment and Change: Two Dissenting Views on American Society and Foreign Policy in the New Revolutionary Age*. New York: Macmillan
Olson, T. 1963 'Who Are These People?' Paper presented at 'The Challenge of Civil Disobedience for the American Police Executive,' New York University, 24–9 March
Orwell, G. 1958 [1937] *The Road to Wigan Pier*. New York: Harcourt Brace Jovanovich
Otto, K. 1977 *Vom Ostermarsch zur APO: Geschichte der ausserparlamentarischen Opposition in der Bundesrepublik, 1960–1970*. Frankfurt-am-Main: Campus-Verlag
Parkin, F. 1967 'A Student Revolution' *New Society* 234: 426–7
- 1968 *Middle Class Radicalism*. New York: Praeger
Paschukanis, E. 1978 [1924] *Law and Marxism: A General Theory*. London: Ink Links

Perlman, F. 1970 *The Incoherence of the Intellectual*. Detroit: Black and Red

Pinner, F.A. 1969 'Western European Student Movements through Changing Times' in S.M. Lipset and P.G. Altbach, eds *Students in Revolt*. Boston: Houghton Mifflin

Podhoretz, N. 1979 'The Adversary Culture and the New Class' in B. Bruce-Briggs, ed *The New Class?* New Brunswick, NJ: Transaction, 19–31

Pohrt, W. 1981 'Ein Volk, ein Reich, ein Frieden' *Die Zeit* 6 November, Canada Edition

Porter, J. 1965 *The Vertical Mosaic*. Toronto: University of Toronto Press

Potter, P. 1963 'The Intellectual as an Agent of Social Change' *Our Generation Against Nuclear War* 2(4):30–6

Powers, T. 1971 *Diana: The Making of a Terrorist*. Boston: Houghton Mifflin

Priewe, J. 1974 'Den Kampf um demokratische Ausbildungsziele als politischen Kampf führen.' *facit* 34:52–62

Quigley, C. 1966 *Tragedy and Hope: A History of the World in Our Time*. New York: Macmillan

Rapoport, A. 1967 'Have the Intellectuals a Class Interest?' *Our Generation* 5(1):31–49

Reich, C. 1970 *The Greening of America*. New York: Random House

Reid, T., and J. Reid 1969 *Student Power and the Canadian Campus*. Toronto: Peter Martin Associates

Renner, K. 1926 *Der geistige Arbeiter in der gegenwärtigen Gesellschaft*. Berlin: Dietz-Verlag

– 1929 *Wege der Verwirklichung*. Berlin: Dietz-Verlag

Repo, S. 1967 'On Being Middle Class' SUPA *Newsletter* 3(10):9, August

Resnick, P. 1977 *The Land of Cain*. Vancouver: New Star Books

Rice, B. 1970 'Down and Out along Route 128' *New York Times Magazine* 1 November

Ringer, F.K. 1978 *Education and Society in Modern Europe*. Bloomington: Indiana University Press

Rodriguez, O. 1978 'Occupational Shifts and Educational Upgrading in the American Labor Force between 1950 and 1970' *Sociology of Education* 51(1):55–67

Rostow, W.W. 1971 [1960] *The Stages of Economic Growth*. New York: Cambridge University Press

Roszak, T. 1969 *The Making of the Counter-Culture*. New York: Anchor

Roth, K.H. 1970 'Jascha Schmierers Marsch in die syndikalistische Sackgasse' *Rotes Forum* 1:37–45

Rothman, S., and S.R. Lichter 1982 *Roots of Radicalism: Jews, Christians, and the New Left*. New York and Oxford: Oxford University Press

Rousseau, J.-J. 1948 [1758] *Lettre à M. D'Alambert sur les spectacles*. M. Fuchs, ed. Lille and Geneva: Librairie Giard, Librairie Droz

Roussopolous, D. 1963 'Radical Analysis' *Sanity* January
- 1966 'Who We Are' *SUPA Newsletter* 3(1):17–19, November

Rowntree, J., and M. Rowntree 1968a 'The Political Economy of Youth' *International Socialist Journal* February
- 1968b 'The Political Economy of Youth' *Our Generation* 6(1–2):155–90
- 1968c 'The Political Economy of Youth' Ann Arbor: Radical Education Project

Sale, K. 1974 [1973] *SDS*. New York: Vintage
- 1975 *Power Shift*. New York: Random House

Satin, J., ed 1960 *The 1950s: America's 'Placid' Decade*. Boston: Houghton Mifflin

Saturday Night 1978 'Fear and Trembling in the Academy' *Saturday Night* Toronto, October
- 1979 'Karl Marx Comes to Canada' *Saturday Night* Toronto, September

Savio, M. 1967 'An End to History' in M. Cohen and D. Hale, eds *The New Student Left*. Boston: Beacon, 248–52

Schäfer, G. 1977 *Studentische Korporationen*. Lollard/Lahn: Verlag-Andreas-Achenbach

Scheler, M. 1961 [1912] *Ressentiment*. L. Coser, ed. New York: Free Press

Schelsky, H. 1977 [1975] *Die Arbeit tun die Anderen: Klassenkampf und Priesterherrschaft der Intellektuellen*. Munich: Deutscher-Taschenbuch-Verlag

Scheuch, E. 1968 'Das Gesellschaftsbild der "Neuen Linken"' in E. Scheuch, ed *Die Wiedertäufer der Wohlstandsgesellschaft*. Cologne: Markus-Verlags-Gesellschaft

Schiffer, I. 1973 *Charisma: A Psychoanalytic Look at Mass Society*. Toronto: University of Toronto Press

Schmierer, J. 1969 'Zur Analyse der Studentenbewegung' *Rotes Forum* 5: 5–14
- 1970 'Die theoretische Auseinandersetzung vorantreiben und die Reste bürgerlicher Ideologie entschieden bekämpfen' *Rotes Forum* 1:29–36

Schnibben, C. 1974 'Das Ende einer Sackgasse in der Studentenbewegung' *facit* 33:45–53

Schumm, W. 1969 *Kritik der Hochschulreform*. Munich: Juventa-Verlag

Schumpeter, J. 1950 [1942] *Capitalism, Socialism and Democracy*. New York: Harper & Row

Scott, M.B., and S.M. Lyman 1970 *The Revolt of the Students*. Columbus: Merrill

SDS 1965 [1961] *Hochschule in der Demokratie*. Frankfurt-am-Main: Verlag-Neue-Kritik

SDS 1964 [1962] *The Port Huron Statement*. Ann Arbor: Radical Education Project

– 1966 'Radical Education Project' Ann Arbor: Radical Education Project
– 1970 'Zur Analyse der Studentenbewegung ...' Mimeograph
Shepherd, H.L. 1967 'Organizing Middle Class Working People: A Proposal'
  SUPA Newsletter 3(4):16–17 February
Shils, E. 1969 'Dreams of Plenitude, Nightmares of Scarcity' in S.M. Lipset and
  P.G. Altbach, eds *Students in Revolt*. Boston: Houghton Mifflin
–1972 *The Intellectuals and the Powers*. Chicago: University of Chicago Press
Simmel, G. 1890 *Über sociale Differenzierung*. Leipzig: Duncker und Humblot
– 1958 [1908] *Soziologie: Untersuchungen über die Formen der Vergesell-
  schaftung*. Berlin: Duncker und Humblot
– 1968 [1882–1918] *The Conflict in Modern Culture and Other Essays*. K.P.
  Etzkorn, tr and intro. New York: Teachers College Press, Columbia Uni-
  versity
Smelser, N. 1962 *Theory of Collective Behavior*. New York: The Free Press
Smith, A. 1863 [1776] *An Inquiry into the Causes of the Wealth of Nations*.
  Edinburgh: Adam and Charles Black
– 1978 [written 1762/63] *Lectures on Jurisprudence*. Oxford: Oxford Univer-
  sity Press
Smith, M.B., et al 1970 'Social Psychological Aspects of Student Activism'
  Youth and Society 1(3):261–88
Snow, C.P. 1960 [1959] *The Two Cultures and the Scientific Revolution*. New
  York: Cambridge University Press
Sohn-Rethel, A. 1978 [1970] *Intellectual and Manual Labour*. London: Mac-
  millan
Solomon, F., and J. Fishman 1963 'Perspectives on the Student Sit-in Movement' *American Journal of Orthopsychiatry* 33:873–4
– 1964a 'Youth and Social Action: An Introduction' *Journal of Social Issues*
  20:1–27
– 1964b 'Youth and Peace: A Psycho-Social Study of Student Peace Demonstra-
  tors in Washington, DC' *Journal of Social Issues* 20:54–73
Sorel, G. 1950 [1901] *Reflections on Violence*. New York: The Free Press
Spencer, H. 1910 [1876–1896] *The Principles of Sociology*. New York and London: D. Appleton
Squires, G.D. 1979 *Education and Jobs*. New Brunswick, NJ: Transaction
Steinfels, P. 1979 *The Neo-Conservatives*. New York: Schuster
'Story of a Science Depression' 1971 *U.S. News and World Report* 25 January
Szymanski, A. 1972 'Trends in the American Working Class' *Socialist Revolu-
  tion* 2(4):101–22
Tessaring, M., and H. Werner 1975 *Beschäftigungsprobleme von Hochschulab-
  solventen im internationalen Vergleich*. Göttingen: Verlag-Otto-Schwarz

Thompson, E.P. 1978 *The Poverty of Theory*. New York: Monthly Review
Tönnies, F. 1979 [1887] *Gemeinschaft und Gesellschaft*. Darmstadt: Wissen-
schaftliche Buchgesellschaft
Touraine, A. 1971 [1968] *The May Movement: Revolt and Reform*. New York:
Random House
Trow, M. 1970 'Reflections on the Transition from Mass to Universal Higher
Education' *Daedelus* 99(1):1–42
– 1973 'Problems in the Transition from Elite to Mass Higher Education' Paris:
OECD
– 1977 'The Second Transformation of American Secondary Education' in J.
Karabel and A.H. Halsey, eds *Power and Ideology in Education*. New York:
Oxford University Press, 105–18
Tuckman, H.P. 1976 *Publication, Teaching and the Academic Reward Struc-
ture*. Lexington, Mass: Lexington Books
Useem, M. 1975 *Protest Movements in America*. Indianapolis: Bobbs-Merrill
Veblen, T. 1957 [1918] *The Higher Learning in America*. New York: Sagamore
Vickers, G.R. 1975 *The Formation of the New Left*. Toronto: Lexington Books
Viorst, M. 1979 *Fire in the Streets*. New York: Simon & Schuster
Wadell, H. 1927 *The Wandering Scholars*. London: Constable
Weber, M. 1958 [1904–05] *The Protestant Ethic and the Spirit of Capitalism*.
New York: Scribner
Weinstein, J. 1972 'The Left, Old and New' *Socialist Revolution* 2(4):3–60
Westby, D. 1976 *The Clouded Vision: The Student Movement in the United
States in the 1960s*. Cranbury, NJ: Associated University Presses
Wetzel, D. 1976 'Marxismus an der Universität' in *Theorie und Organisation*
1:41–100, May
Whicher, G.F. 1949 *The Goliard Poets*. Cambridge, Mass: Cambridge Univer-
sity Press
Wildavsky, A. 1979 'Using Public Funds to Serve Private Interests' in B. Bruce-
Briggs, ed *The New Class?* New Brunswick, NJ: Transaction, 147–53
Wilson, C. 1970 [1956] *The Outsider*. London: Pan Books
*Wir warn die stärkste der Parteien: Erfahrungsberichte aus der Welt der
K-Gruppen* 1977 Berlin: Rotbuch-Verlag
Wolfe, T. 1970 *Radical Chic and Mau-Mauing the Flak Catchers*. New York:
Bantam
Wood, J.L. 1974 *The Sources of American Student Activism*. Lexington, Mass:
D.C. Heath
Woodside, W. 1958 *The University Question*. Toronto: Ryerson Press
Wykstra, R.A., ed 1971 *Education and the Economics of Human Capital*. New
York: The Free Press

Young, N. 1977. *An Infantile Disorder? The Crisis and Decline of the New Left.*
London: Routledge & Kegan Paul
Zinn, H. 1965 [1964] *SNCC: The New Abolitionists.* Boston: Beacon

Index